# MADE TO LAST

*Historic Preservation
in Seattle and King County*

# Made to Last

*Historic Preservation
in Seattle and King County*

## Lawrence Kreisman

Published by Historic Seattle Preservation Foundation
in association with the
University of Washington Press, Seattle and London

Printed in the United States of America

Library of Congress Cataloging-in-Publication Data
Kreisman, Lawrence.
        Made to last: historic preservation in Seattle and King County/Lawrence Kreisman.
            p.   cm.
        Rev. ed. of Historic preservation in Seattle. Seattle: Historic Seattle Preservation and Development Authority, © 1985.
        Includes bibliographical references and index.
        ISBN 0-295-97846-5 (alk. paper)
        1. Historic buildings Washington (State) Seattle—Conservation and restoration.  2. Historic preservation—Washington (State)—Seattle.  3. Historic buildings Washington (State) King County—Conservation and restoration.  4. Historic preservation—Washington (State)—King County.
    I. Kreisman, Lawrence. Historic preservation in Seattle. II. Title.
    F899.S48A2   1999
    363.6'9'0979777—dc21                                                   99-36928
                                                                                CIP

The paper used in this publication is acid-free and recycled from 10 percent post-consumer and at least 50 percent pre-consumer waste. It meets the minimum requirements of American National Standard for Information Sciences—Permanence of Paper for Printed Library Materials, ANSI Z39.48–1984. ♾ ♻

This project has been partially funded by

⬤ King County Landmarks and Heritage Commission
Hotel Motel Tax Revenues
and
Historic Seattle Preservation Foundation

*Realistic hope for the future depends upon public and private awareness, concern, and civic involvement, with a real commitment to human values above material considerations. It is to this commitment, and the vital part that it must play in building a good and livable city, that we must dedicate ourselves.*

*Victor Steinbrueck (1911–1985)*

This book is dedicated to the memory of Victor Steinbrueck, a visionary, articulate, and passionate spokesperson for the value of our built environment. His tireless commitment to Seattle's urban resources and inspiration to fellow citizens led to the preservation of Pioneer Square and Pike Place Market. He was a writer, artist, architect, and, most of all, assertive civic activist of great integrity and outspoken honesty. His efforts reaffirm that people can and do make a difference in determining the values upon which their city builds.

# Contents

# PREFACE

*Historic Preservation in Seattle* was published by Historic Seattle Preservation and Development Authority in 1985 to coincide with the the National Trust for Historic Preservation conference held in Seattle that year. Funded by the National Endowment for the Arts, Historic Seattle, and a number of local firms and organizations, the book outlined the history of the preservation movement in Seattle, its ordinances, historic districts, individual landmarks, and significant rehabilitation and adaptive reuse projects to that point. It was and continues to be a valuable resource for teachers, students, design professionals, and the general public.

The first edition of *Historic Preservation in Seattle* was a collective effort requiring the critical and financial support of many people and organizations. The National Endowment for the Arts Design Arts Program provided initial funds for research, writing, and editing of the manuscript. Local foundations, architecture and development firms, and businesses generously donated funds that were matched by Historic Seattle Preservation and Development Authority. The City of Seattle Urban Conservation Division provided office support and editorial services. Mollie Tremaine, Cindy Hughes, and the council members of Historic Seattle assisted the author in raising funds.

Karen Gordon, City Historic Preservation Officer, and Lawson Elliott, then Executive Director of Historic Seattle, shared their expertise, making themselves available to read and critically evaluate the manuscript drafts. Earl Layman, then City Historic Preservation Officer, outlined the development of the preservation program with which he was so integrally involved for over a decade. The Reverend Dennis Andersen, former archivist at Special Collections and Preservation Division, University of Washington Libraries and an expert in local history and architecture, read the manuscript and provided valuable comment, as did Wayne Dodge, Grant Hildebrand, John Chaney, and Ellen Miller-Wolfe.

Historic photographs from the University of Washington Libraries Special Collections and Preservation Division and from the Museum of History and Industry were complemented by additional photographs taken by Mary Randlett, Kal Malone, and Dick Busher.

Seattle's Landmarks Preservation Ordinance was enacted in 1973 and celebrated its 25th birthday in 1998. The King County Landmarks and Heritage Program celebrated its 20th anniversary of public service in 1998 and, in the year 2000, will celebrate the 20th anniversary of its designating ordinance. Historic Seattle was founded in 1974 and celebrates its silver anniversary in 1999. This second edition is entitled *Made to Last: Historic Preservation in Seattle and King County* to reflect its expanded coverage and to celebrate these milestones.

Since the initial publication, there have been changes to city ordinances, changing levels of support at the federal, state, and local levels for rehabilitation of historic buildings, some major preservation losses for the city and county, and court cases that redefine the abilities of preservation bodies to safeguard landmark properties. Of particular note has been the physical loss of an important downtown theater, from which has come legislation that substantially protects remaining downtown theaters. The removal of two churches from landmarks board review through legal action is a distinct loss, but the willingness of the congregations at St. James Cathedral and other churches to work creatively with the

Seattle Landmarks Preservation Board has produced nationally recognized preservation and rehabilitation projects. After several years of head-to-head disagreements over the preservation, maintenance, and renovation of historic schools, the Seattle School District and the Seattle Landmarks Preservation Board are now efficiently moving ahead with shared goals to preserve and protect neighborhood landmarks while incorporating technical educational specifications.

An outstanding countywide preservation program has been developed that, in addition to designation of properties, offers one of the state's largest grants-in-aid programs, as well as a program of technical assistance that serves property owners, government agencies, and heritage organizations of all types throughout Seattle and King County. In addition to its work in unincorporated King County, the Office of Cultural Resources has established interlocal agreements that permit this preservation program to extend into incorporated cities outside Seattle, thereby broadening the ability of the county to identify, designate, and protect landmark properties in previously unprotected areas.

In both city and county, there have also been excellent projects that successfully balance the economic viability of old buildings with preserving them for continued use by the public. Some of these stories are told in *Made to Last*.

The new edition has been supported by Special Projects grant funds from the King County Landmarks and Heritage Commission Hotel Motel Tax Revenues and additional funds from Historic Seattle Preservation Foundation, Patsy Collins, Allied Arts Foundation, and Carl Smith of Antique Liquidators. Funds supported archival research, oral interviews, preparation of new chapters, revisions and corrections to existing chapters, photographic documentation of projects included in the new edition, and acquisition of photographs and graphic materials. Fees for photographs in chapter 8 were generously waived by the *Seattle Times*.

Direction, documentation quality, and technical accuracy were evaluated by an advisory committee consisting of heritage specialists brought together to help define the scope of the new edition, assist the author in research and development, and review manuscript drafts. Committee members were drawn from Historic Seattle (John Chaney), Urban Conservation (Karen Gordon), Seattle Landmarks Preservation Board (Dennis Andersen, former chair), King County Cultural Resources (Julie Koler, Clo Copass), Allied Arts Historic Preservation Committee (Mimi Sheridan), and the design community (Ron Murphy). Charles Payton, Kate Krafft, and Earl Layman were additional readers. I am most grateful to them for their thoughtful and constructive comments.

I am especially appreciative of the time and attention Julie Koler and Clo Copass devoted to preparing written material on King County programs, and of the editorial thoroughness of Mimi Sheridan, whose expertise in community and neighborhood planning was of great help. Likewise, Dennis Andersen's perspective as architectural historian, author, and former Landmarks Preservation Board member contributed an outstanding critical voice throughout manuscript preparation. He also suggested the title of this new edition. I am blessed by his friendship and support.

The University of Washington Press saw the importance of a new edition and agreed to underwrite production costs—a gesture that has made the project a reality. Allied Arts Foundation provided a grant to Mary Randlett, whose black-and-white photography did so much to breathe life into the preservation story of the first edition, so that she could document additional work for the second edition. Maps were developed by Scott Souchock, whose graphic contributions to the Seattle Architectural Foundation and Historic Seattle have been of great benefit. Pamela Bruton provided invaluable copyediting and a fresh point of view. Virginia Hand, with whom I have collaborated on four books and who gave clarity and visual cohesiveness to the first edition, has extended her talents to the new one.

Finally, for 18 years, my partner, Wayne Dodge, has provided the emotional support, the nurturing and secure environment, and the constructive framework in which I have been encouraged to pursue the work I believe in, regardless of its monetary rewards. I am blessed by his presence in my life and by his personal interest and involvement in my work.

# INTRODUCTION

On September 22, 1998, a celebration was held at the Seattle Asian Art Museum to acknowledge the 25th anniversary of the establishment of the Seattle Landmarks Preservation Ordinance. It recognized the efforts of more than 70 citizen volunteers who served on the Landmarks Preservation Board during that time and acknowledged the stewardship of historic landmarks by local property owners. It was an appropriate time to reflect on the city's accomplishments resulting from its landmarks program and the commitments of individuals and community groups.

Historic preservation accomplishments over the last 25 years have been exemplary. Probably the most telling evidence in support of this statement is the fact that relatively few significant buildings have been demolished. A high degree of community commitment was demonstrated in the early years by strong political support from city hall and more recently by responsive and responsible private sector initiative. The city's initial commitment, including the establishment of successful procedures for creating and protecting historic districts and individual landmarks and the institution of local incentives, was a significant factor in these successes. Fortunately, during the 1980s—just prior to a critical building boom—a number of downtown Seattle's significant buildings were designated under the landmarks ordinance. In Seattle's downtown and neighborhood plans, in unincorporated King County, and, to a lesser extent, in municipalities within the county, the preservation of historic buildings was established as an important public ethic.

Even with this enviable track record, and to some extent because of it, residents of Seattle and King County must be alert. Having such well-established and long-running programs, there is a tendency to rest on laurels and simply maintain what has thus far been achieved. Instead, preservationists must focus their creative energies on using the historic preservation tools that have been established for effective community rebuilding.

If the message at the 25th anniversary celebration was that we have much to celebrate, it also brought to mind many of the missed opportunities, failures, and losses that have gone hand in hand with the successes, both in Seattle and within King County. Demolition—either fast as implosions or painstakingly slow—has been a constant companion. Some buildings, such as a former Presbyterian church and a telephone exchange on lower Queen Anne Hill (part of the Hansen Bakery complex) and the Perry Hotel on First Hill (known as Cabrini Hospital for most of its life), were torn down in virtually no time. They were there one day, and the next day they were reduced to rubble. The weeds growing behind chain-link fence were all that reminded us that something important might have been there. Replacements, when they occur, often have little if any of the character-defining features, well-planned proportions, and distinctive materials that composed the lost buildings.

At the opposite extreme, the Music Hall Theatre took months to bring down because the reinforced-concrete building required a lot of muscle to level. Implosion would have been instant, but the wrecking company wanted to salvage whatever fragments might be reusable and salable. The end result was the same—weeds growing behind a chain-link fence, followed by interim surface parking as financing for a hotel on the site failed to materialize. Six years later, an office building is proposed in its place.

It is no different in King County, where farmhouses, barns, commercial buildings, and mills that epitomized rural life are collapsing from abandonment and neglect or being razed for shopping centers, business parks, and residential subdivisions. Little by little, Seattle and King County residents are watching their architectural, cultural, and social landmarks disappear. It is puzzling that this is happening in a region known for its preservation efforts and the home to an educated and culturally active community.

In 1988, I was asked to reflect upon the state of Seattle preservation for an issue of *Arcade,* a local architecture and design journal. It was a critical piece that found fault in a number of areas. Ten years later, in 1998, I was again asked to offer some perspectives on the local preservation movement. As I reread the earlier piece, I recognized much in the present that has not changed substantially for the better. However, I also saw ways in which, over the past 10 years, the preservation community has successfully weathered challenges, matured, developed methods to cope with growth and change, and educated thousands of old-time residents and newcomers alike to the value of this region's built heritage.

A casualty in the preservation arena has been community leadership. Many people have the attitude, "Why worry anymore? We know better now." Twenty-five years ago preservation was a legitimate "cause" stimulated by Mayor Uhlman's belief that historic and urban preservation was "a task of the highest priority for the City of Seattle," by Earl Layman's enthusiasm and architectural fervor, by Victor Steinbrueck's vocal and organizing spirit, and by Art Skolnik's articulate and frequently stimulating rhetoric. At the time, there was a sense of continuing growth in the field. There was much to do, and federal, state, and local government made a substantial financial commitment to preservation.

These were also times when jurisdictional disputes over city control of state properties made local "landmark" protection of certain properties impossible. Fortunately, buildings of importance—the Skinner Building and its exotic 5th Avenue Theatre and the Olympic Hotel—were protected, not by city ordinance but by committed preservationists in government and the private sector. They were supported by an interested, caring, and sometimes vocal citizenry who convinced the owners of these properties of their value and potential reuse.

Beginning with the fight to save the Pike Place Market in the 1960s, through the Olympic Hotel meetings, and on to the public hearings on Franklin High School, Seattle residents showed that there was a user public with a strong opinion on what private development and public agencies do. There was, of course, a negative side to such public process. Community groups, parks boards, school boards, and the Seattle City Council were sometimes convinced that another set of priorities was more important than preservation. In the past decade, Karen Gordon, the City Historic Preservation Officer, has worked effectively with the Office of the Mayor, the city council, and other city departments to maintain the legitimacy, integrity, and independence of the preservation program as it was originally intended.

Progress in preservation, then and now, is mixed. The controversies surrounding the protection and preservation of Franklin High School, buildings at Fort Lawton, Adams Elementary School, and Martha Washington School in the 1980s have been repeated, with variations, with the Music Hall Theatre, First Methodist Church, First Covenant Church, the Perry Hotel, Ballard High School, and Latona School in the 1990s—to name only a few. The playing out of each of these preservation dramas demonstrates that, regardless of the existence of progressive ordinances and legislation, seemingly rock-solid buildings are, in reality, as fragile as sand castles. Without a concerned and vocal citizenry, they must depend for their survival on how they fit in the modern marketplace.

I am personally disappointed that so few people speak out on preservation and the importance of historic neighborhoods and districts to the city. Rarely do our voices reach the media, stimulate public discussion, and get the message across. If we search for fault in this lack of a preservation constituency, it probably can be traced back to our own education. The value of our buildings traditionally has been lost to generations of students for whom cultural studies and intellectual and arts development have been all but eliminated. There is a great need for broadening the base of awareness and appreciation of architecture and the built heritage in teachers and the children they teach.

Many adults do not understand their world in a visual way. How can we expect a visually alert and concerned citizenry when our teachers and peers have no understanding of buildings or streets or the important part that color, texture, and scale play in the way we perceive our environment? How can we expect them to form a value system in which historic structures and cultural resources have any meaning or traditional neighborhoods are regarded with respect?

The success this region has enjoyed in preserving its heritage continues to be dependent upon a vigilant citizenry. We have the laws, but how do we create the ethic? Those who are concerned about historic preservation and the quality of urban life must continually keep well informed, actively participate in forums and hearings, and remain a visible and vocal constituency. The outstanding preservation program that exists today was created through citizen-initiated litigation, formal petitions, endless lobbying and letter writing, and hundreds of meetings and hearings. There is no easy way!

*Seattle from Elliott Bay, 1985.*

# Chapter One

# THE EVOLUTION OF SEATTLE AND KING COUNTY

*I must not leave the truth unstated, that it is
no question of expediency or feeling whether we
shall preserve the buildings of past times or not.
We have no right whatever to touch them. They
are not ours. They belong partly to those who
built them, and partly to all generations of
mankind who are to follow us.*

John Ruskin, Seven Lamps of Architecture, *1849*

Seattle is 148 years old in 1999—just a toddler by European standards and a brash adolescent compared to its East Coast and Midwest neighbors. During the 17th and 18th centuries, when the thirteen colonies were bringing English and Continental lifestyles to America and clearing land for towns and cities, the Puget Sound area was a center for Native cultures, thriving with an abundance of natural resources, fish, game, land, navigable waterways, and a mild climate. Great longhouses were the first "mixed-use" buildings in the Northwest.

During the 19th century, the Industrial Revolution and the development of railroads pushed settlements westward to the goldfields of California and northward to Oregon Territory. But with the excep-

tion of Hudson's Bay Company trappers and early explorers, Puget Sound remained largely the province of Native American tribes because of its inaccessibility by overland routes.

The Federal Oregon Donation Land Act of 1850 did much to encourage settlement, particularly along waterways that were accessible by boat or canoe. In 1850, John Holgate navigated the Duwamish River to Elliott Bay. In 1851, Luther Collins, Henry Van Asselt, Jacob Maple, Samuel Maple, and their families settled along the Duwamish, followed by others who farmed the White River valley. In December 1852, King County was designated a governmental entity while still a part of Oregon Territory. At that time, it extended all the way to the Pacific Ocean. Shortly thereafter, on March 2, 1853, the U.S. Senate passed the law that created Washington Territory. In 1889, Washington became a state.

The first Euro-American settlers in "New York Alki"—the Denny, Terry, Boren, and Bell families— traveled overland to Oregon and sailed north to reach the shores of the Sound in 1851. They moved to a more protected location the following spring, naming it Seattle after a tribal chief.

*Seattle from Denny Hill, 1882. Prominent building at top center is the territorial university.*

*Yesler Wharf during major snowstorm, January 1880.*

Seattle represents a particularly western phenomenon—the boom town. Like Denver, Salt Lake City, and San Francisco, Seattle's growth into a major metropolis has been extraordinarily rapid. Unlike its older East Coast counterparts, such as New York or Philadelphia, the longhouses and communal meeting grounds of the Duwamish, Snoqualmie, Puyallup, Skykomish, Muckleshoot, Suquamish, and Tulalip peoples were within the recollections of the parents or grandparents of Seattle's oldest residents, reflecting the swiftness with which settlers moved onto the land and adapted it for their own uses. With the exception of county archaeological sites that contain the remains of Native American villages and meeting grounds, Seattle's residences, churches, and commercial buildings do not date from a time earlier than the late 19th century.

Nevertheless, these buildings are as significant as 17th- and early-18th-century buildings might be to older cities that can claim earlier settlement. In fact, the local awareness of the relevance of Seattle's late-19th and early-20th-century buildings has protected these resources. In some other cities, such relatively new additions to the cityscape tend to be neglected or ignored as insignificant when compared to the seeming importance of saving resources that testify to an older heritage or of making a grand civic gesture. One case in point is Philadelphia, which protected its Society Hill townhouses but cleared much of its late-19th-century warehouse district to make way for a great plaza fronting Independence Hall. Another is St. Louis, which cleared blocks of its 19th-century cast-iron front and brick riverfront, stockpiled its salvage for future use, and lost it in flood before it could be reused in later projects. Consequently, the city has little to remind people of that river front's role in developing the West apart from a glistening arch to symbolize its role as a "gateway to the West." New York, with 69 historic districts, has done much to recognize and protect areas of importance, although it has lost some of its greatest mansions, significant early skyscrapers, and important churches to the rapid northward expansion, shifts in use, and increasing density of Manhattan.

Seattle's contemporary skyline, set against an incomparable backdrop of mountain ranges and water, only hints at the city's dramatic and colorful

*Denny Renton Clay and Coal Company, Renton, 1907.*

*Weber's Shingle Mill, Redmond.*

*View of David Thomas Denny at his cabin. He supervised repair work in September 1899 on the Snoqualmie Pass Wagon Road east of North Bend.*

history. Indian wars, railroad and lumber barons, gold rush fever, maritime competition, ethnic settlements, and dramatic earthmoving and waterway rechanneling have all left their mark upon the physical shape of the city.

The founders of Seattle were optimistic, calling their 1851 settlement New York Alki—the latter being Chinook Jargon meaning "by and by," "after a while," or "in the future." The fledgling community that developed along the shores of Elliott Bay in 1852 centered its economic, social, and political existence on the steam-powered sawmill operated by Henry Yesler. From that strategic point, land was gradually logged and cleared as the town expanded north and east, limited in its growth by the nearly impassable hills adjacent to the waterfront settlement. Timber was sawn into boards at Yesler's mill and shipped out to other West Coast ports. This stimulated the growth of the shipbuilding industry as well.

Much of the lumber was destined to feed the enormous construction appetite of 19th-century San Francisco. That appetite spurred the development of mills throughout King County to produce shingles and sawn boards, as well as major logging operations to provide the raw materials. As land was cleared, agriculture, hops growing, and dairy farming became important livelihoods. The discovery of coal at Black River near modern-day Renton in 1853 stimulated the building of a road to Lake Washington, where coal could be barged to Seattle. But roads came late. Early settlements and supply centers were initially serviced only by small steamboats that regularly transported people, goods, and supplies to communities that sprang up along the shores of lakes, rivers, and Puget Sound.

Seattle's first real spurt of growth resulted from the construction of several important rail lines. By 1890, the Northern Pacific, the Columbia & Puget Sound Railroad, and the Seattle, Lakeshore & Eastern had formed vital links to lumber, farming, and coal mining communities in western King County. The influx of settlers from the East and Midwest stimulated a thriving business center in Seattle, nearly all of it constructed from the local material of choice—wood. An 1889 fire destroyed the central business district. Fortunately, the fire occurred at a time of prosperity, and businessmen immediately rebuilt the commercial core in brick, stone, cast iron, and heavy timber. Architects from the East, the Midwest, and California flocked to Seattle to take advantage of the building opportunities. They designed

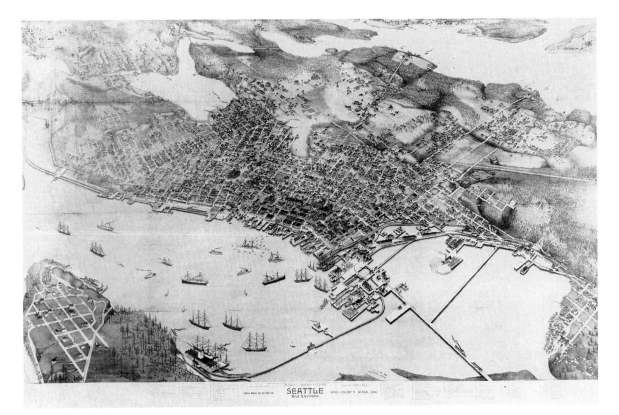

*Seattle and environs, King County, Washington, 1891. From* The West Shore.

*C. C. Calkins resort hotel (1890) on Mercer Island became the Murray Institute. It burned in 1908.*

brick and stone buildings that, with early-20th-century brick warehouses and commercial blocks, constitute today's Pioneer Square Historic District.

The nationwide Panic and Depression of 1893 slowed growth in Seattle and King County. But the discovery of gold in the Yukon in 1897 prompted a second and greater influx of people to the shores of Puget Sound. Seattle became the major banking, outfitting, and departure point for Alaska and, subsequently, the settling place for many of those return-

ing from the goldfields. The population grew from 42,837 in 1890 to 237,194 in 1910, according to contemporary census figures.

The Seattle, Renton & Southern ushered in an era of transportation lines that spurred development of Columbia City and neighboring communities. The construction of the Puget Sound Electric Railway (commonly referred to as the Interurban) beginning in 1902 established a fast, low-cost passenger and freight link between Tacoma in Pierce County and Seattle. Service was extended in 1910 north to Everett, in Snohomish County, and branches to Renton and other outlying King County communities furthered suburban development because of the ease with which people and goods could reach Seattle markets.

The city's heightened prosperity during the second decade of the 20th century was evidenced in handsome brick- and terra-cotta-faced skyscrapers, banking headquarters, and department stores that arose north of the older business district. A major theatrical district was also established that, if one can believe local civic boosters, was second only to New York in the quantity and variety of its offerings.

As if to announce to the world that Seattle had come of age, the city staged the Alaska-Yukon-Pacific

*Railroad Avenue (now Alaskan Way) in 1908 was a tangle of tracks and traffic.*

Exposition in 1909. Its gleaming white classical buildings, fountains, and axial panoramas drew visitors from around the world and was a financial success. The fair was also a gesture to the Pacific Rim countries to promote Seattle as the commercial "Gateway to the Orient." Evidence of the national City Beautiful ideal in Seattle can be found in the exposition buildings and grounds; the development of an extensive park and boulevard system recommended by the Olmsted Brothers in 1903; the master planning of a commercial and retail district on the original university grounds by the Metropolitan Building Company beginning in 1907 (of which the Cobb Building is the only remaining piece by New York architects Howells & Stokes); and the failed proposal for a civic center and major transportation and harbor improvements by Virgil Bogue in 1911. Collectively these designs signaled the growing influence of design professionals in city planning, as well as the acceptance of the City Beautiful philosophy that aesthetic and physical solutions could resolve many urban problems.

But it was as the City Practical that Seattle really showed its muscle. J. D. Ross developed City Light and committed the city to improved utilities. Largely because of the leadership of two engineers, R. H.

*Second Avenue (view north from James Street) became a major thoroughfare, parade ground, and banking headquarters as skyscrapers, such as the Alaska Building (right), were erected.*

The Hiram Chittenden Locks opened Lakes Washington and Union to Puget Sound. Ballard shingle and saw mills are a part of this c. 1920 vista.

Lake Washington Boulevard in 1914. In the distance, below Mount Rainier, is Bailey Peninsula (now Seward Park).

Aerial view of the Alaska-Yukon-Pacific Exposition on the grounds of the University of Washington in 1909.

Denny Hill regrading well under way, c. 1905. The prestigious Denny Hotel, completed in 1903, would soon be demolished as the hillside was lowered.

Thomson and George Cotterill, the city established an effective water and sewer system. Engineering feats on a scale seldom attempted in an American city produced extensive regrading (raising and lowering of streets using hydraulic hoses and excavating equipment), filling of tide flats, and cutting of canals to provide shipping lanes and building sites for the expanding city. In the process, the water level of Lake Washington was lowered, adding significantly to shoreline parks and boulevards proposed by the Olmsted Brothers.

These projects increased access to newly developing residential districts to the north and east of the downtown while creating new land to the south and west for shipping, railroads, and industry. Unfortunately, regrading also eliminated parts of existing neighborhoods and razed much of what remained of the city's early buildings, including simple frame residences and row houses.

After World War I, the principles espoused in the City Beautiful movement were dismissed as belonging to a more romantic and increasingly distant era. The preoccupation with aesthetics was to be increas-

*Puget Sound Electric Railroad served the Everett to Seattle interurban run.*

*Mike's Service Station in Renton, on the old Issaquah highway.*

ingly replaced by more pragmatic issues of health, safety, and development pressure. By 1915, Pacific Highway had become the first major highway in a developing system of paved roads that eventually would enable automobile and truck transportation to erode the effectiveness of the Interurban system. Ultimately, the move led to its shutdown (1929 for the Tacoma-Seattle run and 1939 for the Everett-Seattle run).

The Great Depression brought downtown commercial construction to a standstill. Few privately initiated architecture and planning projects during the 1930s came to fruition. But federally funded Works Progress Administration projects, including dams, highways, and other public-works projects, supported the local workforce. By 1939, a prototypical public-housing project—Yesler Terrace—began to take

shape on the site of a decaying residential district that ran along Yesler Way. In the downtown, a new and elegant Woolworth's filled the corner of Third and Pine Street in 1940, signaling confidence in economic recovery. World War II stimulated military industries and brought workers to Puget Sound to work in the defense industry, including the Naval Shipyards in Bremerton and at Boeing in Seattle and Renton. With them came some federally funded wartime housing. The post–World War II shortage of housing spurred developments in expanding suburban areas outside Seattle city limits and the annexation by the city of suburban areas. The postwar "baby boom" and job opportunities stimulated further growth.

The opening of the Lacey V. Murrow Bridge across Lake Washington in 1941—the world's first concrete floating bridge and its longest—stimulated residential growth on Mercer Island and the Eastside. A freeway system and a second bridge across Lake Washington in the 1960s led to further dramatic changes in King County that shifted it from rural to suburban and urban. Although municipalities had begun to form in King County as early as the 1890s and the first decade of the 20th century, additional periods of incorporation took place between 1947 and 1961 and again beginning in 1989 and into the present.

Seattle manifested a prevailing spirit of optimism about the future in preparing for the Century 21 World's Fair in 1962. The fair left a permanent legacy to the city in the form of a major cultural and recreational complex at the edge of the downtown that signaled the growing maturity of local performing arts groups—the Seattle Symphony, Seattle Opera, and Seattle Repertory Theatre. The establishment and growth of the Seattle Arts Commission, Seattle Design Commission, and Allied Arts during this period were significant and have led to the rich and varied arts and cultural opportunities that are offered in the region today.

At the same time, the city ushered in a comprehensive plan that focused public attention on key issues. New interests in historic preservation, adaptive reuse of older buildings, revitalization of old neighborhoods, and the creation of new environments for living in downtown were beginning to surface. Efforts in these areas, particularly in the 15-year period from 1970 through 1985, resulted in the establishment of Seattle's international and national preservation reputation. The city established historic

*Yesler Terrace Housing Project was a progressive locally generated design for multifamily housing on First Hill.*

*The completion of Interstate 5 through Seattle divided neighborhoods and destroyed residential buildings that knit communities together. High-rise buildings constructed in the 1980s pushed the community to control height and mass of new construction.*

district protection for Pioneer Square in 1970 and for the Pike Place Market in 1971. Other districts followed. The city adopted its Landmarks Preservation Ordinance in 1973 and set up an 11 member review board and an Office of Historic Preservation that year, setting the stage for nominating and designating individual landmarks. In 1974, the Historic Seattle Preservation and Development Authority was established to do meaningful preservation projects.

In terms of its built resources, Seattle has been fortunate. The regrading efforts undertaken in the city destroyed a great many of its early buildings, but they also continually opened up new areas to development, leaving some of the oldest sections of the city, such as Pioneer Square, untouched and preserved, in their neglected state, until a time when their potential could be realized. Moreover, economic recessions during the late 1960s and early 1970s prevented the then "American dream" of urban renewal from replacing the older urban fabric of streets and buildings that are now a source of pride for their visual and economic contributions to the city.

During the 1970s, as the nation approached its Bicentennial Celebration, King County residents focused attention on their local history, finding in their community roots a source of pride and accomplishment. The built reminders of this past were important; they reflected the contributions that had been made by settlers to the development of Northwest agriculture, industry, transportation, and communities.

Coinciding with this interest in community heritage was increasing concern about the rapid changes occurring in King County. Growth was no longer confined to Seattle city limits but spread outward to embrace less dense, less expensive lands on the periphery. Farmlands in the rich, fertile valleys surrounding Seattle were particularly vulnerable because of the ease with which they lent themselves to industrial, business, and housing development. Much irreversible damage was done to the fragile components of rural King County—active farmlands, significant pioneer

*Pacific Coast Condensed Milk Company, Carnation, was part of a large dairy industry that packed and distributed its products far further than the Northwest.*

homesteads, and town centers. The built reminders of its history were being razed at an alarming rate or simply collapsing from neglect and natural decay. With a mind toward preserving those elements of value, concerned citizens and King County officials encouraged the county to undertake an inventory and evaluation of significant historic sites beginning in 1972 and continuing to the present.

The community's interest in rediscovering and promoting its heritage led to the formation of the Association of King County Historical Organizations (AKCHO) in July 1977 to provide a forum for the interests of the many heritage groups and activists around the county. Since its incorporation, it has become one of the most effective heritage groups in the state and continues to be a sustaining force behind public history and historic preservation in King County. The county established an Office of Historic Preservation in 1978 and adopted a Landmarks Ordinance in 1980 with a nine-member commission to designate sites. A Heritage Resource Protection Plan was begun in 1983 and prepared in 1985 to better understand and evaluate cultural resources in the county.

While there have been losses, with nearly 30 years of preservation planning and implementation to their credit, Seattle and King County have protected a significant number of visual reminders of history and have acted as catalysts to encourage the restoration, rehabilitation, and reuse of these resources. The

*Ghosts of the county's agricultural heritage abound. Barn near Carnation, 1979*

following chapters describe the events that led up to the establishment of city and county policies toward preservation and the resulting designation of individual landmarks and historic districts.

Both the city and the county have done much in this regard. But it is, in fact, the efforts of individual property owners with pride in their businesses, homes, gardens, and farmlands that, while often overlooked, provide the major contribution to local preservation. Their stories are also told in this publication. Ultimately their efforts create the all-important base of encouragement and support that furthers preservation and conservation goals in the community.

| | |
|---|---|
| Native American presence, prehistory–1850 | Longhouses |
| King County Anglo-American settlement, c. 1850 | Log houses |
| Henry Yesler's sawmill, 1853 | Sawn lumber for building |
| Discovery of coal near Black River, 1853 | Natural resource puts county on map |
| Shipbuilding and port development | Sail and steam vessels; the development of the "Mosquito Fleet" |
| Railroads to Tacoma, Seattle, and rural areas, 1873–96 | Ease of access to finished materials for construction; cast iron; elevators; terra-cotta as ornament; rapid growth of small communities |
| Seattle fire and rebuilding, 1889–92 | City requirements for brick, stone, and "slow-burning" timber construction; terra-cotta as fireproofing material |
| Nationwide Depression, 1893 | Construction standstill |
| Interurban development, 1896–1939 | Stimulates and focuses town growth |
| Yukon Gold Rush, 1897–98 | Hotels, service, retail |
| Regrading of downtown areas, 1898–1930 | New development areas downtown result in demolition and reconstruction |
| Growth of forest products industry | Mills and wood-processing plants |
| Rise of dairy industry to national prominence | State-of-the-art dairy farms |
| Olmsted Park plan, 1903 | Provision for public open space |
| Alaska Building, 1903–4 | First steel-frame skyscraper |
| Pike Place Market founded, 1907 | Efficient food distribution and sanitation |
| Metropolitan Center Plan, 1907 | Prototype for large-scale urban commercial developments |
| Alaska-Yukon-Pacific Exposition, 1909 | Site planning for the university campus by Olmsted Brothers; grand classical revival presence and promotion of city business |
| Development of the Highlands, 1909 | Exclusive residential enclave with Olmsted-designed plan |

| | |
|---|---|
| Bogue Plan, 1911 | Broad-reaching civic plan (unrealized); implementation of harbor |
| Smith Tower, 1914 | Tallest building outside New York |
| First Seattle zoning ordinance, 1922–23 | Local government controls building size, scale, and location of use |
| Northern Life Tower, 1928–29 | Local response to new zoning law |
| CCC (Conservation Corps), WPA projects, 1930s | Construction of rural and vernacular public buildings in county |
| Yesler Terrace Housing, 1941 | Planned public-housing development |
| Lacey V. Murrow Bridge opens, 1941 | Development of Eastside communities |
| Postwar expansion | Suburban development in King County |
| Northgate Shopping Center, 1950 | Prototype for regional shopping center |
| Century 21 World's Fair, 1962 | Promotes science, technology, and modular housing |
| Interstate 5 completion, 1964–65 | Expansion of suburban communities |
| National Historic Preservation Act, 1966 | Recognition of the importance of preserving built heritage |
| Seattle First Bank headquarters, 1969 | Significant scale change in downtown; 50 floors, 609 feet |
| Pioneer Square Historic District, 1970 | First local government commitment to preservation |
| Landmarks Preservation Ordinance, 1973 | City able to designate and protect individual properties |
| King County Landmarks Ordinance, 1980 | County begins to designate properties |
| 76-story Columbia Sea-First Center, 1985 | Generates controversy over heights |
| CAP limits on heights, 1989 | Height, mass, and square footage controls to reduce impact of future downtown development |
| Growth Management Act, 1990 | |

*The Exchange Building is the backdrop for Elmer Fisher's Burke Building (1889–91), which was demolished in 1971 to make way for a new federal office building.*

# Chapter Two

# THE HISTORIC PRESERVATION MOVEMENT IN SEATTLE

## BUILDING THE FOUNDATIONS

The internationally known British architect and planner Graeme Shankland noted that "a country without a past has the emptiness of a barren continent; and a city without old buildings is like a man without a memory." Former Seattle Mayor Wes Uhlman, a guiding force behind the initial recovery of Pioneer Square, echoed these sentiments: "The old buildings that remind us of the past are the signposts pointing toward a better, richer, more stable future for us all." These attitudes reflect the philosophy that engendered, guided, and continue to direct Seattle's preservation efforts.

The foundations upon which Seattle's preservation program are built evolved from local citizens' pride in their surroundings, their concern for the preservation of significant physical aspects of Northwest heritage, and their interest in maintaining a degree of historic continuity in the downtown and surrounding neighborhoods. These concerns were amplified when important physical elements of that heritage were threatened with destruction for proposed parking garages, traffic arterials, and high-rise

developments. Many of these threats came from within city government itself, under the guise of progress and economic improvement.

As early as the late 1950s and 1960s, architect and teacher Victor Steinbrueck directed the attention of his University of Washington students to studying, drawing, and recording buildings in Pioneer Square. His *Seattle Architecture, 1850–1953,* published in that year, *Seattle Cityscape* (1962), *Seattle Cityscape #2* (1973), and *A Visual Inventory of Buildings and Urban Design Resources for Seattle, Washington,* which he and Folke Nyberg undertook in 1975, did much to publicize and popularize the value of local resources.

During the 1960s, a number of local property owners identified the intrinsic qualities of craftsmanship and character of derelict Skid Road buildings and sought to rehabilitate these properties sensitively. Architect Ralph Anderson and owner/developer Alan Black took financial risk in initially rehabilitating the Capitol Brewing Company Building at First Avenue S. and S. Jackson Street and the Union Trust Building on Occidental Avenue S. and S. Main Street. While several small projects followed,

*From left to right, Ralph Anderson, Al Bumgarder, Ibsen Nelsen, Fred Bassetti, and Victor Steinbrueck in front of the Pioneer Building.*

recommendations to the National Register. That bill also established the Washington State Register of Historic Places (now called the Washington Heritage Register) to recognize regional properties of significance and value. Over 200 properties are listed on the Washington Heritage Register (see Appendix D), and over 20,000 properties are included in the State Inventory of Cultural Resources. The National Register, State Register, and State Inventory are programs administered by the Washington State Office of Archaeology and Historic Preservation. Over 140 of Seattle's historic and cultural resources have been placed in the National Register. More than 80 additional Seattle properties and districts have been identified and formally determined to be eligible for National Register Listing.

The Office of Archaeology and Historic Preservation administers the National Register of Historic Places and the Washington Heritage Register. It provides expertise, services, and training for the protection and preservation of Washington's historic places and is staffed by specialists in history, architectural history, restoration architecture, preservation planning, archaeology, and historic records management.

The National and Washington State Registers are authoritative listings of those properties which deserve to be recognized as significant and protected from destruction or defacement. The National Register of Historic Places is intended to include not only places of national significance but also places of state and local importance. The National Register is a legal instrument that ensures that registered properties will be subject to review if threatened by federal or federally assisted undertakings. Nevertheless, it does not ensure protection from demolition or changes initiated by property owners or other agencies. For this reason, cities, towns, and other political entities throughout the country have found it necessary to offer a greater degree of protection under law to their most valuable built resources and to ensure a public process.

Federal and state actions occurred at a very propitious time with respect to the preservation concerns of some Seattle citizens and officials. In 1968 and 1969, the Seattle Planning Commission hired consultant Victor Steinbrueck to conduct a survey of the historic structures in the Pioneer Square/Skid Road area and to make recommendations for boundaries for a possible historic district. At the time, city officials were concerned primarily with Pioneer Place and its immediately surrounding

historic preservation as a concerted effort supported by government did not occur in Seattle until 1970, when it began to be encouraged by national and state legislation.

The National Register of Historic Places was established in 1966. Through the Historic American Building Survey, the federal government had been recognizing historically and architecturally significant buildings since the Depression years. But the passage of the National Historic Preservation Act of 1966 initiated a broad nationwide effort to identify American cultural resources, to recognize their value, and to provide for or assist in their restoration and protection whenever possible. This legislation also provided for State and National Registers of Historic Places, determined the criteria and procedures for nominating property to those registers, and created the means for distributing federal funds (and, later, tax advantages) to registered properties through matching grants.

In 1967, Washington State Senate Bill Number 363 created the Washington State Advisory Council on Historic Preservation as a review body to evaluate

*The unrestored portal of the Maynard Building frames the east side of First Avenue S. prior to restoration, 1968.*

buildings at First Avenue and Yesler Way. However, the final recommendation included approximately 30 acres of harmonious and contiguous structures, largely constructed in the years immediately following the Great Fire of 1889. In 1969, a nomination for a Pioneer Square/Skid Road Historic District was forwarded to the Washington State Office of Archaeology and Historic Preservation for consideration on the State and National Registers. The nomination was accepted as proposed at both state and federal levels. At the time, it was one of the first and largest districts to be entered in the National Register.

The city recognized that register entry alone would provide insufficient protection for buildings in the district. Consequently, the City Planning Commission and a number of interested citizens drafted a proposed municipal ordinance to establish a historic district locally. After well over a year of struggle and debate, and encouraged by Wes Uhlman, the newly elected mayor, and a newly formed Department of Community Development,

differences were resolved. James D. Braman Jr., director of the department, played a very important role in guiding, developing, and implementing the historic programs. His experience in preservation planning in Denver helped forge more progressive attitudes that countered the prevailing "knock down" philosophy of the planning department and the planning commission at the time. The Pioneer Square Historic District ordinance was passed by the city council and approved by the mayor in May 1970.

As Seattle's first historic preservation legislation, this ordinance established a review board to approve applications for external changes to buildings or public spaces within the district. Several years later, the district was amended by expansions to include approximately 10 additional acres of buildings, including two railway stations, and the district was further protected by the establishment of a special review district with its own review board to act upon changes in height, mass, or use. Much more recent-

*Unrestored window bay and cornice of the Pioneer Building, 1971.*

ly, the two review boards, two ordinances, and two districts were combined into one preservation district encompassing all the salient elements of the previous two ordinances. With over forty square blocks of buildings, 90 percent of which are late-19th- and early-20th-century structures, Pioneer Square has been and, to some extent, continues to be the centerpiece of Seattle's preservation efforts.

Because the district was recognized on the state and national levels very early in terms of the nationwide preservation movement, Seattle had little competition in the early 1970s in applying for and receiving available preservation grants for rehabilitation of Pioneer Square buildings. Even more importantly, the district gained credibility. Banks that had turned away from providing real estate loans for rehabilitation changed their policies once they observed the positive results of these early risk-taking ventures. Private investors and property owners were able to raise the required moneys to accomplish large-scale projects, such as renovating the Pioneer and Grand Central Buildings. The city and other agencies provided additional funds for improvements to public right-of-ways and public spaces. Recently, a second renaissance within Pioneer Square has occurred, occasioned to a great extent by federal tax credits (see chapter 4).

In late 1971, following a heated public debate that culminated in a successful public initiative spearheaded by Victor Steinbrueck, Friends of the Market, Allied Arts, and other local community groups, the city council passed an ordinance establishing the Pike Place Market Historic District. The district is administered by its own historic commission, which carefully monitors and oversees changes in both use and appearance. The case of the Market

was quite different from that of Pioneer Square, where there had been no overall development plan and where nearly all projects have resulted due to private initiative. The original seven-acre Pike Place Market Historic District was part of a larger 22-acre Pike Place Urban Renewal Project. Due to its local designation status, the project goals were redirected to rehabilitation and restoration rather than demolition. The city, using federal urban renewal funds, gradually acquired most of the privately owned properties within the historic district and formulated a systematic plan for rehabilitation and adaptive reuse, as well as new construction. A public nonprofit development authority was established for the purpose of owning, managing, maintaining, and operating the market as a quasi-public institution.

The creation of two local historic districts stimulated the city and its citizens to define their preservation goals in a comprehensive manner. The result of many conferences and community meetings was the drafting of the first Landmarks Preservation Ordinance in 1973, modeled after similar programs in New York City and Denver. It established a citywide landmark preservation/conservation program with a review board to act upon nominations for designation and to process applications for changes to designated properties. It offered a public forum for discussion and a process by which arguments for and against designation could be presented and evaluated.

The 11 volunteer members of the Landmarks Preservation Board are appointed by the mayor and confirmed by the city council for three-year terms. They represent the fields of architecture, history, engineering, finance, law, and real estate management, as well as citizen interests. They have the authority to designate and protect individual landmark properties, sites, objects, and districts, to establish design controls, and to protect significant structures from major alterations and demolition. For specific nomination and designation procedures and guidelines, see appendix B.

To date, approximately 200 individual properties—including commercial and industrial buildings, single- and multifamily residences, fire stations, churches, clubs, parks, clocks, statues, ships, and bridges—have been designated by the Board and approved by the city council. In addition to the initial landmark districts, the board and council approved creation of the International Special Review District, Ballard Avenue, Columbia City, Harvard/Belmont, and Fort Lawton Historic Districts.

*Signs, lights, posted notices, and cobblestone streets make the Pike Place Market a familiar place for those who remember its earlier years.*

The visible sign of the city's legislated commitment to preservation was the establishment, in the summer of 1973, of an Office of Historic Preservation within the Department of Community Development. The lead staff person in this office, Earl Layman, was one of the nation's first municipal historic preservation officers. This action set the direction that other cities would soon take in adding a professional arm to already existing volunteer and grassroots efforts.

As the responsibilities of the Office of Historic Preservation (now the Urban Conservation Office in the Department of Neighborhoods) expanded and as budgets permitted, professional staff was hired to administer the several historic districts and the city-wide landmarks preservation program. Office staff consults with civic groups, public agencies, and individuals, inspects and investigates potential preservation sites, disseminates public information, and recommends proper methods for the restoration and rehabilitation of properties throughout the city. Initially, inventory, research, and preparation of landmark nominations were functions of the office. In order to establish a more orderly and legitimate base for considering landmark nominations, the city conducted a survey of historic resources in 1978 and 1979.

In the early 1970s the city passed enabling legislation for the establishment of public development authorities to accomplish specific public functions which the City of Seattle cannot undertake. Of these, the one with the broadest influence has been Historic Seattle Preservation and Development Authority, created in 1974 as a public non profit development authority dealing with historic properties. The authority has acted as a catalyst to identify significant local landmarks that are neglected or threatened with destruction but which possess the potential to be reused and again successfully compete in the marketplace. Using capital initially provided by the city—$600,000 in federal revenue-sharing seed money—the agency managed to complete 22 projects by 1985, generating $22 million in private capital. These projects included surplus schools, fire stations, residences, commercial buildings, a street clock, and a steam ferry.

In recent years, Historic Seattle has had to contend with the reality of the expense of preservation projects, the volatility of the marketplace, and the limited number of private backers for projects. Consequently, the agency has used its unique position to assemble public/private partnerships in which private investors and lending institutions work cooperatively with local government to finance and carry out large- and small-scale projects. In this way, it has completed some outstanding low-income housing and commercial projects in cooperation with Seattle Housing Resources Group and others. Its feasibility studies have helped save Fourth Church of Christ Scientist from sale to developers, and its education programs have turned thousands of residents and newcomers into preservation supporters and activists.

## DEVELOPING INCENTIVES

Many of the restoration, rehabilitation, and adaptive reuse projects initiated in the 1970s and early 1980s were prompted by a favorable federal system of tax credits and depreciation that made "affordable" the relatively expensive process of refurbishing older buildings and bringing them up to code. The Tax Reform Act of 1986 changed the method by which these benefits were figured. Property owners and potential developers had to serious-

*The Stimson/Green residence was one of the earliest projects of Historic Seattle. Timely purchase and local landmarks protection of the exterior and significant interior spaces were key to its preservation.*

*The Dexter Horton Building, Arctic Club, Rainier Club, and First United Methodist Church (left to right) hold their own against the encroaching high-rise office towers of the Central Business District.*

ly weigh the cost of rehabilitating their buildings in relation to the return on their investments.

Coincidentally, new construction in the Central Business District in the late 1980s led to an overbuilt office market. That, coupled with a recession and high interest rates, contributed toward foreclosures, bankruptcies, and high vacancy rates for recently restored buildings in Pioneer Square and important early skyscrapers, such as the Alaska, Arctic, and Dexter Horton Buildings. In the latter cases, the City of Seattle made an outstanding decision to purchase these for municipal offices.

As explained in the city's *Historic Preservation in Seattle: A Guide to Incentives and Procedures,* prepared in 1991, the State of Washington sought ways to counteract the lack of incentives to developers by passing a law in 1985 allowing a "special valuation" for certain historic properties. Prior to its passage, owners rehabilitating historic buildings were subject to increased property taxes once the improvements

were made. The primary benefit of the law is that during the 10-year special valuation period, property taxes do not reflect substantial improvements made to the historic property. Eligible properties, as defined by the Seattle City Council, are designated landmarks or contributing buildings located within National Register or local historic districts. More than 100 property owners have used this program since its inception. Their rehabilitation projects represent hundreds of millions of dollars of private reinvestment throughout Seattle and have produced rehabilitated commercial and residential spaces, including hundreds of units of affordable housing.

Current Use Taxation, a program initiated by the state in 1992, continued to encourage rehabilitation by allowing city and county landmarks and properties listed on the National Register of Historic Places to qualify for a 50 percent reduction in the taxable value of the land portion of the assessment. This and other incentives within King County, such as low-interest loans and grants, are discussed in chapter 5.

Other incentives offered by the city include zoning and building code relief. For a designated landmark, the director of the Department of Design, Construction, and Land Use may authorize a use not otherwise permitted in a certain zone. This provision provides flexibility of use to encourage the preservation and use of historic buildings. At the same time, the Seattle Building Code, which is adopted by the city council to accompany the Uniform Building Code, allows the director of the Department of Design, Construction, and Land Use to modify specific requirements of the building code for landmark buildings. The director is given the discretion to request alternative requirements that will still result in a reasonable degree of safety to the public and occupants of the building.

The Downtown Zoning Chapter of the Land Use and Zoning Code established a mechanism for the transfer of development rights for designated landmarks in office, retail, and mixed-use areas. To encourage building preservation, rehabilitation, and restoration, a property owner is permitted to sell unused development rights to other developers.

As a disincentive for razing or altering historic properties, the city also identified 15 buildings in the retail core for which bonuses for a major retail store or performing arts use would not be granted unless the buildings' facades were preserved. It also was made clear that development on a site that resulted in the destruction of a designated Seattle landmark was not allowed to acquire additional development rights through a floor area bonus.

Preservation interests often follow the ebb and flow of economics and development. The construction boom in downtown Seattle in the early 1980s resulted in demolition of numerous buildings that were part of the city's historic fabric. Their loss increased awareness of preservation's importance to our city. Both the Seattle 2000 report and the 1985 Downtown Land Use Plan addressed these challenges to some extent. As the city enters a new period of building development in the late 1990s and into the next millennium, residents need to be vigilant or the last vestiges of small-scale independent retail and residential structures in central and neighborhood business districts will disappear, just as many of the farms and outbuildings that defined King County have been razed for residential development, business parks, and shopping malls.

Ironically, growth management's emphasis on focusing growth in developed areas is one of preservation's largest challenges. Many of Seattle's oldest neighborhood commercial areas are threatened with redevelopment. Increased housing density brings in new residents to help these businesses prosper, but existing housing and early small-scale commercial buildings are often demolished to build larger apartment or mixed-use structures. These areas are zoned for 30- to 65-foot buildings, but the existing older structures are only 10–20 feet in height. New ways are needed to encourage economic use of older buildings to retain neighborhood character.

The lack of sufficient economic incentives for preservation on the federal, state, and local levels encourages demolition. Preservation is still largely a matter of personal dedication and investment. Economic incentives, such as "highest and best use taxation," discourage preservation of existing buildings, giving preference to the hope of making large profits by demolishing the old and building new structures. The inadequacies of economic incentives for property owners, combined with the tremendous potential profits, mean that many owners can claim economic hardship as a reason for demolishing historic structures.

New methods for protection and preservation of these fragile neighborhoods are being explored, not limited to the traditional landmark review process. One potential option being discussed is the formation of conservation districts, recognition given a historic area but with criteria and controls less stringent than those for a historic district.

## Challenges

There have been numerous new challenges in the legal, financial, and regulatory arenas over the past two decades. Some of these simply ended in the demolition of important parts of our history. Others proved to be the impetus for new approaches to preservation and the adoption of new legislation that will be the foundation of preservation efforts into the 21st century.

The fight to save the Music Hall Theatre was the primary rallying point for Allied Arts, preservation groups, and individuals during the 1980s. After this outstanding building was demolished in 1992 despite strong public support for its preservation, the city worked with these groups to develop an ordinance that encouraged the preservation of the

*Demolition of the Music Hall Theatre spurred the community to develop a method to preserve remaining downtown theaters.*

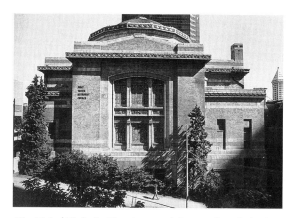

*First United Methodist Church contested city control over its landmark site and won its case in the courts.*

remaining historic theaters by using transfer of development rights. This ordinance allows the city to buy development rights from the owner of a historic theater in exchange for preserving the building. The city will then sell these rights to another downtown property owner wanting to build a larger building than would otherwise be allowed on the site.

Less publicly conspicuous was the legal challenge posed against Landmarks Preservation Board jurisdiction by two churches in the downtown area. First United Methodist Church took its landmarks designation to the courts, arguing interference in its practice of religion, although it had never dealt with the board in any controls issues. The decision of the Washington State Court in favor of First United Methodist was based on the strict interpretation of the state constitution's articulation of church/state relations. It weakened the ability of the city to oversee changes and will enable future demolition of church properties in an economic market that favors high-rise office construction on this prime downtown site. A similar ruling was made in favor of First Covenant Church on First Hill. While neither ruling took a broader approach regarding all religious structures, each made it clear that the power of government to legislate preservation on the basis of its public good was in jeopardy in regards to certain groups.

However, the cooperation and excellent working relationship between the city's Landmarks Preservation Board and the congregation of St. James Cathedral in an award-winning renovation and restoration demonstrate some of the benefits of preservation legislation to churches, as well as to the general population. Father Michael Ryan's comments at a 25th anniversary celebration for the Landmarks Preserva-

tion Ordinance illuminate the role that preservation can have in shaping projects for the better.

> *There are those who see a preservation ordinance as an unfortunate encumbrance and even unwarranted restriction on ownership rights. For us, I believe it worked the opposite way. Were it not for the fact that St. James was listed on the landmark registry, I honestly believe we would never have received the enormously helpful cooperation we routinely received with city planning officials and fire officials. . . . We were not only well served by the stipulations of the ordinance, we were also inspired and challenged by its underlying wisdom.*

Neighborhood congregations, such as Bethany Presbyterian and Immanuel Lutheran, also materially benefited from board expertise as they planned additions and renovations.

Another major challenge has centered on public schools, which are a focal point for many neighborhoods, as the heart of their community. Educational change, technological and life safety upgrades, and shifting school-age populations have forced the Seattle School District to reevaluate existing structures. Deferred maintenance by the School District has left many older schools in a condition that puts into question the value of repair over replacement. In addition, nationally adopted policies regarding open space, classroom size, teaching methodology, and disabled accessibility have shaped redesign and additions to older buildings, often compromising their integrity.

The School District resisted city control over its buildings, contending that educational specifications must be a primary consideration in preserving or razing older buildings. Designated landmarks, such as Green Lake Elementary, were razed to provide open space. Significant neighborhood schools that were not designated landmarks, such as Ballard High School and Adams Elementary in Ballard and Bailey Gatzert Elementary at the eastern edge of the International District, were demolished for new buildings on-site or nearby.

One casualty, the 1917 brick addition to the 1906 Latona School site, was designated by the Seattle Landmarks Preservation Board. In December 1995, the board denied a Certificate of Approval for demolition and that ruling was supported by the City Hearing Examiner. However, the city council, in a 6-3 vote, sided with the School Board and removed the brick school from control. A positive result of that process has been to change the Landmarks Preservation Ordinance so that city council approval is no longer required once the board has designated a property.

Recently, the School District and the Seattle Landmarks Preservation Board have forged a workable, efficient review of nominations, designations, and Certificates of Approval ensuring that the historic structures will maintain their integrity and continue to be valued fixtures in their communities, and that additions and new construction will be sensitively planned with appropriate scale and materials. In 1998, the Landmarks Preservation Board and its Architectural Review Committee had major impact upon the design of historic and new buildings at Seward, Bryant, Concord, Stevens, Dunlap, and Coe Elementary Schools and West Seattle High School.

Through its review process, the 11-member board has also improved the final design outcomes of large and small projects throughout the city, including Franklin High School, the Space Needle, Smith Tower, Frederick and Nelson Department Store, Ford Assembly Plant, and Log House Museum. These projects reinforce the value of review and critique in extending the use of landmark properties without severely compromising their architectural and historic integrity. Since the 1970s, hundreds of Seattle residents have served voluntarily as members of the Seattle Landmarks Preservation Board and District and Special Review Boards. Their generous donation of time and thoughtful critical reviews have made a great difference. None of the city's preservation programs could have been accomplished or continued without their dedication.

In the past decade, efforts to weaken the power of the landmarks ordinance and to place the landmarks program in other departments with potentially conflicting goals have been halted by an astute Urban Conservation Office staff, headed by Karen Gordon, the City Historic Preservation Officer.

## New Approaches

But what can be done to preserve the city's unprotected buildings? There is growing awareness that historic preservation is not just about saving buildings and other specific landmarks. It is also about a sense of place and community—preserving those features that make a place unique and special to residents and visitors.

Preservation has increasingly become a part of the planning of our communities. In 1990, Washington became one of the first states to require comprehensive growth planning for most cities and counties. The Growth Management Act identified 13 goals for these plans, including "Identify and encourage the preservation of land, sites and structures that have historical, cultural and archeological significance." In the following years, both the City of Seattle and King County developed comprehensive plans as required, making historic preservation a priority. With vigilance from the Urban Conservation Office staff and comments by the Seattle Landmarks Preservation Board and local organizations, Seattle adopted a Cultural Resource Plan in 1997 that included historic preservation. This recent addition to the city's 1994 Comprehensive Plan sets goals and policies that, for the first time, give focus to this philosophy and commit the city to developing and promoting cultural resources. The plan acknowledges the importance that historic buildings play as visible statements of community identity and the value of preserving the integrity of these resources.

After completion of the Seattle Comprehensive Plan, individual neighborhoods throughout the city turned to planning their own futures. Thirty-seven communities took on the challenge. As each one developed a vision of how they wanted to grow and be in the future, preservation of their existing neighborhood character was typically a very high priority. Ballard and Queen Anne did surveys of portions of their neighborhoods. Other areas emphasized design guidelines to ensure that new development would be compatible with the old.

Historic preservation has been incorporated at numerous levels of government, requiring that buildings scheduled for demolition or change be evaluated for their historic significance. Both the national and state environmental policy acts, which require environmental studies before projects are done, include historic review as an important element. Both Seattle and King County require that buildings over 50 years old be assessed for historic significance before permits are issued. If a building is determined to have potential significance, a landmark review can occur.

On the federal level, before any project assisted by federal funds (or permits, etc.) may proceed, it must undergo a specific review to determine if any historic resources will be affected. Through this process, known as Section 106 Review, properties that are listed on the National Register or found to be eligible for listing are provided some degree of protection, and mitigation is required if they are adversely affected by the undertaking.

Several important federal initiatives have proved to be useful for Seattle and King County preservation efforts. Perhaps the most important has been the Intermodal Surface Transportation Efficiency Act of 1991, known as ISTEA (now TEA-21), which provides funds for the preservation of transportation-related buildings and structures. One of these programs was Washington's Heritage Corridor Program, which has supported several preservation efforts in rural King County.

All of the above approaches are healthy signs of the maturity of the preservation movement and its integration into government and community life. As preservation moves beyond its early focus on saving particular landmarks through regulations, educating the general public to preservation's importance becomes increasingly vital. The best protection is to develop a strong preservation ethic among the general populace rooted in a sense of shared values. People can learn how to get involved at the local level to save not only major landmarks but smaller things that are important to them and their neighbors. The Urban Conservation Office has sponsored educational programs and community outreach. Historic Seattle and more than 47 historical societies and heritage groups throughout Seattle and King County are individually and collectively concerned and involved in preserving historic buildings and their programs educate thousands of County residents.

Statewide, the Washington Trust for Historic Preservation is a nonprofit membership organization that disseminates information about preservation successes, failures, and issues to the preservation community, primarily through an annual conference and awards ceremony and a quarterly newsletter, the Trust News. Its Ten Most Endangered Properties list calls attention to properties throughout the state of Washington that are threatened, through either imminent demolition or neglect.

## SLIPPING THROUGH THE CRACKS

The Seattle Landmarks Preservation Board evaluates nominations submitted by individuals and groups for a wide range of buildings that represent various types, styles, periods, materials, and methods of construction. They come from virtually every neighborhood in the city. Many recent nominations have been generated by owners themselves because of the tax credits for rehabilitation of designated properties or by concerned tenants and neighborhood groups who wish to safeguard buildings from change. In both cases, the architectural, economic, social, and cultural significance of the building may be secondary in the applicants' efforts to primary interests that have little to do with the intrinsic value of the potential landmark.

A number of properties are also brought before the Landmarks Preservation Board for mandatory review as part of the State Environmental Policy Act (SEPA) review process, which is triggered during development planning. These nomination sessions are valuable opportunities to rule on the significance of property that might otherwise be adversely affected. To adequately evaluate a building, board members need to review the broader physical and cultural context in which a nominated buildings exists and to examine that building or site in relationship to buildings of a similar period, style, type, and method of construction. Without such background, it is difficult for board members to determine whether, in fact, a nominated building represents the integrity, quality, and significance that warrant a place on the Landmarks list. This information is generally not provided.

The intent of a citywide survey effort conducted by the Urban Conservation Office in 1978–79 was to identify and prioritize significant buildings of all types in most neighborhoods. Little of that material has formed the basis for landmark nominations in

*The collegiate Gothic entrance to Suzzallo Library at the University of Washington.*

the past 20 years. Of particular value in light of former Mayor Rice's Urban Village policies and the recent preparation of neighborhood community development plans would be research and preparation of nominations for the city's best multifamily housing and its most intact and best designed large- and small-scale commercial buildings in neighborhoods outside downtown, areas that are increasingly threatened. These nominations should be an important part of implementation of neighborhood plans.

Over the course of 26 years, the nomination and designation process has produced a broad-based but uneven group of designated properties that are, first and foremost, architecturally distinctive. The list underrepresents sites that are not distinctive architecturally but are associated with important contributors to Seattle's social, economic, ethnic, and cultural development; vernacular buildings important to inner-city neighborhoods; and important "background" building types. One example of a building type that has totally eluded landmark status is the automobile showroom, which had a profound effect upon the development of the city. Only a small number now retain integrity of exterior and interior.

The University of Washington campus, which includes both significant buildings and landscape, is exempt from city control because it is under state jurisdiction (see chapter 7 discussions of the Olympic Hotel and the 5th Avenue Theatre). Changes to the campus are overseen by advisory architecture and landscape commissions or committees within the aca-

demic structure. The relocation and refurbishment of the Penthouse Theatre and the rehabilitation of Old Architecture Hall, Denny Hall, and Parrington Hall exemplify sensitive approaches and good stewardship of historic properties. But that has not always been the case. Additions to the jewel-like box of the Henry Art Gallery have effectively destroyed its integrity and blighted its surroundings.

Other organizations have made efforts toward recognizing valuable resources in the city and finding avenues for their protection. Allied Arts conducted a survey from which emerged *Impressions of Imagination: Terra Cotta Seattle* in 1986. A thematic district nomination—residential architecture on First Hill—was prepared for the State and National Registers in 1980 but was not accepted. The group that developed it was urged to reevaluate the boundaries of the district, do further research, and resubmit a revised nomination. That work was not pursued. Subsequent demolition of entire blocks of housing for parking lots, hospital and medical facilities, condominiums, and apartment blocks has left only four major homes intact from a much larger number extant at the time of the survey and nomination.

The mayor and city council could take a proactive role by budgeting and supporting Urban Conservation Office staff to update and expand their initial survey, using revised criteria; review extant buildings that were indicated as being of primary importance in early surveys; establish a prioritized list of these buildings based upon the Seattle landmarks designation criteria; prepare nomination materials and documentation; and submit these with staff recommendations to the Seattle Landmarks Preservation Board for consideration. Without this kind of evaluative system in place, many of the best buildings in city neighborhoods will remain unprotected as the city's density increases and as the historic commercial cores of these neighborhoods are redeveloped.

With the passage of time, many post–World War II skyscrapers and commercial buildings enter the "historic" category. It is important to evaluate their architectural, structural, economic, and cultural worth and offer protection to those meeting designation criteria. For example, the Norton Building and the Seattle First National Bank headquarters (now 1001 Fourth Avenue Plaza) represent important symbols of progress, growth, and structural sophistication. As tastes changed, they were maligned for their vacant and inhospitable plazas (both of them now altered to be "friendlier" to pedes-

*The Seattle First National Bank designed by Naramore, Bain, Brady & Johanson in 1969 may be Seattle's most elegant interpretation of International modernism. It is not a city landmark.*

trians). To the public, and to design professionals as well, their slender boxlike forms and glass curtain walls seemed dated and plain compared to the granite and colored glass facades, bays, and setbacks of late 1980s Postmodern structures, such as the Washington Mutual Tower and Pacific Bank Centre (now U.S. Bank Centre). In a nation where the festival marketplace formula has taken over office and commercial buildings as well as retail districts, the intended purity of design form and function of these elegant International style buildings has been compromised. Limited consideration was given to safeguard that through landmarks protection.

There is growing interest in varied types of landmarks—ones that are not yet generally accepted as historically significant, such as neighborhood store-

fronts, postwar housing, and reminders of Seattle's culture in the 1950s, 1960s, and 1970s. It is easy to recognize and support designation of the Space Needle from the Century 21 World's Fair as a landmark structure. But can the same be said for a popular culture icon such as an Elephant Car Wash sign or Dick's Drive-In? In February 1999, when a major sale of brewery holdings threatened the closure of Rainier Brewery, the front pages of the Seattle Times asked what would become of the landmark red "R" that commuters used as their milepost every day on Interstate 5.

The Blue Moon Tavern—Seattle's answer to New York's Greenwich Village and San Francisco's North Beach, a gathering place and watering hole for artists, writers, and political activists—provided an early test case. The threat of its demolition brought a large group of supporters to press for its protection. Questions about its architectural integrity and its use spurred debate; it failed to receive sufficient votes by the Seattle Landmarks Preservation Board for designation as a Seattle landmark. Fortunately, the property owner agreed to incorporate it into future development on the site.

Another growing interest is the heritage of ethnic minorities and the lesbian and gay community. The state and county have acknowledged the importance of responding to diversity by developing "context documents" specifically addressing the question of preservation of sites related to the heritage of African Americans and Asian/Pacific Island Americans. The City of Seattle acknowledged the importance of Asian/Pacific Island heritage in its designation of the International Special Review District and nomination of the district to the State and National Registers. If individual sites are not well represented in the designated landmark list, that has little to do with the ordinance itself or with those who serve on the Landmarks Preservation Board. Rather, it has to do with the lack of publicity or knowledge about the landmarks program citywide. Educational outreach and technical assistance could have valuable positive impacts. Increasingly, safeguarding heritage requires the involvement of local organizations and the building of a preservation constituency.

*Terra-cotta walruses stand guard over the landmark Arctic Club at the corner of Cherry Street and Third Avenue.*

# Chapter Three

# Designated Landmarks in Seattle

Seattle's individually designated landmarks encompass many facets of the region's architectural, cultural, economic, social, and civic history and nearly every era as well. They range from 19th-century Romanesque Revival commercial buildings to Art Deco skyscrapers; from onion-domed Russian Orthodox churches to Italian Renaissance Revival cathedrals; from ornate 1920s motion picture palaces to innovative steam power generating facilities; from palatial mansions to modest Victorian farmhouses; from institutions of learning to automobile and overall factories; from Gothic-inspired bridges to the reminders of the age of sail and steam on Seattle's waterways; from street clocks and statues to parks and open spaces that soften the built surroundings.

Some of the landmarks listed below are also listed on the State or National Register. They are included in the list provided in appendix D, which also lists properties that are not city landmarks but are on one or both registers. Some buildings that are listed as individual landmarks may also be within the boundaries of a designated historic district that is also a National Register District, such as Pioneer Square or Harvard/Belmont.

The landmarks described in this chapter are listed geographically by neighborhoods and, within these sections, alphabetically by name. The earliest or commonly referred to name of the building is listed first, followed by later or recent names. That may pose some challenges for newcomers to the city—and even for those who have lived in Seattle all their lives and for whom the original name of the building is unfamiliar. Refer to the index, where recent names are cross-referenced to original names.

The architects are those initially responsible and those responsible for early major changes to each building. The dates reflect dates from design to completion, when known, and dates of significant additions or changes in the building's history. In some cases, recent research has revealed discrepancies in dating and architects since preparation of the original landmark nomination and designation materials. In those cases, the more accurate dates provided in the 1994 publication *Shaping Seattle Architecture,* edited by Jeffrey Karl Ochsner, are presented.

The firms responsible for recent additions and rehabilitation efforts are mentioned in the text. Where a significant rehabilitation has occurred that is discussed in chapter 4 or 7, the description and history of the landmark will be found in that chapter.

Readers will realize how the history of our city and our region is told in the buildings we have built and saved.

Nevertheless, some losses have occurred since the Seattle landmarks designation program began in 1973. Landmarks that have been demolished or significantly altered, or buildings for which controls no longer exist, are described more fully in appendix A, "Obituaries."

## CENTRAL BUSINESS DISTRICT/ PIONEER SQUARE/INTERNATIONAL DISTRICT

### John B. Agen Warehouse
1203–7 Western Avenue
*John Graham Sr., 1910; 1911*

John Agen has been called the father of the dairy industry in the Northwest, founding creameries at Mount Vernon and eventually operating businesses throughout the state. Agen's tin packaged butter was a staple in the Klondike goldfields, and his waterfront warehouse and processing plant shipped goods throughout the United States and to foreign lands from his own dock at Pier 6 (now 56). The warehouse accommodated his expanding butter, egg, and cheese business; the four story building of 1910 was increased by two additional floors the next year, with both designs coming from the offices of John Graham Sr. Structurally, the building sits on concrete footings over timber pilings, with brick bearing walls and heavy timber posts and beams sized to reflect the diminishing loads of the upper floors—typical of this type of structure. The warehouse was one of Graham's earliest large-scale industrial buildings and may account for his being hired by Henry Ford in 1913 to design an automobile assembly plant in Seattle (later Craftsman Press and now Shurgard headquarters), which led to his designing over 30 assembly plants for Ford between 1914 and 1917. The building was adapted to office and retail in 1986–87 by the firm of Hewitt Daly.

### Arctic Club Building
700 Third Avenue
*A. Warren Gould, George Lawton, 1913–17*

See chapter 7.

### Bank of California/Key Bank
815 Second Avenue
*John Graham Company, 1923–24*

The last major banking headquarters built along lower Second Avenue—the Wall Street of Seattle— this building's finely detailed and well-proportioned Neoclassical facade is sheathed with terra-cotta with a speckled glaze that appears to be granite, called "granitex." Its Roman temple facade is impressive, with four Ionic order fluted columns and two related pilasters. The exterior is equaled by a splendid skylit interior with fluted Corinthian columns supporting balconies and a polychrome coffered plaster ceiling that was described at its opening as being "semi-Pompeian." This building shows the architect's fine eye for classical detail and nuance. The building was restored in 1982 by the Callison Partnership (now Callison Architecture). At that time, the skylight, which had been blacked out since World War II, was reconstructed.

*The Bon Marché before 1953 addition.*

### Bon Marché
300 Pine Street
*John Graham Company, 1928–29*

The Bon Marché represents a significant milestone in the development of a homegrown business and in the shift of retail to its present center at Pine Street. In 1890, Edward Nordhoff named his fledgling dry goods store in Belltown the Bon Marché after a Parisian emporium with a reputation for fine service and integrity. In 1896, he moved the store to Second and Pike, where the company continued to expand into adjoining buildings. Architect John Graham Sr. designed a six-story building in 1912 at the corner of

Union Street to provide additional space. Following the lead of major competitor Frederick and Nelson, in 1929, the Bon Marché moved to another Graham-designed store—this one costing $5 million and taking up an entire city block. Influenced by modernistic design trends, the beige-limestone-faced building is embellished with low-relief geometric and floral motifs derived from the French decorative arts movement later termed Art Deco. Its wraparound cast-copper marquee depicts underwater flora and fish appropriate to the seaport nature of the city. Interior spaces, from wavelike coffers and decorated column capitals to mahogany trim and cast-metal grills and balusters, complement the modernistic style of the architecture. A much simpler three-story addition in 1953 did away with the incised ornamental banding that crowned the building and filled in corner windows. A rehabilitation in 1990–91 by NBBJ respected its interiors while making a number of changes to upscale spaces. In 1998, the facade was cleaned and sealed, and plans proceed on additional interior upgrades, which, unfortunately, will remove a 1939 central stair and mezzanine designed by Graham in harmony with the original interiors.

**Brooklyn Building**
1222 Second Avenue
*Designer unknown, 1890 (altered)*

This four-story masonry building in the popular Romanesque Revival style housed a residential hotel and commercial space. It is typical of construction in postfire Seattle and one of the few remaining late 19th century commercial buildings outside the Pioneer Square Historic District. Others include the Austin Bell Building, Barnes Building, and Holyoke Building. It symbolizes the evolution of Second Avenue from a residential street prior to the fire to the principal business thoroughfare of the city in the first decade of the 20th century. The Brooklyn and other residential hotels provided housing for laborers who lived and worked in the downtown area. Within two blocks of the Brooklyn arose the city's major department stores, the Bon Marché, McDougall and Southwick, Rhodes, and Frederick and Nelson. Despite its landmark status, only the two principal facades were saved and incorporated into the development of Washington Mutual Tower.

**Camlin Hotel**
1619 Ninth Avenue
*Carl Linde, 1926*

This 11-story building was designed as an apartment hotel to house well-to-do residents at the eastern edge of the business district and developed by Adolph Linden and Edmund Campbell. Linden was president of Puget Sound Savings and Loan Association and Campbell was vice president and secretary. The Camlin has a distinguished brick and terra-cotta facade designed by a prominent Portland architect, Carl Linde. Its stylistic references derive from the English Jacobean and Elizabethan periods, and include Tudor and ogee arches, quatrefoils, quoins, gargoyles, and niches. The Camlin's parapet showcases one of the city's most exuberant applications of the style.

**Coliseum Theater/Banana Republic**
1506 Fifth Avenue
*B. Marcus Priteca, 1914–16 (altered)*

See chapter 7.

**Colman Block**
801–21 First Avenue
*S. Meany, 1889–90; A. Tidemand, 1904–6;*
*A. Loveless, 1929*

A six-story brick-faced commercial building with cast-iron, stone, and marble trim, the Colman Block is an excellent and early example of the influence of the Chicago commercial style on Seattle architecture. Designed as a six-story building with central tower, only the basement and first two floors were constructed by early 1890. Additions and a new facade by August Tidemand in 1904–6 significantly changed its appearance. With its large pivoting windows, brownstone base, and absence of most classical ornamentation, the building reflected Louis Sullivan's belief that 20th century American buildings should honestly express their function without adhering to historical decorative principles. In 1929, the remodeling of the south corner for Peoples Bank & Trust Company and renovation of the building lobby were accomplished by architect Arthur Loveless in the Art Deco style with remarkably fine cast-bronze panels and doors designed by artist Dudley Pratt (now removed).

### Community Bulletin Board
505 Seventh Avenue S.
*Chinese Community Service Organization, c. 1960*

The Chinese were brought to the Northwest to work on construction of the railroads and in the lumber and fishing industries in the 1870s. During the depression of the 1880s, they faced discrimination and deportation, but returned to build an even stronger, more stable community with its cultural and commercial center located in a newly regraded section south and east of the central business district. The bulletin board, located on the east wall of a three-story hotel building near the heart of Chinatown, follows a long-standing tradition. The earliest posting board in the Chinese section of the city was established in the 1890s to provide information to the largely non-English-speaking population. The present board, installed in the 1960s, provides a public forum for news and messages, particularly for senior citizens who do not read English. Because the district is ethnically diverse, the bulletin board also serves Japanese, Filipinos, Vietnamese, Thai, and other groups living or working in the International District.

### Decatur Building
1521 Sixth Avenue
*Henry Bittman, 1921–22*

The Decatur Building was built for Louisa Denny Frye, daughter of one of the city's founders and herself one of the first settlers in 1851. The architect, Henry Bittman, established a reputation for highly detailed, well proportioned, and structurally innovative commercial and public buildings in downtown

Seattle. The Decatur represents one of the finest classically ornamented terra-cotta facades extant. Its floral relief panels, pilasters, acanthus leaf capitals, and entablature and cornice iconography of spirals, ovals, flowers, and rosettes are molded in a warm, golden terra-cotta, further embellished by acanthus and acroterion crests that crown the parapet. The gracious way in which its eight retail bays provide a continuous and harmonious street front makes this one of the city's most successful smaller commercial buildings. Through a Transfer of Development Rights program (TDR), the developer of a building on Sixth Avenue and Pike Street was able to purchase the developable space above the landmark; the intrusive height and mass of the new building above the southern portion of the Decatur calls into question design solutions using this potentially valuable development tool.

### Dexter Horton Building
710 Second Avenue
*John Graham Company, 1921–24*

The office building that served as the headquarters of the Dexter Horton Bank (later Seattle First National Bank) accommodated a thousand offices in 5 3/4 acres, making it one of the largest office buildings in the country at the time of its construction. It included every modern innovation at the time, including high-speed elevators grouped at the north end of the building, with four wings projecting south, separated by light courts. Its builders prided themselves on the use of local materials, including cream white terra-cotta from Northern Clay Com-

pany in Auburn. John Graham embellished the facade and the main banking hall with Beaux Arts classical finishes, monumental granite columns, and richly colored Roman coffered barrel vaulting in the Second Avenue entrance lobby.

## Eagles Temple Building
1416 Seventh Avenue
*Henry Bittman, 1924–25*

The Eagles is one of the best preserved of Seattle's terra-cotta facades. Designed by local architect Henry Bittman, the handsome Italian Renaissance palazzo was erected by the Fraternal Order of Eagles, Seattle Aerie No. 1, and was intended to be the most splendid fraternal building in the country. The fraternal organization had been formed as early as 1898 by a group of Seattle theater managers to foster brotherhood and to "make human life more desirable by lessening its ills and promoting peace, prosperity, gladness, and hope." It was hugely successful and grew in ten years to 1,800 member lodges throughout the United States, Canada, Mexico, Hawaii, and the Philippine Islands, with membership exceeding 350,000. The Seattle facility housed retail on the ground floor, rental apartments on the

perimeter, and a lavish ballroom and lodge rooms within. The exterior was restored and the interior was adapted to low- income housing, two theaters and a cabaret space by two local firms, Callison Architecture and GGLO.

## Eastern Hotel
506–510 Maynard Avenue S.
*David Dow, 1911*

The Eastern Hotel was constructed for the Wa Chong Company, a Chinese Benevolent Society, to house transient workers and provide retail in the expanding Chinatown that developed south of S. Jackson Street after the regrades of 1906–7. The red brick and stone-trimmed facade, with two floors of arched windows, is especially noteworthy for the unusually fine use of decorative brick. A diamond-shaped brick trompe l'oeil type relief fills the recessed second floor window arches. Two toned, alternating bricks fill third-floor window arches. A modified Greek key patterned band embellishes the upper part of the facade below a bracketed copper cornice. The Eastern was refurbished and turned into subsidized housing in 1998 for Interim Community Development Association (ICDA) by the firm of Kovalenko Hale Architects.

## El Rio Apartment Hotel
1922–28 Ninth Avenue
*John Alfred Creutzer, 1929*

The five-story masonry-clad El Rio is an early example of the efficiency apartment, which offered a growing population of urban workers the opportunity to live affordably adjacent to the Central Business District. Each of the 47 studio apartments contains a living room with steam heat radiator, dinette, kitchen, bath, and spacious dressing room (some large enough to accommodate a double bed). Interior finishes included mahogany woodwork and terrazzo and concrete floors.

In addition to its apartments, the building housed retail at the street level. The stylized ornament in cast stone that embellishes the exterior of the building is typical of late 1920s modernistic "Art Deco" treatments more commonly seen in commercial buildings. The building points in the direction that might have been taken had the Denny Regrade area been developed as planned into an up-to-date commercial and residential section. The Great Depression put plans on hold indefinitely.

**Exchange Building**
821 Second Avenue
*John Graham Company, 1929-31*

The Exchange Building, built to house Northwest commodities and stock exchanges, opened its doors, ironically, in the year of the stock market crash. This Art Deco building is sheathed with a warm colored cast-concrete product called "Romanite" that resembles sandstone in appearance. The 23 story building was the second-tallest reinforced-concrete structure in the nation when built. Most of its design vocabulary was borrowed directly from stylized floral designs from the International Exposition of Modern Decorative and Industrial Arts held in Paris in 1925, including baskets of stylized flowers and geometric and spiral borders and fill. However, John Graham Company also created ornamental reliefs in cast stone, bronze, plaster, and sandblasted wood that represented the produce and commodities for which Washington State was known. Sheaves of wheat, grapes, peaches, tulips, roses, and wildflowers appear at every turn. The Second Avenue entrance lobby offers one of Seattle's most theatrical experiences. The gilt plaster diamond and triangle reliefs of

the ceiling, set off by the curving black marble and bronze elevator bays, lend an ambiance of enchantment and drama more in keeping with King Tut's treasury than with a modern-day office building. Bronze ornament surrounding the directory highlights tulips that were grown locally prior to the development of the Skagit tulip fields. Wildflowers radiate from the mailbox, and the great wheat fields of central and eastern Washington are depicted prominently above the elevator doors. The central Washington fruit-growing region is represented in the bronze surrounds of the elevators and in the vine and grape panels that originally decorated the exterior of the elevator doors. Wood stencil treatments around interior lobby doors and telephone booths consist of incised ornament of native flora and fauna.

**Fire Station No. Two**
2318 Fourth Avenue
*Daniel Huntington, 1920*

While it isn't the oldest building in the city designed as a fire station, Fire Station No. Two does have the distinction of being the oldest still operating for its original purpose. The station replaced two earlier station houses built for horse-drawn wagons. It is an excellent example of industrial architecture that exceeds the bounds of pure function through skillfully detailed brick inlay to the concrete frame— recalling earlier public works on the West Queen Anne Retaining Walls (1913) by W. R. B. Willcox. The building had a maintenance shop and also functioned as the principal meeting place for the department, providing a large auditorium.

**First Avenue Building Group/Waterfront Place**

In the years following the fire of 1889, the First Avenue business district was rebuilt and expanded northward. Many modified Romanesque brick and stone commercial and hotel buildings were designed by architects who moved to Seattle because of the obvious opportunities after the fire. With the discovery of gold in the Klondike in 1896 and the influx of newcomers to Seattle, new transient lodging, restaurants, and commercial buildings were built along upper First Avenue, close to the railroad depot and steamship terminals. These turn-of-the-century buildings were designed in a more refined, sophisticated Beaux Arts classicism, reflecting the changes in architectural taste over the decade. This particular group of buildings along the west side of First Avenue between Madison and Spring Streets was rehabilitated and the interiors adapted to new hotel, office, and residential purposes as part of a much larger project by the Cornerstone Development Company. Bumgardner Architects was responsible for the First Avenue group during 1982–83. Hewitt/Daly refurbished the National Building on Western Avenue. For the reconstruction of the Alexis Hotel and rehabilitation of the Arlington and Grand Pacific Buildings, see chapter 7. Waterfront Place includes:

### Globe Building
1001–1011 First Avenue
*Max Umbrecht, 1901*

### Beebe Building
1013 First Avenue
*Max Umbrecht, 1901*

### Hotel Cecil
*1019–23 First Avenue*
*Max Umbrecht, 1901*

### Grand Pacific
1115–17 First Avenue
*Designer unknown, date unknown*

### Colonial Building
1119–23 First Avenue
*Max Umbrecht, 1901–2*

### Coleman Building
94–96 Spring Street
*Bebb & Gould, 1915*

### National Building
1001–24 Western Avenue
*Kingsley & Anderson, 1904*

### First United Methodist Church
811 Fifth Avenue
*James Schack & Daniel Huntington, 1907–10*
*(no longer listed)*

See appendix A.

### 1411 Fourth Avenue
1411 Fourth Avenue
*R. C. Reamer, 1928–29*

The last major project developed by lumberman and real estate entrepreneur C. D. Stimson was neither the largest nor the tallest Seattle office building, but at 15 stories, it was claimed to be the tallest in the city sheathed in stone, while its contemporaries were faced in brick with terra-cotta trim or in glazed terra-cotta alone. The stone complements two other Reamer-designed buildings nearby, the Great Northern and Skinner Buildings. Its boxlike modernistic style is defined by recessed spandrels, unadorned vertical piers, gently setback parapet pillars, and a vocabulary of French Art Deco and Celtic ornament at both base and crown. The Honduran mahogany lobby, polished-brass elevator doors and surrounds, and sandblasted glass fixtures were inspired by the French decorative arts vocabulary. Located directly across from the Great Northern main ticket office, the building housed many of the city's railroad and steamship lines, making Fourth and Union Street a transportation hub. A 1998 refurbishment of storefronts and lobby by the firm of Fuller Sears has removed some of the damage caused by inappropriate changes made in recent years by certain retailers.

### Frederick and Nelson/Nordstrom
500–524 Pine Street
*John Graham Company, 1916–19; 1952*

See chapter 7.

### J. S. Graham Store/Doyle Building
119 Pine Street
*A. E. Doyle, 1919–20*

Built as the home of J. S. Graham, Inc., a women's apparel store, this four-story commercial and office block is an outstanding Italian Renaissance styled block recalling Florentine and Venetian palaces. It is a rare local work by the distinguished and prolific Portland, Oregon, architect, A. E. Doyle. Its terra-cotta facade is graceful in its proportions, with a rhythmic repetition of paired narrow windows and arched top-floor windows with spiral columned surrounds. The wide overhanging cornice crowns the building. In terms of the city's economic development, the store represents the expansion of retail north along Second Avenue to Pine Street, following the move of Frederick and Nelson in 1918 to Pine Street and preceding the major relocation of the Bon Marché a decade later.

## Great Northern Building

1404 Fourth Avenue
*R. C. Reamer, 1928–29*

The Great Northern Building housed the ticket office and headquarters for the Great Northern Railway. It is the earliest effort to design a modernistic medium-rise building in Seattle by merging common Beaux Arts design elements, such as cornices, fluted pilasters, and dentil molding, with up-to-date incised French stylized floral and geometric motifs placed to be subordinate to the unadorned Indiana limestone box of the building. Its symmetry and its graceful, almost lyrical ornament form a well scaled relationship to its larger, taller, and Beaux Arts classical inspired neighbors in the Metropolitan Center and bridges the gap between historic eclecticism and modernism.

## Joshua Green Building

1425 Fourth Avenue
*John Graham Company, 1913*

This 10-story retail and office building joined the Northern Securities Trust Building to establish the corner of Fourth Avenue and Pike Street as an important commercial location in the north end of downtown. It shared characteristics with the McDermott Building of the same year (demolished) and prefigured the design of the Frederick and Nelson Department Store (1918) by the same company; all three shared light-colored terra-cotta facades and similar cornices, pilasters, and fenestration (unfortunately, this building no longer has its cornice). The building is named for Joshua Green, who arrived in the city in 1886 from Mississippi and established a lucrative steamboat business that merged with Puget Sound Navigation Company and finally became the Washington State Ferry system. He also took charge of stabilizing an ailing local bank, turning it into the profitable People's National Bank, for which he served as Chair of the Board until 1962.

## Hoge Building

705 Second Avenue
*Bebb & Mendel, 1909–11*

Built on the site of the first white settler's cabin, that of Carson Boren, this 18 story office tower was the city's second skyscraper, following the Alaska Building (1904) diagonally across the street. It was also the second Seattle structure to employ structural steel cage construction with light-colored brick and terra-cotta veneers. It broke all world's records for the rapidity with which the steel frame went up—the entire 18 stories were in place in 30 days. Prompted by the 1906 San Francisco earthquake, the Hoge Building was also a pacesetter in using design and materials which met seismic requirements, Its facade fits easily into what Louis Sullivan termed the tall building "triumphant." Its base and crown are heavily ornamented in the Beaux Arts style—Corinthian pilasters, cartouches, medallions, and lion head corbels and a substantial cornice, all of molded terra-cotta. Contrasting sharply with the flamboyance of the lower floors and the topmost floors is a simple brick faced shaft of office floors. The Hoge and Alaska Buildings and the Smith Tower epitomize the new building forms made possible by structural steel, concrete, and the technology of the elevator. A 1994 renovation by GGLO led to removal of a later marble-faced entrance and reconstruction of the lobby and banking hall, with the unfortunate necessity of visible girders to seismically reinforce it.

## Holyoke Building

1018–22 First Avenue
*Bird & Dornbach, 1889–90*

The Holyoke Building is a dignified red-brick, cast-iron, and rusticated stone building in the Romanesque style characteristic of its neighbors along First Avenue and in the Pioneer Square Historic District. Its upper facade along First Avenue is unified by seven continuous pilasters, each with carved stone capitals below the entablature, and six sets of bays with horizontally expressed spandrels. Each bay contains a pair of windows. The Spring Street facade repeats the rhythm of brick pilasters and bays, with the added interest of a triple window in the westmost bay. Aside from its architectural interest, the building site played an interesting role during the Seattle fire of 1889. Excavation was in progress when the fire broke out near Madison Street. The hole provided a firebreak and prevented the flames from crossing Spring Street and destroying the wood structures to the north.

### Leamington Hotel & Apartments/Pacific Hotel
317 Marion Street
*W. R. B. Willcox & Julian Everett, 1915–16*

The brick- and masonry-faced Leamington was originally built to house both a hotel and an apartment building that shared hotel services—an unusual approach at this time and one that accounts for its outward appearance as two distinct buildings. The apartments featured French window forms at mock balconies, while the hotel boasted a cornice-level balustrade and pressed terra-cotta quatrefoils. In 1995, rehabilitation of exterior and interior was overseen by the firm of Stickney & Murphy Architects for the Plymouth Housing Group to provide 112 permanent housing units for formerly homeless and very low income tenants.

### Liggett/Fourth and Pike Building
1424 Fourth Avenue
*Lawton & Moldenhour, 1927*

One of a number of concrete and structural steel office towers rising in downtown during the 1920s, the Liggett was distinguished by one of the city's finest Gothic-styled terra-cotta facades, replete with arches and multifoil tracery crowned by miniature turrets and parapet finials. The historic style and period are carried into the lobby's ribbed ceiling, colored stenciled borders, and bronze lattice chandeliers. The design of the Liggett Building was nearly repeated a block away in the Republic Building at the corner of Third Avenue and Pike Street, with the

only change being the adaptation of a French Renaissance vocabulary for its facade.

### Lyon Building
607 Third Avenue
*Graham & Myers, 1909–10*

This six-story brick and classical period terra-cotta-faced commercial building was built for the Yukon Investment Company, whose president, R. Auzias–de Turenne, was probably responsible for the shield and lion rampant above the entry and the motto "Toujours avant." It was one of a number of major commercial buildings that rose along Third Avenue in the first decades of the century after widening and regrading occurred there. It was also financed—as were many such projects—by local businessmen whose resources had been vastly improved by investments spurred by the Klondike Gold Rush. Despite 1950 period alterations of the ground-floor entrance, the lobby retains a marble staircase, walls, pilasters, and boxed beams with Greek key patterns, rosettes, and floral medallions that reflect exterior terra-cotta details. The building has been converted to housing for AIDS Housing of Washington.

### Main Street School Annex
307 Sixth Avenue S.
*Designer unknown, 1903; James Stephen, c. 1910*

By 1910, the corner of S. Main Street and Sixth Avenue S. had become the commercial center of a thriving Japanese community. This early two-room frame school building was built as an annex to the South School (1873). The property was donated by Mrs. Bailey Gatzert with the stipulation that it be used to develop a kindergarten, a progressive educational concept she had learned about on a trip to Switzerland. The first kindergarten in Seattle was a gable-roofed building with shiplap wood siding, wooden cornices, and a shed-roofed porch. The present front porch, probably designed about 1910 under school architect James Stephen's supervision, features Ionic columns supporting a dentiled pediment that forms a formal portico to the street. For many years, the school annex functioned as a Chinese restaurant. The building was one of the earliest projects of Historic Seattle Preservation and Development Authority. It now provides office space.

## Mann Building/Embassy Theatre

1411 Third Avenue
*Henry Bittman, 1926*

The terra-cotta-clad Mann Building housed offices on the second floor and retail stores along Third Avenue and in its lower level formed by the slope of Union Street. The theater, which originally housed film and live musical entertainment, is the sole surviving remnant of a thriving district of vaudeville and film houses that occupied the surrounding streets. Because of its hillside location, it had box offices and entrances on both Third Avenue and Union Street. The site also made its interior a labyrinth of hallways, staircases, and ramps leading to the auditorium. The building's English Gothic decoration is elaborate high-relief design work that came out of the office of Henry Bittman, which was responsible for a great many downtown terra-cotta facades, including the Eagles Temple Building, the Decatur Building, Terminal Sales Building, and the United Shopping Tower (now Olympic Tower). The building is being refurbished for nightclub, restaurant, and office space designed by NBBJ.

## McGraw Place

Fifth Avenue at Westlake
*Richard Edwin Brooks, sculptor, 1913*

One of very few public monuments erected in Seattle, this statue of John Harte McGraw (1850–1910) was dedicated in 1913 in memory of the second governor of Washington State (1893–97). The sculpture, done in the realistic manner popular early in the century, was executed by Richard Edwin Brooks of Paris, New York, and Washington, D.C., whose bronze statues of prominent public figures grace many public squares and buildings on the East Coast, including the U.S. Capitol. The triangular setting was designed by the Olmsted Brothers to provide an appropriate background for the statue.

## Moore Theatre and Hotel

1932 Second Avenue
*E. W. Houghton, 1903–7*

The Moore Theatre and Hotel were designed and engineered partly to accommodate tourists to the 1909 Alaska-Yukon-Pacific Exposition with a hotel, sports, and entertainment complex complete at one location. Its innovations even included a basement

swimming pool. The theater was the leading cultural house in the city prior to the opening of the Metropolitan Theatre in 1911. It hosted such celebrities as Marie Dressler, Ethel Barrymore, Anna Pavlova, Sergei Rachmaninoff, and Feodor Chaliapin. Constructed with reinforced concrete and faced with white ceramic glazed tile and beige terra-cotta trim, the building's simple and stylistically neutral exterior belies an opulent lobby and auditorium that borrow freely from Italianate and Byzantine styles. The foyer, richly adorned with gray and red marbles and onyx, was said to be influenced by Pompeii. It has a patterned mosaic floor, walls of paneled gray marble, and double columns of mottled red marble. Allegorical figures representing the arts of music and dance support the beams below a central dome. The auditorium originally had 26 private boxes. Indirect lighting was achieved by colored glass set behind scrollwork bands. The innovative structure called for a huge steel girder that extended the width of the house and supported the weight of the balcony in the steel and concrete side walls. This eliminated support columns that might block views of the stage.

## Music Hall Theatre

702 Olive Way
*Sherwood Ford, 1927–28 (demolished)*

See appendix A.

## New Washington Hotel/Josephinium

1902 Second Avenue
*Eames & Young, 1906–8*

The New Washington replaced the original Washington Hotel, doomed to be demolished in the massive regrading of the north business district in 1906.

The New Washington, built slightly west and south of its namesake (and about 125 feet lower), opened its doors in 1908. Its 14 stories contained 250 guest rooms and a marble-finished lobby and dining room with exquisite plaster ornamentation that made it the city's premier hotel prior to the opening of the Olympic Hotel in 1924. Among its guests, it housed Presidents Theodore Roosevelt, William Howard Taft, Woodrow Wilson, and Warren G. Harding. J. Crawford Marmaduke, the hotel's developer, was responsible for erection of Seattle's first steel-framed skyscraper, the 15-story Alaska Building, in 1904, designed by the same St. Louis architects. From 1963 until 1991, the hotel was a residence for seniors operated by the Catholic Archdiocese. Renovation in 1991 was done under the supervision of Stickney & Murphy Architects to provide low income housing.

**Northern Bank & Trust/Seaboard Building**
1506 Westlake Avenue
*William D. Van Siclen, 1906–9*

Planned as early as 1906 and completed in 1909, this 10-story, trapezoidal building responds to the angular conversion of Westlake and Fourth Avenues. It was one of the earliest substantial office buildings in this end of downtown and reflects the community's confidence in northward and eastern expansion of commercial and banking activity from lower Second Avenue, the headquarters of major banks at the time. While the base of the building and its interiors have been significantly altered, the entablature and cor-

nice at the top of the building continue to feature some of the most elaborately devised Beaux Arts period ornament in cream-colored terra-cotta, replete with vines, flowers, oval shields, garlands, swags, and lion heads.

**Northern Life Tower/Seattle Tower**
1212 Third Avenue
*Albertson, Wilson & Richardson, 1927–29*

The first and finest example of the Art Deco skyscraper in Seattle and one of the showpieces of that style on the West Coast, the Northern Life Tower's setback form and accentuation of verticality resemble Saarinen's famed submission for the 1922 Chicago Tribune Tower competition. Designed to convey the impression of lofty aspirations, strength, durability, and solidity, the 27-story tower form suggests the rock mass of Mount Rainier, both in form and in the gradations of earthy-colored brick with which it is sheathed. The lobby was conceived as a tunnel, carved out of solid rock, its sidewalls polished, the floor worn smooth, and the ceiling incised and decorated as a civilized caveman might have done it. Marble, intricate incised bronze panels, and a gilt ceiling with low relief abstract patterns share a consistent set of motifs suggestive of Northwest Indian, Mayan, and Chinese cultures. Throughout the interior, symbols of the evergreen forest of the Pacific Northwest are stylistically represented in bronze and plaster. The building itself is crowned by three metal spires representing evergreens.

## Paramount Theatre

901 Pine Street
*Rapp & Rapp; B. Marcus Priteca, 1927–28*

See chapter 7.

## Rainier Club

810 Fourth Avenue
*Cutter, Malmgren & Wager, 1902–4; Bebb & Gould, 1928–29*

A rare example of Jacobean Revival style, the distinguished facade of Seattle's premier gentlemen's club (founded in 1888) was inspired by Aston Hall, a 17th-century stately home in Warwickshire, England. The curvilinear multigabled facade designed by the prominent Spokane firm of Cutter, Malmgren & Wager was capably expanded 54 feet southward by Seattle's leading firm of Bebb & Gould. Interiors reflected these two building periods, with a large brick fireplace and inglenook in the main lounge echoing the Arts and Crafts period (altered), while the new lobby lighting fixtures, brass railings, and elevator doors mirror up-to-date French decorative arts that came to be referred to as Art Deco. Bumgardner Architects has upgraded the building in recent years and removed a number of insensitive design treatments from previous remodel efforts.

## Shafer Building

515 Pine Street
*James E. Blackwell, 1923–24*

The Shafer is an excellent example of the Chicago style of commercial office tower, with minimal struc-

ture and large window expanses, its honest expression of structure and function, and its adept application of English Gothic style to the terra-cotta surfaces—a stylistic treatment that broke with the Beaux Arts classicism represented in other downtown office buildings up to that time. Its Gothic facade reflected the lightweight, open feeling achieved by the steel frame and emphasized the verticality of the building. Blackwell's approach was followed in the Medical and Dental Building by John Creutzer and the Liggett Building by Lawton & Moldenhour. The building also represented the strength of the local business community in the north end of the central business district and the shift in major retailing and commercial space, probably encouraged by the establishment of the Frederick and Nelson Department Store at Fifth Avenue and Pine Street in 1918.

## L. C. Smith Building (Smith Tower)

502–508 Second Avenue
*Gaggin & Gaggin, 1910–14*

Lyman Cornelius Smith of Syracuse, New York, had made a fortune in a prosperous typewriter manufac-

turing company (now Smith Corona) and Smith & Wesson revolvers. Having invested in property in Seattle in 1890, Smith decided to erect a 12-story office tower in 1909. Learning that the Hoge family was planning an 18-story building at the corner of Second Avenue and Cherry Street, Smith was encouraged by his son, Burns, to build a skyscraper that would be the tallest outside New York. Smith commissioned a Syracuse design firm to generate plans for a 600-office, 522-foot-high tower costing $1.5 million that would become the fourth-tallest building in the world, topped only by the Singer, Woolworth, and Metropolitan towers in New York.

The building's steel frame is covered in white glazed terra-cotta with a minimum of ornament and maximum expanses of windows with copper casings. In form, it consists of a 21-floor base structure surmounted by a 14-floor tower. The Second Avenue lobby is paneled with Mexican onyx walls and pilasters. A beamed ceiling appears to be supported by 22 hand-carved and richly painted Indian heads. Ornate brass grille elevator cages line the south wall of the lobby. Eight operator-assisted elevators originally served the building; two of them serve the tower portion, and one rises to the Chinese Temple Room at the 35th floor. This remarkable room, with its oriental-inspired interiors, provided the public with a spectacular outside observation deck. A balustrade has been removed from the deck, changes have occurred to office space and shopfronts, and the Smith Tower is no longer the tallest building outside New York. However, its distinctive white form is still a very welcome and familiar landmark despite the many taller glass boxes north and east of it in the central business district. Infill and alterations made during 1998–99 have turned the building into first-class office space and upgraded life safety systems. NBBJ and Mithun Partners did the design work.

## Terminal Sales Building
1932 First Avenue
*Henry Bittman, 1923*

The Terminal Sales Building presented an innovative marketing solution for the growing commercial enterprises that were turning the Pike and Pine Street corridor into the major retailing section of the city: to group together under one roof the sales and display rooms of the manufacturers and jobbers serving department and general stores. This concept proved a success and led to contemporary merchandise

marts and design centers for trade use. Its function as a loft building and warehouse for goods is reflected by industrial sash windows that maximize daylight for display of merchandise. Its setback form (it was one of the first buildings erected under the new Seattle building code that encouraged setbacks) and Gothic terra-cotta piers and spandrels contrast with more traditional Beaux Arts designed office buildings of the same period.

## Times Square Building
414 Olive Way
*Bebb & Gould, 1913–15*

Begun as the Press Times in 1886 and taken over by Colonel A. J. Blethen in 1896, the Times became the largest circulation daily in the region. By 1915, with a circulation of 70,000–80,000, the old headquarters proved inadequate and a triangular site was selected for a new building between Fourth and Fifth Avenues bordered by Stewart and Olive Streets. The site became known as Times Square, due to the building's resemblence to the famous New York Times Building in New York City. The building's Renaissance Revival design reflects Gould's training at the Ecole de Beaux Arts in Paris and his associa-

tion with the firm of McKim, Mead & White. The six-story building rises from a polished granite base to a stonelike terra-cotta skin with handsome voussoirs and lintels. Rich embellishments include molding courses, three-story-high arches outlining window bays, and a corbelled cornice with pale blue coloring. Over the entrance is a bas-relief that depicts the printing process.

**Triangle Hotel**
551 First Avenue S.
*C. A. Breitung, 1908–10*

This three-story eight-room hotel was constructed on a small triangular lot by businessman Victor Hugo Smith. In 1929, the "flatiron" building housed the first branch office of Western Union in the United States, linked by pneumatic tubes to the main office at Second Avenue and Cherry Street. The hotel has brick masonry bearing walls and a corbelled para-

pet. The facades are composed of two-story-high square bay windows clad in sheet metal.

**United Shopping Tower**
217 Pine Street
*Henry Bittman; Harold Adams, 1928–31*

The United Shopping Tower (now Olympic Tower) is a fine example of Art Deco commercial building design by a local architect whose signature works, such as the Eagles Temple, the Decatur Building, and the Terminal Sales Building, were richly faced in terra-cotta. Above a two-story retail and office base, a ten-story tower rises to setbacks at the twelfth floor forming corner terraces and encompassing a covered open loggia and projecting balconies. Graceful, uninterrupted piers, narrow window mullions, and recessed, vertically ribbed spandrels accentuate the building's verticality. Art Deco stylized floral ornament enriches the terra-cotta wall surfaces and pier caps at the polygonal crown of the building.

**U.S. Immigration Building**
84 Union Street
*Bebb & Gould, 1915*

This dignified masonry building with cast stone trim and cream-colored terra-cotta ornament has been associated with the U.S. Immigration Service, the Cannery Workers and Farm Laborers Union, the Federal Public Housing Authority, and the International Longshoremen's and Warehousemen's Union. Retail occupied the Western Avenue side of the building, while the immigration functions were carried out in the floor above and approached from Union Street, which originally housed an application room, dining, kitchen, and bathroom spaces. The third floor housed sleeping rooms and the fourth floor was divided into the headquarters offices. The Immigration Service occupied the building until 1931, when they relocated to a much larger facility on Airport Way. Subsequently, the building was a key gathering place for trade unionists. It now houses a youth hostel.

**YMCA Central Branch, South Building**
909 Fourth Avenue
*Albertson, Wilson & Richardson, 1929–31*

The Young Men's Christian Association movement was introduced to Seattle as early as 1876 by Catherine Maynard, Dexter Horton, Roland Denny, and other leading citizens as a way of civilizing and providing alternative diversions for the young men arriving in town. In its maturity, it became an important civic institution by promoting civic, moral, and religious values through its programming. The north building was completed in 1907 and designed by James Stephen, the Seattle Public Schools architect. A successful fundraising campaign made it possible to erect a new, Collegiate Gothic style building in 1930—an appropriate idiom given the ecclesiastical and educational mission of the organization. Despite its traditional appearance, the virtually flat brick veneers and punched-out window and door openings reflect the move into modernism by architects whose Northern Life Tower and St. Joseph's Church would become icons to modernistic design. The north building (which is not designated) was recently demolished to make way for new commercial development.

## REGRADE/BELLTOWN/CASCADE/ EASTLAKE

### Barnes Building
2320–22 First Avenue
*William Boone, 1889*

### Austin A. Bell Building
2326 First Avenue
*Elmer Fisher, 1889–90 (altered)*

The four-story Barnes Building was originally an Odd Fellows hall in Belltown, a separate community north of pioneer Seattle. Promoter and developer Austin Bell commissioned Elmer Fisher to construct a four-story apartment building adjacent to the hall. Fisher was Seattle's premier architect during the reconstruction of the downtown following a disastrous 1889 fire. Fisher's particular handling of red brick, terra-cotta, pressed brick, and stone are evident in this free adaptation of Victorian Gothic. The buildings are physically and historically pivotal structures in Belltown; they represent the nucleus of a development effort that never materialized in the way their pioneer builder envisioned. A fire in the Bell Building and subsequent failed proposals for new uses left it derelict. A 1998–99 design by Snell Partnership preserves the facade and builds condominiums behind it and in new construction to the north. Unfortunately, the intact interiors, which

included an unaltered atrium, were judged structurally unsound and were razed for the project.

### Ford Assembly Plant/Shurgard
1155 Valley Street
*John Graham Sr., 1913*

See chapter 7.

### Guiry Hotel
2101–5 1/2 First Avenue
*Designer unknown, 1903–4*

The Guiry, originally called the Hotel Desimone, provided transient housing for workers to the mills and factories along the waterfront in the community north of Seattle called Belltown. It advertised "All outside rooms, finely furnished. Transients 50 cents and up–by the week $2.50. Hot and cold water in rooms. Free baths. Brick building; steam heat and electric lights." Its present name is for the hotel manager who took over in 1926. The building's four-story brick facade features Romanesque arched windows grouped in pairs and surrounded by two-story high superimposed brick arches. Its dignified facade reflects the characteristic style, scale, and use of materials of other commercial buildings in the Belltown area, and it is one of the few that remain intact and vital in the face of continuing high-rise apartment and office development pressures.

## Hull Building

2401–5 First Avenue
*Elmer Fisher, 1889*

Alonzo Hull, president of a local furniture and upholstery company, built this building to house his business and provide hotel space. Along with the Bell and Barnes Buildings nearby, the Hull reflects the pre-20th century character of Belltown. It is a three-story brick commercial building with cast-iron columns and large shop windows on the ground floor and a richly detailed brick facade with a metal cornice.

## Immanuel Lutheran Church

1215 Thomas Street
*Watson Vernon, 1907–12*

Organized in 1890 by 33 Norwegian immigrants, Immanuel Lutheran Church was designed in a style strongly reminiscent of architecture in Scandinavia and northern Germany, particularly its massive, square-based tower, tapered buttresses, and spire with diminutive dormered vents. Although completely constructed with wood siding and shingle, these materials are handled to imitate masonry construction throughout. A simple pitched roof broken by clerestories shelters the main portion of the church. Semiround arched colored-glass windows and a front rose window embellish the simple building form. The interior combines characteristics of a Protestant meeting hall with a nave and side aisle arrangement. Structurally, the nave is expressed by a ribbed barrel vault supported by four square piers. Half-round clerestory windows filter light into the aisles below.

## Jensen Block

601–611 Eastlake Avenue E.
*F. F. Travis, builder, 1906*

The three-story Jensen Block was one of the earliest masonry veneer buildings in the Cascade neighborhood and still maintains its original commercial and residential uses. The building is very simple, but ground-floor stores are embellished by arched entrances, brick voussoirs, and ornamental tile work. The apartment sections have multiple entries. Originally housing 12 apartments, the building was reconfigured in 1944 into 26 housekeeping units. In 1996–97, Tonkin/Hoyne/Lokan, Inc., supervised

refurbishment of the building for the Low Income Housing Institute.

## Lake Union Steam Plant and Hydro House

1179 Eastlake Avenue E.
*Daniel Huntington, 1912, 1914, 1917–18, 1921 (altered)*

The buildings that compose the Steam Plant and Hydro House tell the story of Seattle's establishment of municipal power facilities, largely through the vision of City Engineer R. H. Thompson and J. D. Ross, superintendent of City Light from 1911 to 1937. Architecturally, the charming Spanish Colonial Revival Hydro House is residential in character. The later steam plant reflects functional needs above style. Only in the final addition of 1921 does the exterior attempt a more formal, civic appearance through the use of terra-cotta decorative panels. The buildings as a group reflect the design virtuosity of Daniel Huntington, who served as the City Architect from 1911 to 1925. The steam plant generated electric power until the 1980s. Its utilitarian building style was expressed with poured-in-place concrete walls punctuated with great expanses of metal sash windows that filled the plant with natural light. Its size, expansive windows, and towering smokestacks were as much a landmark and symbol of industrial progress for the city as the Smith Tower was a symbol of commercial success. The steam plant was closed in 1984. In 1993, it was turned into a biotechnology research and development laboratory for ZymoGenetics by Daly & Associates and NBBJ. Unfortunately, the original industrial sash windows were replaced with proportionally inappropriate new sash and tinted windows, and the original stacks were removed and replaced with fewer and shorter replicas.

### Old Norway Hall
2015 Boren Avenue
*Sonke Englehart Sonnichsen, 1915*

Norway Hall was built to house the Sons and Daughters of Norway cultural and fraternal societies, organized on the Pacific Coast between 1903 and 1906 by immigrants to the area. The building is an architectural effort to express traditional forms and details that would be familiar to transplanted Norwegians. The architect had trained and practiced in Norway during a period that witnessed a nationalistic or romantic revival movement; the forms stimulated by this revival focused upon the assumed Norwegian medieval structural forms and ornament particular to the loft-type house, which provided ground-floor storerooms and living and sleeping quarters above. The social hall Sonnichsen designed in Seattle borrowed elements of these vernacular Scandinavian farmsteads while at the same time incorporating elements of the dragon style seen in early stave churches. The dragon style was expressed in the carved dragon head which once enhanced the major gables of Norway Hall. Currently it serves as a dance hall.

### Owings Residence
2819 Franklin Avenue E.
*Charles Owings, 1898*

This house represents a vernacular residence style of the turn of the century that was quite common but has become a rare survivor as new development encroaches upon older neighborhoods. Built by a carpenter who worked on the house in his spare time, adding ornament as he saw fit and his budget allowed, it is decorated with turned posts, fancy butt shingles, scroll-sawn verge boards, and post brackets. Its front and side bays, gabled roofs, and stained-glass edged front door are typical of such homes, the elements of which often came directly from catalogues and pattern books.

### Pacific Hospital/New Pacific Apartments
2600–2604 First Avenue
*Designer unknown, 1904*

Built as a 25-bed hospital and training school for nurses, this three-story building conformed to the design of turn-of-the-century apartment buildings, particularly in its use of curved bay windows to allow

generous openings for light and cross-ventilation. Although quite simple and restrained in its use of ornament, there are some classic or Italian elements, including cornice details above the storefronts and at the parapet. When this building opened its doors, it was one of the city's earliest hospitals. By 1915, Seattle General Hospital had located two blocks away. By 1919, as health care increasingly began to center on First Hill, Pacific Hospital was relocated and the building was converted to the New Pacific Apartments.

### Schillestad Building
2111 First Avenue
*Andrew McBean, 1907*

This restrained brick building with cast stone lintels and sills opened the same year the Pike Place Farmers Market was officially established nearby. It provided space for needed retail services and modest housing for factory workers and waterfront laborers in the early part of the century and represents an early mixed-use structure in Belltown.

### Seattle, Chief of the Suquamish Statue
Tillicum Place, Fifth Avenue at Denny Way
*James Wehn, sculptor, Gorham & Company, foundry, 1912*

This gilt bronze life size statue, placed on a granite pedestal and originally set in a drinking trough for horses, forms the centerpiece of a fountain at Tillicum Place, a small park north of the Central Business District. The statue and fountain commemorate the ties of friendship between the white settlers and the Suquamish and Duwamish peoples, who greeted them in peace when they arrived in 1851. *Tillikum* is Chinook Jargon meaning "tribe, people, relations, and friend." The statue was commissioned by the City of Seattle and designed by a local sculptor to honor the man for whom the city was named, a tribal leader noted for his friendship, his philosophy of acceptance, and benevolence. The landscape architecture firm of Jones & Jones was responsible for the present parklike setting, developed in 1975.

## Seattle Times Building
1120 John Street
*R. C. Reamer, 1930–31*

In 1916, the *Seattle Times* flatiron building faced in ornamental terra-cotta and designed by Carl Gould reflected the best qualities of American Renaissance architecture. When the newspaper expanded to its new location, European and East Coast modernistic design aesthetics influenced R. C. Reamer to develop a headquarters building that emphasized mass and proportion with smooth-faced Indiana limestone above a granite base. The window spandrels are faced with decorative cast-aluminum panels in abstract motifs, and there are occasional references to traditional classicism with fluted piers and simple cresting at the parapet. A handsome aluminum entrance door grill decorated with octagons and floral, spiral, and wave motifs was inspired by contemporary French decorative metalwork, and incised floral ornament in limestone is used discretely in the vestibule. The printing plant to the north uses exposed concrete and industrial windows to echo the scale and proportions of its refined office building neighbor.

## St. Spiridon Cathedral
400 Yale Avenue N.
*Designer unknown, 1937–38*

Similar in plan and form to St. Nicholas Cathedral, St. Spiridon has a square main sanctuary approached through a small west portico and rectangular vestibule. The entrance porch, framed with twisted columns, supports a roof with an octagonal spire adorned with five small pointed gables, a central onion dome, and four corner domes. The roof of the vestibule has two onion domes, and an adjacent bell tower is also embellished with similarly sized domes. The main sanctuary is defined by a large central dome and four corner domes, all painted blue.

## Steinbrueck/Nelson Residence
2622 Franklin Avenue E.
*Designer unknown, c. 1891*

A two-story cross-gabled Victorian residence of frame construction with a wraparound verandah, this house is a well preserved example of late Victorian residential architecture. The form is enriched by a tower at the left of the front, a fan gable brace, acorn newel post finials, turned balusters, porch posts, and brackets. A colored glass transom and fish scale shingles also decorate the facades. Victor Steinbrueck, considered by many to be Seattle's foremost protector of vernacular architecture, was a leading civic activist whose efforts spearheaded the movement to save the Pike Place Market and preserve Pioneer Square as a historic district.

## Troy Laundry Building
311–329 Fairview Avenue N.
*V. W. Voorhees, 1927; Henry Bittman, 1944, 1946*

This ornate brick- and terra-cotta-faced industrial building was the home of Troy Laundry, the Northwest's largest laundry, with the largest automatic, self-loading washer in the Northwest, capable of handling 900 pounds at a time. The handsome entrance includes a terra-cotta surround with a cable molding around the semicircular arched opening. Above the entrance is a decorative cartouche with a woman's head that may represent Helen of Troy— the namesake of the company. Patterned brick pilasters with ornamental capitals embellish the facade.

# First Hill

## Fire Station No. Three
301 Terry Avenue
*Designer unknown, 1903*

Seattle's oldest extant firehouse was used for only eighteen years and was never adapted for motorized equipment. Consequently, it retains all its original interiors, reflecting the era of horse drawn fire fighting equipment. A hay loft and hoist beam for loading hay, stables and horse stalls, and a brick floor complete with steel rails that gave the wagons a faster start and aided the firemen when backing the wagons into the station are some of the building's preserved features. Like other early firehouses, this one was designed in a modified English style, with brick ground floor and stucco and half-timbered upper floor and pitched roofs. Set back from the street and with its landscaped lawn, the building respected its residential neighbors with an appropriately residential character.

**Fire Station No. Twenty-five**
1400 Harvard Avenue
*Somervell & Coté, 1908–9*

See chapter 7.

**Seattle First Baptist Church**
1121 Harvard Avenue
*U. Grant Fay; Russell & Babcock, 1908–12*

The First Baptist Church is an impressive example of English Gothic ecclesiastical architecture. The church, and particularly its tower and spire, create a dramatic, almost medieval cathedral image, contributing to the richness and variety of First Hill's urban townscape. The present church represents the third house of worship for one of Seattle's earliest congregations, established in 1869. Its composition is dominated by a 160-foot-high tower and spire, correctly proportioned and detailed in the English

Gothic idiom. Color and contrast are introduced to the building with the use of dark red oriental brick exterior walls, light colored granite and terra-cotta details, slate roofing, and a copper clad spire. At the time of its construction, the church was regionally recognized for its early and innovative use of structural steel. The 1990 renovation of the sanctuary by the firm of Cardwell/Thomas resulted in an open chancel and improved lighting and was inspired by a desire to return to its Gothic tradition—including the restoration of a central pulpit.

**St. James Cathedral**
Ninth Avenue and Marion Street
*Heins & LaFarge/W. Marbury Somervell, 1903–7;*
*John Graham Sr., 1916–17*

See chapter 7.

**Stimson/Green Residence**
1204 Minor Avenue
*Cutter & Malmgren, 1898–1901*

This English Tudor styled brick, stucco, and half-timber mansion was one of a large number of stately homes for the city's foremost businessmen and civic leaders that once occupied First Hill. Most of these homes have been replaced by apartment buildings, hospital and health care facilities, and parking lots. This home, which took two years to complete, was built for lumber and real estate developer C. D. Stimson and was designed by Kirtland Cutter of the Spokane firm of Cutter & Malmgren. Charles Bebb was the local supervisor. It was purchased in 1914 by shipping and banking magnate Joshua Green. Because the Greens occupied the house into the 1970s, the interiors, including the furnishings, hon-

estly represent lifestyles of the affluent at the turn of the century. While the exterior of the residence is predominantly English Tudor or Elizabethan, the interior contains rooms of baronial and Turkish styles, as well as a beautiful reception chamber whose plaster moldings and friezes recall the work of French designers Percier and Fontaine. In danger of demolition, the house was purchased by Historic Seattle in 1975 and resold with protective covenants. It currently is owned by the granddaughter of C. D. Stimson, has been meticulously restored, and provides meeting, wedding, and party space year-round.

**Summit School/Northwest School**
1415 Summit Avenue
*James Stephen, 1904–5*

Summit School is the oldest extant school building built to serve the central city at the turn of the century, when First Hill was an active neighborhood of well-to-do families and less affluent laborers living in dwellings ranging from mansions to boardinghouses within blocks of one another. While school architect James Stephen had developed a model school plan in 1901 that allowed for easy expansion of buildings, his plan for a 16-classroom schoolhouse at Summit deviated from the model in the location of stairways and the number and location of classrooms. His plan, in conjunction with the design demands of the sloping site and the use of a stucco exterior finish and Mission style parapets, resulted in a unique schoolhouse that accommodated additions in 1914 and 1928. The Northwest School, which has occupied the building since 1980, has upgraded the facility while preserving the interior spaces and finishes.

**Swedish Tabernacle/First Covenant Church**
1500 Bellevue Avenue
*John A. Creutzer, 1906 (no longer listed)*

See appendix A.

**Trinity Episcopal Church**
609 Eighth Avenue
*Henry Starbuck; John Graham Sr., 1891; 1902–03*

The first Episcopal congregation in Seattle was organized in 1855. The first church building, constructed at Third and Jefferson Street in 1870, was destroyed in the 1889 fire. The vestry purchased three lots at Eighth Avenue and James Street

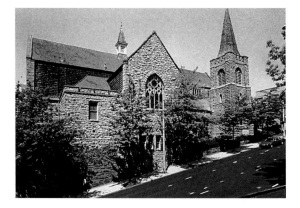

"removed from the business district," and in 1891, a stone church was built in the English parish Gothic style. It was designed with local stone, its interiors defined by heavy timber beams and plaster-finished walls. A fire of unknown origin gutted the church in 1901, but a new interior with some enlargements was accomplished within the original stone walls by English-born architect John Graham Sr. At that time, the spire and narthex were added. Stained-glass windows were made by the firm of Franz Mayer of Munich, Germany.

**U.S. Assay Office**
613 Ninth Avenue
*John Parkinson, 1893*

Built by civic leader Thomas Prosch for offices and an entertainment hall, the federal government rented the building in 1898 to serve as the assay office to process the flood of gold arriving daily from the Klondike. During the early years of the gold strike, annual deposits in the office reached $20–22 million. The building had its own melting department, and gold bars produced here were stamped and shipped to the U.S. Mint in Philadelphia. By 1928, deposits had declined to $6 million and in 1932, the office moved. In 1935, Deutsches Haus purchased the handsome brick building, with its Roman arched windows, classical columns, and cast-stone cornice. Since that time, it has functioned as the social center for the German Club.

**Wintonia Hotel**
1431 Minor Avenue
*Bebb & Mendel, 1909*

Pioneer lumber man Cyrus Walker arrived in Puget Sound in 1853. He was an early partner in the Port Gamble mill of Pope & Talbot and one of the largest landowners in Seattle by the time of his death in 1913. He developed this 6-story hotel—originally named the Walker—at the northern edge of First Hill along the route of the Pike Street streetcar line to house tourists, businessmen, and permanent residents. It was completed in time to welcome visitors to the Alaska-Yukon-Pacific Exposition. The architects incorporated masonry and terra-cotta ornament to make the building a distinctive visual landmark. Converted into a rooming house in the 1940s, the building was rehabilitated in 1994 by Kovelenko Architects into low-income housing.

## Capitol Hill/Stevens Neighborhood

### Anhalt Apartment Buildings
1005 and 1014 E. Roy Street
*Anhalt Company, 1929–30*

Fred Anhalt was a prolific designer, developer, landscaper, and promoter of many uncommon apartment buildings constructed within a four-year period

*Fred Anhalt stands at the entrance to the tower 1005 E. Roy Street*

(1926–30). Their number and the remarkable quality of their craftsmanship make these Mediterranean and French Norman styled buildings some of the most admired in Seattle. Promoted as apartment homes, they broke away from the traditional apartment form, eliminating long hallways and providing front and rear entrances, balconies, fireplaces, and main living areas facing onto beautifully landscaped courtyards. The Roy Street pair are exemplary of Anhalt's best French Norman designs executed in clinker brick, leaded and stained glass, cast stone, oak flooring, cedar shake, slate, and wrought iron. The building at 1005 E. Roy, one of his largest, also includes what Anhalt claimed to be the first underground parking garage designed for a Seattle apartment building. Organized around three stair towers, the building's most striking element is a freestanding circular staircase that rises, shell-like, to a roundel colored-glass lantern at the third-floor level.

### Art Institute of Seattle/Seattle Art Museum/ Seattle Asian Art Museum
1400 E. Prospect Street
*Bebb & Gould, 1931–33*

This "art moderne" art museum was constructed to the designs of Bebb & Gould to replace a band pavilion in Volunteer Park. The sandstone-faced building was a progressive departure from the traditional Beaux Arts styled art museums being built throughout America in the first quarter of the century and was especially avant-garde for Seattle. Its aluminum grill entrance bay reflected the metalwork of French designer Edgar Brandt popularized by the International Exposition of Modern Decorative and Industrial Arts held in Paris in 1925. The galleries were symmetrically placed on either side of a streamlined and gilt-trimmed lobby and central skylit fountain courtyard. When the Seattle Art Museum moved into its new Venturi Brown–designed building downtown, Olson/Sundberg and David Leavengood were responsible for restoration of the facade and interior renovation to turn the facility into the Asian Art Museum.

### Capitol Hill United Methodist Church
128 Sixteenth Avenue E.
*J. C. Fulton, 1906*

Built by the second-oldest congregation in the city, this sandstone structure is an excellent example of Gothic Revival design. The plan is particularly interesting since the main auditorium space is cleverly located on the bias within the external cruciform massing. The treatment of stonework and arches, the high roofs, corner tower, and adjoining parsonage make an important ensemble in the neighborhood. A stained-glass dome and stained- and leaded-glass windows incorporate in their structural design the major symbols of the world's major cultures, such as the yin yang of the Far East, the wheel of fortune of the Middle East, and the pillars of heaven of Eastern Europe. The architectural firm of Arai/ Jackson has made the church its offices with minimal structural changes, so that it can be restored to its original use at a later date.

### Pierre P. Ferry Residence
1531 Tenth Avenue E.
*John Graham Sr.; Alfred Bodley, 1903–5*

Built for Pierre Peyre Ferry, son of Elisha Ferry, one of Washington Territory's governors and the first governor of the new state, this English styled stucco and half-timbered country home is an excellent example of the influence of the English Arts and Crafts movement upon American residential design. Its designer may have been influenced by the works of Charles Voysey and William Morris in the informal massing, the large chimneys, and the banks of windows that characterize the exterior and in the creation of a variety of large and intimate interior spaces. The fixtures, tiles, ceiling decoration, woodwork,

windows, and fireplaces are splendid examples of the Art Nouveau style, executed by that style's foremost American artist, Louis Comfort Tiffany. Tiffany was invited to complete the interiors, and came to Seattle to personally supervise the installation of a four-paneled autumn foliage stained-glass window, a magnificent colored mosaic and gold leaf tile wisteria mural for the dining-room fireplace, and other decorative pieces.

### First Church of Christ Scientist
1519 E. Denny Way
*Bebb & Mendel, 1909; 1914*

Built in two stages as funds became available, First Church of Christ Scientist is one of a number of Neoclassically inspired churches built with centric forms and cubic massing. It has a flattened octagonal dome. Externally this design expresses very well the volumes and functions of interior spaces. The exterior is executed in stone with granite steps leading to the marble-floored main entrance portal and foyer. The focal point of the auditorium is its impressive stained-glass dome and stained-glass windows, accented by finely crafted cornice moldings and pilasters.

### Harvard Mansion
2706 Harvard Avenue E.
*Edward J. Duhamel, 1903*

Located on a prominent site in the Roanoke neighborhood, this three-story Colonial Revival mansion is fronted with imposing Corinthian columns and a top-floor railed belvedere. Decks that wrap around the first and second floors with Ionic columns were added by the second owners beginning in 1910. Elaborate decorative eaves, cornices, brackets, friezes, and moldings in the Greco-Roman style and leaded beveled-glass panes make this one of the most flamboyant homes in the area. Its architect-owner, Edward J. Duhamel, established a building/contracting firm that constructed many important buildings for Kirtland Cutter, C. H. Bebb, A. Warren Gould, Saunders & Lawton, Max Umbrecht, and other important local firms. Second owner William Parsons was a financial leader whose Washington Trust Company merged with Dexter Horton National Bank in 1910, for which he served as president beginning in 1922.

**Hillcrest Apartments**
1616 E. Howell Street
*Designer unknown, 1909*

Appropriately named, this apartment building was constructed at the top of Capitol Hill in one of Seattle's newly developing and desirable residential neighborhoods, made more accessible by frequent streetcar service from downtown along Madison Street. A shortage of housing during the early part of the century meant that not everyone could afford to live in single-family homes. Yet apartment living was not easily accepted as an alternative for the middle classes. Developers of such buildings had to offer amenities and a high degree of craftsmanship in their products. The Hillcrest is an exceptionally well preserved and maintained example of an early-20th-century apartment building. Its bright, naturally lit interiors, good cross ventilation, high ceilings, and practical floor plans were and are desirable qualities in a living space. Architecturally, the tan brick and stucco building is compatible with its commodious neighboring residences. The mass of the building is broken into a central section and two side wings; exterior wall planes are broken down by a rich undulation of square and angled bay windows, projecting balconies, and deeply recessed fire escapes. The building's classically derived scroll brackets, entablature, and dentiled cornices reflect the Beaux Arts style of other nearby buildings.

**Lincoln Park/Lincoln Reservoir and Bobby Morris Playfield**
1000 E. Pine Street
*R. H. Thomson 1897–1901; Olmsted Brothers, c. 1904–1909*

Lincoln and Volunteer Park reservoirs were the first reservoirs developed as part of the city's municipal water supply system. Designed in 1897 under the direction of R. H. Thomson, the City of Seattle Engineer, the Lincoln Park reservoir has cast- in-place concrete walls in the Renaissance Revival style and with the appearance of cut stone, a style repeated in the gatehouse on the southwest edge of the reservoir wall. It was constructed beginning in 1899 and was put into service in 1901. Lincoln Park was an integral element of the Olmsted Brothers' 1903 plan for a system of parks and boulevards in Seattle. In his 1904 plan for improvements to the site, John Charles Olmsted of the Olmsted Brothers landscape

architecture firm proposed both pastoral park and active recreation areas for the 11-acre site. The paths, open lawn, deciduous trees, and playfields remain largely intact and used as they were intended despite nearly a century of growth and change in the surrounding neighborhood. Now more than ever, the park, reservoir, and playfield provide valuable and needed physical, mental, and emotional relief in the densely populated community.

**Maryland Apartments**
626 Thirteenth Avenue E.
*Henderson Ryan, 1910–11*

This four-story apartment block is distinguished by its rich use of cut sandstone, multicolored brick, sheet metal, terra-cotta, ceramic tile, marble, and wood to present a handsome and individualized interpretation of Italianate design to the street. A large two-story entrance portico is composed of four brick pilasters capped with a sheet metal cornice embellished with egg and dart moldings. Two two-story-high composite wood columns support a curved front exterior balcony. Brick veneer bays of five windows each are laid in large-radius curves on either side of the entrance. The idiosyncratic style of this building reflects upon an architect whose body of work is stylistically varied, including the Ballard Library, Waldorf Towers Apartments (recently demolished to make way for expansion of the Washington State Convention and Trade Center), and numerous small apartment buildings throughout the city.

**Moore Mansion**
811 Fourteenth Avenue E.
*W. D. Kimball, 1902*

The French Empire styled sandstone and brick mansion James Moore had built on what at the time was dubbed "millionaire's row," reflected his increasing power and influence from his first encounters with the city in 1886. An enterprising industrialist and capitalist, whose reach extended far outside of the city, he incorporated the Moore Investment Company in 1897 and developed housing tracts on Capitol Hill, Madison Park, Renton Hill, Rainier Beach, Latona, Brooklyn, University Heights, and University Heights Addition. His progressive methods included installing all the infrastructure (water and sewer lines, drainage, paved streets and sidewalks) prior to platting the tracts and selling the lots. He also developed the Moore Theater and Hotel building, the New Washington Hotel (now the Josephinium), and a number of other downtown properties along with his own home.

## Parker-Fersen House
1409 E. Prospect Street
*Frederick A. Sexton, 1909*

One of the most impressive Colonial Revival styled homes in Seattle was built at the north end of millionaire's row for George H. Parker, a fiscal agent for an East Coast telegraph company. His name generated front-page headlines when he was convicted on stock fraud charges shortly after completion of the $100,000 house. In 1929, Baron Eugen Fersen, a Russian nobleman, purchased the 7,500-square-foot house and made it the center of an international religious group he founded called the Lightbearers. Though the original clapboard siding has been replaced by stucco, and balustrades on the second and third floor have been removed, the residence is largely intact inside. It features outstanding Tiffany windows and fixtures, mahogany and oak woodwork, stenciled walls and ceilings, and art tile fireplaces by major American manufacturers, including Henry Chapman Mercer and Rookwood. See chapter 8 for further details.

## East Republican Street Stairway
Between Melrose and Bellevue Avenue E.
*City Engineering Department, 1910*

This public stairway is less than half of a major pedestrian link that originally consisted of nine flights of stairs (three of them split into pairs), a paved circle, and two semicircular overlooks or belvederes. With the intrusion of the interstate freeway, the upper three flights and a single overlook are the only remaining elements. Construction took place during an era when Seattle was placing an increasing emphasis on urban amenities and public improvements, influenced by the national City Beautiful movement. This stairway solved the functional problem of vertical circulation along the hillside in an aesthetically pleasing way. Although the stairs and retaining walls are entirely of unadorned reinforced concrete, they are scored and modeled after their cut stone European counterparts. Traversing a parklike slope 35 feet in height, the extant stairway creates a significant open-space amenity within a landscape of mature maples, ash, and laurels.

## Russian Orthodox Cathedral of St. Nicholas
1714 Thirteenth Avenue
*Ivan Palmov, 1932–38*

The Russian community in Seattle established a church, St. Spiridon, on Lakeview Boulevard in 1898. Most of its members were emigrants from Russia after the death of Alexander III in 1894. After the Bolshevik Revolution, more conservative members of the congregation, joined by new refugees from Russia, split from the more moderate faction, who supported the Soviet takeover. By 1933, the disagreement had led to the establishment of another church, St. Nicholas. A court battle over ownership of the St. Spiridon property forced its closing and the relocation to a new site nearby. The St. Nicholas congregation acquired property on Capitol Hill and a church member designed a church as a memorial to Nicholas II, last czar of Russia. The church follows the model of 16th-century Russian Orthodox cathedrals, a square plan with a small rectangular portico at the west front entrance. Faced with tan brick, the building's arched portico has a tiny onion dome and an octagonal brick tower and spire adorned with small gables behind it. Atop the sanctuary is a large central gold onion dome, surrounded by four blue onion domes at each of the four corners. These domes represent Christ and the four apostles. Each dome is capped by an Eastern cross.

### San Remo Apartment Building

606 Thirteenth Avenue E.
*William D. Van Siclen, 1907*

The four-story San Remo was among the first of dozens of apartments and residential hotels built on Capitol Hill as the city expanded east. Its design reflected contemporary concerns for adequate natural lighting, ventilation, and quality interior living and social spaces. Its facade is composed of clinker brick, buff colored brick, and stucco with Mediterranean revival ornament at the entry. The facade curves gently along a property line that defines E. Thomas Street. The architect's early practice in California may have inspired his introduction of Italian and Spanish Revival touches into his Seattle works such as this building, which originally was capped with a tile roof and an ornamental raised parapet wall with classical ornamentation and urns.

### Semple/Bystrom Residence

1022 Summit Avenue E.
*Designer unknown, 1890*

Originally, this house was leased to Eugene Semple, the last governor of Washington Territory. Located within the Harvard/Belmont Historic District, it is one of several late-19th-century Victorian homes among a much larger grouping of early-20th-century residences. Its characteristic gabled roofs, angled bay windows, and milled porch with open brackets reflect a late 19th century vernacular style that was once commonplace but has all but disappeared from this metropolitan area. Architect Arne Bystrom has made modifications to the building to provide modern conveniences; changes have been accomplished with a sensitive understanding of Victorian decora-

tion. The porch has been rebuilt using several original turned balusters and posts as models for the rest. Throughout the house, stained-glass edging has been added to windows and doors in the manner of the originals.

### Seward Public School

2515 Boylston Avenue E.
*Chamberlin & Siebrand, 1894; 1899;*
*James Stephen, 1905; Edgar Blair, 1917*

The Seward School consists of three separate buildings from different periods that are grouped to form a small campus illustrating the development of public school architecture from the end of the 19th century through the first two decades of the 20th century. The earliest school on the site, the Denny-Fuhrman School, was completed in 1894 and added to in 1899. It is a hipped-roof frame building with a round arched entry. In 1905, a second frame building, one of a number of model eight room frame schools by James Stephen, was built on the site. Its exteriors are finished with clapboard siding at the first story and simulated half-timber and stucco treatment at the second story to present an English Tudor appearance. A third building, designed by Edgar Blair, reflects new approaches in the design of fireproof brick schoolhouses. This building is essentially nonstylistic, with the exception of some Beaux Arts styled terra-cotta detailing at the entrances. Duarte/Bryant was responsible for a recent renovation of the historic buildings and a new gymnasium on the north part of the site.

### St. Joseph's Church

732 Eighteenth Avenue E.
*Albertson, Wilson & Richardson, 1929–30*

St. Joseph's Church was one of the most technically progressive religious edifices built in the United States in its time. It was widely recognized for its early and expressive use of reinforced-concrete technology inspired by work in the material by such pioneers in the modern idiom as Auguste Perret in France and Werner Moser and others in Switzerland. The church had been designed in the Gothic style and the foundation had been poured when, lacking the funds to continue as planned, the architect provided a creative and inexpensive solution. The uplifting form and verticality of this modernistic church and its cruciform plan recall the Gothic tradition with-

out the restrictions of literal interpretation. Rather, it attempts to express a 20th-century church in terms of the skyscraper idiom—a form for which Albertson and his partners, Joseph Wilson and Paul Richardson, had received accolades in their Northern Life Tower of the same period. The bell tower, with its vertical piers rising to a three-tiered, setback crown, is an especially powerful symbolic image executed in the Art Deco style. Replacing the traditional rose window is an octagonal window with a tightly ordered geometric pattern in keeping with the refreshing simplicity of the overall design. The church interior has been embellished since its completion by the addition of beautiful stained-glass windows and mosaics that contribute color and warmth.

## St. Nicholas School
1501 Tenth Avenue E.
*Bebb & Gould, 1925–26*

St. Nicholas School was the first nonsectarian private school in Seattle. Its founders were well-established pioneer families who wished to create a learning environment modeled after the best academies on the East Coast to provide their children with a privileged education without leaving the area. Named after the patron saint of children, the school operated out of the R. D. Merrill home at first, moving to a new building in 1910. In 1925, a Jacobean styled

brick school was designed for a site on Tenth Avenue E. by the firm of Bebb & Gould, whose other commissions had included the University of Washington campus plan and several major buildings, including Suzzallo Library and the Henry Art Gallery. The school's Elizabethan and Norman form and detailing fit easily into this traditional residential neighborhood. In 1971, St. Nicholas School merged with Lakeside, another private academy. The building now houses several departments of the Cornish Institute, a school for visual and performing arts.

## Isaac Stevens School
1242 Eighteenth Avenue E.
*James Stephen, 1906*

Built from Stephen's standardized plan, this school—named for the first governor of Washington Territory—differs from others in the school district in that it was not expanded with north and south wings; instead, a small single-story frame wing was added in 1928. The west, or primary, facade of Stevens School is distinguished by a central two-story colossal Ionic columned entrance portico with pediment. The main entrance within the portico is a scaled down version, replete with pediment and columns. Other

wood decorations include quoined corners and a cornice supported by attenuated brackets. Arai/Jackson is the firm responsible for refurbishment of the 1906 building and new additions. The 1928 wing will be demolished.

**Ward Residence**
1025 Pike Street; 1423 Boren Avenue
*Relocated to 520 E. Denny Way*
*Attributed to George W. Ward, 1882*

The Ward residence is the oldest surviving structure in central Seattle, having escaped the fate of similar wood frame buildings that burned or were razed for new construction. It is an excellent example of the Italianate villa style so popular during the later part of the 19th century. The tower, bay windows, decorative shingles, low-pitched roofs, and numerous decorative eave brackets and window and door casings are typical of the style. Most of the decorative elements of the facade were machine produced and offered through catalogues. George W. Ward was a building contractor and manufacturer of sashes and doors who, by 1882, had become president of Llewellyn and Ward Company, doing business in real estate, insurance, and loans. In that year, he had a handsome Italianate residence built on Pike Street surrounded by a green lawn covering the southwestern half-block of Boren Avenue and Union Street. In 1905, the property was sold to a hotel development company and the house was turned so

that the front, originally facing north onto Pike Street, faced east fronting Boren. This provided more space for a new hotel that rose adjacent to the residence. During the 1909 Alaska-Yukon-Pacific Exposition, the house became a hotel annex to accommodate the large number of tourists visiting Seattle. When it was threatened by proposed new construction in 1985, Historic Seattle Preservation and Development Authority sought and found new owners willing to move it to a new location. It has been refurbished for law offices on East Denny Way.

## QUEEN ANNE HILL

**Ballard Residence**
22 W. Highland Drive
*DeNeuf & Heide, 1901*

Built for a prominent Seattle family, the Ballard residence represents one of the finest Colonial Revival facades found locally. The building's columned verandah is typical of that style, and the architects combined a number of more ornate architectural details, such as curved balcony railings and arches over windows, with the more austere geometry to generate a lively and unique composition. In the early 1930s, the residence was converted to apartments, the east and west wings were added, and the roof balustrade and other embellishments were removed. Nevertheless, the front of the house has been generally maintained as it was in 1901.

**Bethany Presbyterian Church**
1818 Queen Anne Avenue N.
*Charles Hay, 1929–30*

Designed in the English Gothic style, this red-brick-faced building with light-colored cast-stone trim has a distinctive and well-proportioned tower with a spire rising from the intersection of its pitch roofed wings. The tower is detailed with cast-stone pilasters and finials at the corners and crenellations at the top. Gothic arched openings with cast-stone tracery casings and quoins occur near the tower's crown. An octagonal spire sheathed with square, diagonally set copper plates rises to a height of approximately 80 feet above the tower. In terms of the composition and detailing, this church represents one of Seattle's most successful adaptations of English Gothic architecture and provides an important visual element for the neighborhood.

## C. H. Black Residence
615 W. Lee Street
*Bebb & Mendel; Olmsted Brothers, 1907–9*

Built by the founder of the Seattle Hardware Company on 1.7 acres, this home is an outstanding mixture of English manor styling with characteristics derived from the Arts and Crafts movement. Its asymmetrical form, expressed with a heavy masonry base and stucco/half-timbered upper floor, boasts many gables, gabled bays, balconies, large expanses of window, and broad eaves. Designed by the prominent local firm of Bebb & Mendel, the 33-room house has 11,600 square feet of living space. Its richly appointed reception and living rooms feature oak and mahogany paneling and beams, marble and tile fireplaces, and hand painted wall panels. The Olmsted Brothers prepared drawings for the grounds and landscaping between 1906 and 1908. Grading, driveways, retaining walls, gates, stable, and belvedere were carried out, and the grounds were extensively landscaped with many varieties of evergreen and deciduous plant material. A formal rose garden and a pond are some of the more notable landscape features.

## Bowen Bungalow
715 W. Prospect Street
*Harris & Coles, 1913*

This bungalow is a design of Harris & Coles, a firm that also sold plans under the name The Bungalow Company. Its exterior form is characterized by a complexity of roofs; verge boards are raised at the peak and turned slightly upwards at their ends in the Japanese manner to give a soaring feeling. Other features include widely spaced shakes laid up in biased courses and diamond-paned windows of leaded glass. Located on a brick and cobblestone cul-de-sac with an expansive view of Puget Sound and the Olympic Mountains, the house and its richly landscaped site are an important community landmark. It was the home of Betty Bowen (1919–77), a noted Seattle arts patron. As founder and supporter of a number of leading organizations that encouraged and lobbied for artists, Ms. Bowen is credited with having promoted the careers of many famed Northwest artists, among them Mark Tobey, Richard Gilkey, and Morris Graves.

## Brace Residence
170 Prospect Street
*Kerr & Rogers, 1904*

Built for a prosperous lumber magnate, John Stuart Brace, this is one of the earliest and best examples of the Mission style in Seattle. The house is architecturally unique in several respects. Its river rock foundation is designed to give the appearance of dry-wall construction. The first story exterior treatment imitates masonry with board and batten wood construction. The building's most outstanding feature, however, is a recessed verandah extending the full length of the south facade; enhanced by seven round arches, it is detailed with exceptional Sullivanesque styled casings. The house's strong unity of composition and excellence of detailing contribute significantly to the Queen Anne Boulevard system of which Prospect Street is a part.

## Chelsea Apartments
620 W. Olympic Place
*Harlan Thomas, 1907*

The first of a number of apartment hotels developed along major streetcar lines to serve visitors to the Alaska-Yukon-Pacific Exposition in 1909, the

Chelsea is a four-story U-shaped building with stucco and clinker brick detailing and tiers of projecting bay windows. Its most striking feature is the spatial treatment of the entrance; a triple arched loggia with stained-glass panels leads into a forecourt from which a stairway rises to the portal. Architect Harlan Thomas had traveled extensively throughout Italy and was an admirer of Italian styles; his almost baroque treatment of the stairway and balustrades of the Chelsea are evidence of his interest, as are his designs for the Sorrento Hotel, Amalfi Apartments, and Chamber of Commerce in Seattle. Originally, a roof garden with pergola, palm trees, and arbors overlooked the magnificent views of Puget Sound.

## Coe Elementary School
2433 Sixth Avenue W.
*James Stephen, 1907; Edgar Blair, 1914*

Coe was built according to Stephen's standardized eight-room wood-framed model school plan, with Colonial Revival stylistic treatments. The west, or primary, facade is distinguished by a central two-story Ionic columned entrance portico with pediment similar to the architect's Isaac Stevens School on Capitol Hill, built a year earlier. The main entrance within the portico is a scaled-down version, replete with pediment and columns. Other wood decorations include quoined corners and a cornice supported by attenuated brackets. Blair's 1914 north wing, which contains an auditorium and kindergarten, as well as classrooms and offices, uses similar materials and fenestration. Mahlum Architects is currently working on plans for renovation of the historic building, a new library wing to the south, and a new gymnasium in a separate building to the north.

## Cotterill Residence
2501 Westview Drive W.
*Designer unknown, 1910*

George F. Cotterill was a civil engineer and Seattle's mayor from 1912 to 1914. His most important contribution was the establishment of the Cedar River watershed to secure a major water supply system for the city. The nine-room home he had built for his family on the west slope of Queen Anne Hill successfully combines features of the shingle and bungalow styles. Its use of rough-sawn cedar siding, bay windows, wide dormers, and recessed porches antic-ipates the development of an indigenous Northwest regional residential style.

## Delamar Apartments
115 W. Olympic Place
*Schack & Huntington, 1908–9*

This four-story U-shaped apartment building was built by a major Queen Anne Hill landowner, George Kinnear, to house friends and visitors to the Alaska-Yukon-Pacific Exposition in 1909. The formality of this modified Italianate palazzo is expressed with yellow brick and simulated masonry of molded terra-cotta and ivory terra-cotta pilasters and fluted capitals crowned by a three-part entablature and dentiled cornice with terra-cotta balustrade. A wrought-iron gate with arched canopy leads into a well-scaled courtyard with a sunken Roman pool, further decorated with a late Victorian cast iron lamppost and the statue of a maiden. The lobby is a blend of Italianate and late Victorian elements with ochre-colored marble columns and wainscoting, cast-plaster ceiling, ornate wall sconces, and a tiled floor featuring a multicolored coat of arms. Damage to the terra-cotta-extended cornice has required its removal and reconstruction of a shallow cornice in sheet metal.

## Fourteenth Avenue West Residences
2000–2016 Fourteenth Avenue W.
*Designers unknown, 1890–1910*

See chapter 7.

## Handschy Residence
2433 Ninth Avenue W.
*Willatsen & Byrne, 1910*

Andrew Willatsen and Barry Byrne apprenticed with Frank Lloyd Wright in his Oak Park studio. Their four-year partnership in Seattle enriched the area with second-generation Wright architecture. Their residences, derived directly from Wright's Prairie Style, nonetheless made adjustments for the Northwest terrain and climate. The Frederick Handschy residence demonstrates a sculptural quality in both the use of materials (rough sawn siding, light colored stucco, and dark stained fir trim boards) and the composition of forms (a low horizontal massing enriched by the incorporation of dramatically pitched gables). The residence is located at the rear of two city lots, providing a strong horizontal form while creating a wide front yard to buffer the house from the street. Characteristics of this house that are familiar Wrightian expressions are the one-story open verandah entry porch that extends from the body of the house, the horizontal emphasis of its shingle siding, the deep eaves of its gabled roof forms, and the contrast of light-colored stucco upper facade and eaves against the dark-stained wood accent moldings.

## John Hay School
2100 Fourth Avenue N.
*James Stephen, 1905*

An excellent and virtually unaltered eight-room school built from Stephen's model, John Hay is remarkably free of Beaux Arts influence. Whereas other neighborhood frame schools were cloaked with eclectically designed facade elements, Hay is particularly meritorious for its honest expression of function and lack of eclecticism.

## McFee Residence
524 W. Highland Drive
*Spalding & Umbrecht, 1909*

This impressive formal Tudor residence of brick with half-timbering occupies a prominent corner site on West Highland Drive, one of the city's major view boulevards. A brick retaining wall surrounded by a brick terrace serves as a pedestal base for the house, noted for the sensitive organization of windows within the modulation of half-timbering and stucco. The interiors reflect and carry through the formality and balance of the exterior, with excellent woodwork and trim and a number of Art Nouveau fixtures.

## North Queen Anne Drive Bridge
Spans ravine at Wolf Creek
*Clark Eldridge, City Bridge Engineer, 1936*

This vehicular bridge represents the convergence of high-quality design and engineering excellence under the Works Progress Administration. Drawing from an awareness of 20th-century European technology in the application of ferroconcrete, the bridge is a 238-foot-long reinforced concrete open spandrel arch bridge with a 45-foot-wide deck. It includes two 5-foot-wide sidewalks and carries foot and vehicular raffic across a very deep wooded ravine formerly called Wolf Creek. The simple concrete forms are

embellished by regularly spaced groups of rectangular indentations and by tulip-shaped ornamental lighting fixtures mounted on projecting pier headings. The bridge is striking for its unusually high (85 feet) parabolic arch and the minimal dimensions of its network of supporting members. The arch is constructed of curved and riveted I beam sections and the form they create provides a stunning backdrop to the modest residential scale at the base of the hill on which it is located.

## Parsons Residence
618 W. Highland Drive
*W. Marbury Somervell, 1905*

Designed by a well-established residential architect for Seattle businessman Reginald Parsons, this two-story stucco clad Dutch Colonial styled residence was part of an estate that included gardens to the west (given to the city in 1956) and land to the east on which a later addition was built. The slate-covered gambrel roofs shelter a handsome home that includes fireplaces in every bedroom, a gymnasium on the third floor, a large library, a tile-floored conservatory, and a large sunroom. In 1994, architect Brandt Hollinger oversaw additions to the house, a new garage, and a brick perimeter wall.

## Queen Anne Boulevard
Queen Anne Hill
*Seattle Engineering Department and Parks Board, 1911–16*

In 1903, when the prestigious Olmsted firm generated a comprehensive park and boulevard system for Seattle, Queen Anne residents were disappointed to find that their hill had not been included. Consequently, the Queen Anne Club, with the leadership of prominent civic leaders and businessmen, lobbied the city to provide a complementary scenic drive surrounding the top of the hill. Their 1906 proposal was finally approved by the Parks Board, Engineering Department, and the community. Condemnation was used to acquire land, acquisition costs were shared, and improvements were undertaken by the city Engineering Department. Ownership of most of the route was transferred to the Parks Department for planting and maintenance. Actual construction took place in six phases, during which a variety of tree species were planted, handsome concrete and brick infill retaining walls were built (known as the

Willcox Walls for their designer, W. R. B. Willcox), and promenades with custom-designed lampposts were provided. Over time, donations of private land along or near the boulevard have added gardens and viewpoints that enhance its character, such as Parsons Gardens and Betty Bowen Lookout. In recent years, decaying lighting fixtures were repaired or replaced by replicas.

## Queen Anne High School
215 Galer Street
*James Stephen, 1909; F. Naramore, 1929*

Queen Anne High School's monumental design and prominent hilltop location make it a distinctive visual landmark. The school also provided a central focus socially and academically for the Queen Anne community, helping to make it one of the most cohesive of Seattle neighborhoods. The 1909 building was the work of distinguished school architect James Stephen, whose model elementary schools were focal points of many Seattle neighborhoods. He utilized refined decorative masonry to generate an English late Renaissance palace form with handsome pedimented entrances and prominent ornamented cornices and parapets that may have been inspired by Blenheim Palace. The roof is hipped and gabled; its original glass skylights, bracketed cupolas housing ventilation louvers, and terra-cotta coping have either been removed or covered over. Additions to the four-story main building have included a gymnasium, assembly hall, and classroom wings constructed in 1955. The school, closed since 1981, was rehabilitated and converted to apartment use under the auspices of Historic Seattle Preservation and Development Authority. Lorig Associates was developer with Bumgardner Architects. See chapter 7.

*Rendering of Queen Anne High School by James Stephen, 1909*

QUEEN ANNE HIGH SCHOOL

## Queen Anne Water Tank No. 1
1410 First Avenue N.
*R. H. Thomson, supervisor, 1899–1901*

After a drought in 1899 that lasted several weeks, during which time two privately owned water companies were unable to supply water to Queen Anne Hill, the residents petitioned city government to form a municipal water company. Because of the height of the hill, it was selected for one of the city's three first in-town storage facilities. The steel cylinder was encased in a 69-foot-tall concrete shell that resembled a medieval fortress tower, with the appearance of rusticated stone, pointed arched windows, and a crenelated parapet. With the installation of a counterbalance streetcar in 1902 along Queen Anne Avenue, the city named the property Observatory Park and the storage tank, wrapped with an exterior stairway, doubled as a popular observatory for unobstructed views. Despite the second water tank and fire station that fill the small site, the tower is still a romantic marker from many locations on Queen Anne Hill.

## Space Needle
219 Fourth Avenue N.
*John Graham & Company, 1962*

Anchoring the southeast corner of the Century 21 exposition site, the Space Needle embodied a futuristic form and height that immediately made it an emblem for the city of Seattle, both locally and internationally. Despite high-rise construction in downtown, the Needle continues to be a significant landmark and geographical marker to residents and visitors alike. Design of this visionary piece of architecture that would embody the spirit of the theme "Century 21" was the result of conceptual work by John Graham Jr. and design refinements by Art Edwards, John Ridley, and Victor Steinbrueck. It was constructed by Howard S. Wright, a co-owner whose firm also was responsible for construction of the Coliseum, Monorail, and Skyride at the exposition. Three pairs of slender steel legs curve inward from a 102-foot diameter base to the 373-foot "waist" level and flair out into an hourglass form to hold a disc-shaped structure at the top, which comprises a revolving restaurant, a mezzanine, and an observation deck. The top 50 feet of the structure was originally a flame of natural gas, which was ignited from a tripod of stainless steel. (The flame was subse-

### West Queen Anne Elementary School
515 W. Galer Street
*Skillings & Corner; Edgar Blair, 1895–96; 1900; 1902; 1916 (altered)*

See chapter 7.

quently dismantled and replaced by an aircraft warning beacon.) Visitors to the top of the Needle ride one of three 29-passenger elevators traveling at the speed of up to 800 feet a minute. Some of the construction techniques were revolutionary at the time and set construction industry records. The foundation consisted of a 30-foot-deep Y-shaped pit filled with 2,819 cubic yards of concrete and 250 tons of reinforcing steel. It was the largest continuous concrete pour on the West Coast. Rising a total of 607.88 feet, the Space Needle was deemed the highest structure west of the Mississippi in 1962. Modifications include a postfair enclosure at the ground level, a 100-foot-level addition in 1981–82, and elevator replacements in 1993.

### Stuart Residence
619 W. Comstock Street
*A. H. Albertson, 1926*

DeEtte McAuslan Smith Stuart amassed a $23 million estate and was a patron of Seattle arts, schools, and charities until her death in 1979. From its prominent Queen Anne Hill location, her modified Georgian brick home is a showplace of terraced formal gardens and splendid views of the city. Designed by architect A. H. Albertson, the house is united and articulated vertically by a handsome spiral staircase of oak treads and dogwood motif metal railings and horizontally by a spacious gallery leading through arched French windows onto a loggia with a superb view. Below, on the garden level, is a large ballroom and library.

### West Queen Anne Walls
Queen Anne Boulevard
*Willcox & Sayward, 1913*

These retaining walls, a part of the Queen Anne Boulevard improvements proposed by the community and accomplished by the City Engineering Department and the Parks Department, are outstanding examples of the use of poured in place reinforced concrete and decorative brick infill. The walls, crowned by a handsome balustrade and cast metal light fixtures (recently replaced with replicas) and featuring a number of stairways and pullouts, provide an outstanding scenic promenade on the west side of the crest of Queen Anne Hill along Eighth Avenue W. near W. Galer Street. The walls were designed by W. R. B. Willcox, whose personal acquaintance with Louis Sullivan and Frank Lloyd Wright influenced his design of structures for the city, including that of the Arboretum Aqueduct.

## CENTRAL AREA/BEACON HILL

### Beacon Hill First Baptist Church
1607 S. Forest Street
*Ellsworth Storey, 1910*

This church was designed by a locally prominent architect who was strongly influenced by the Swiss chalet style and the works of architects and designers in both the European and American Arts and Crafts movement. Storey's work inspired the Northwest

Regional style in residential design. One of three Seattle churches designed by Ellsworth Storey, Beacon Hill First Baptist Church expresses his concern for originality within the confines of function and the eclectic styles popular at the time. In particular, he chose inexpensive materials that honestly expressed interior functions. Although the building's original stained shingles and white trim are now covered by asphalt shake, much of the original exterior detailing is still revealed, including various geometric forms of gable bracing, shallow gable roofs, and Tudor arched windows.

### Frank D. Black Gatehouse

1319 Twelfth Avenue S.
*Designer unknown, 1914*

Although the 1896 Swiss chalet styled Craftsman residence no longer exists, improvements to this estate made in 1914 by its prosperous owner are protected. The most notable is a cobblestone gate lodge consisting of one large room and a seven-foot-wide verandah that took advantage of a panoramic view of the city and Puget Sound. Although cobblestone was used in a decorative manner in Seattle, in no other extant building was it used as extensively, authentically, or as carefully graded as at the Black estate. The walls of the gate lodge are laid up in faultless horizontal courses of uniform stones that gradually diminish in size from bottom to top. The same precision and craftsmanship are evident in the cobbled walls, gateposts, and an unusual beehive-shaped milk cooler that are among the protected site elements now incorporated into an apartment complex.

### Congregation Bikur Cholim

104 Seventeenth Avenue S.
*B. Marcus Priteca, 1912–15 (altered)*

Chevra Bikur Cholim was Seattle's first Jewish congregation, organized in 1889; its Hebrew name means "Society for the Visitation of the Sick." The group's traditional role in Old World communities had been to provide a wide range of services to the sick and disabled and their families, including burial. In keeping with these goals, Bikur Cholim established a cemetery in 1890 and incorporated in 1891, becoming a full congregation the following year. Several frame buildings preceded the E. Yesler Way temple, which is one of a small group of domed, centric-plan religious structures extant in Seattle.

Representing an eclectic synthesis of Neoclassical and Byzantine forms and massing, the temple was designed by prominent theater architect B. Marcus Priteca. His expertise in theater design is evident in the axial progression of interior spaces. The external form is that of an expanded octagon covered by a shallow dome. The facade is faced in smooth, tan colored brick enriched by white glazed terra-cotta trim. The north and south facades are dominated by large Roman arched window openings. The west, or front, entrance facade is distinguished by five round arched windows above a three-door portal that was originally reached from a monumental stairway framed with ornate cast iron lamps. The two tablets of the ten commandments crown the parapet. Certain stairway, window, and interior spatial alterations occurred when the synagogue relocated and the building was turned into the Langston Hughes Cultural Center in 1971.

### Fire Station No. Twenty-three

722 Eighteenth Avenue
*Everett & Baker, 1909*

This two-story red-brick firehouse with Flemish bond facing and green tile roof honestly reflects its purpose and function without the trappings of a particular eclectic style. Although built for horse-drawn equipment, the station housed motorized vehicles as early as 1918. In the 1970s, the building was converted to the Cherry Hill Neighborhood Center in a highly successful adaptive reuse venture. Having firmly established its physical identity with the neighborhood, the firehouse's role as a neighborhood center served to reinforce and continue its service to the community. It currently houses the offices of Central Area Motivation Program (CAMP).

## First African Methodist Episcopal Church

1522 Fourteenth Avenue
*A. Dudley, 1912*

This congregation was the first black mission to have been established in Seattle, begun in 1885 and incorporated in 1890. The present church replaced an early frame building. Architecturally, it is similar to many others built in Seattle during the first decade of the 20th century for "establishment" Protestant denominations. The building is relatively nonstylistic, with the exception of some Gothic arches and allusions to the Mission style in the form and detailing of its tower roof. Although architecturally without significance, it is important as one of Seattle's oldest and most substantial church structures built for and continuing to serve a black congregation.

## Immaculate Conception Church

820 Eighteenth Avenue
*Williams & Clark, 1904*

The oldest extant Catholic church in Seattle was completed and dedicated in 1904. The parish was founded by Jesuit priests who came to the Northwest to open a school for boys and later were persuaded to

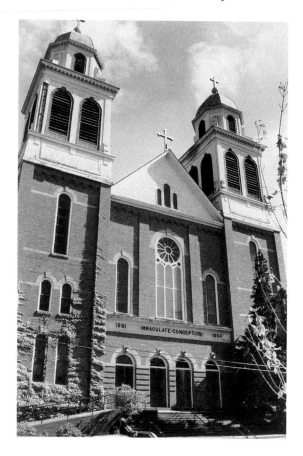

open a college, which eventually became Seattle University. The Parish of Immaculate Conception was created in 1891. In 1904, with the oversight of Rev. Adrian Sweere, S.J., the parish raised a new church of modified Italianate design executed in red brick and wood and exhibiting a high degree of symmetry. Two wood bell towers capped by gold cupolas and crosses frame a pedimented wood gabled central entrance. The exterior walls incorporate slender Romanesque windows of stained glass; a rose window is placed above the entrance. The interior seating capacity of 950 made the church the largest gathering place in Seattle at the time. In addition to its hand carved communion rails, pulpit, and alter, the nave ceiling contains frescoes painted by the Jesuits who originally administered the parish. The interiors were refurbished by Bumgardner Architects after fire damage in 1982.

## Italianate Victorian Pair

208–210 Thirteenth Avenue S.
Now at 1414 S. Washington Street
*Designer unknown, 1901 (one burned; one moved)*

The area directly east of the Central Business District was the site of many handsome large and small Victorian homes at the turn of the century. Most have disappeared or been radically altered. This pair of two-story frame residences was virtually untouched, though fragile and decaying examples of the Italianate Victorian style. Nearly identical in floor plans and window arrangements, both houses had bays supported by decorative brackets and bracketed cornices. However, porch treatments varied; 210 had a covered entry supported by turned columns with ornate brackets evocative of Corinthian capitals; 208 had two porches, one on each floor. The second floor porch was enclosed by columns and arches with sawn decoratives. After designation, one building burned and the other was relocated during redevelopment for the new Bailey Gatzert Elementary School.

## Seattle Buddhist Church

1427 S. Main Street
*Pierce Horrocks; A. K. Arai, 1940–41*

Replacing a 1908 temple that was demolished for the Yesler Terrace Housing Project, the 1941 building is both a temple and a community cultural center, housing a gymnasium, auditorium, and library and

providing dance, music, drama, sports, and cultural enrichment to the Asian community. The building translates traditional Japanese architectural elements into contemporary construction and materials. The exterior of the brick-faced building displays wood trimmed eaves with upturned corners, a decorative roof ridge, and ornamental gables. Carved open brackets frame the portal. Inside the building, the shrine and altar consist of elaborate carved and gilded posts, beams, and brackets. A gilded wood canopy shelters the statue of Buddha. Screens, lanterns, furniture, and religious artifacts further embellish the sanctuary.

**Temple de Hirsch Sinai**
Fifteenth Avenue E. and E. Union Street
*J. F. Everett, 1907–8 (demolished)*

See appendix A.

**Twenty-third Avenue Row Houses**
812–28 Twenty-third Avenue
*Designer unknown, 1892–93*

These six row houses of similar "pullman" floor plans and exterior trim are fine examples of low-income speculative housing of the late Victorian period. Built in the popular Carpenter Gothic idiom of stick style or balloon frame construction, they are sheathed in narrow siding laid horizontally on the first-floor facades and vertically in upper-floor dormers. Houses have small entrance porches on their northwest corners and there are slight variations in roof line and porch width. Some have small-paned window glass and wood friezes below the gables, and

some porches have turned posts. Historic Seattle Preservation and Development Authority purchased and refurbished four of the six to their original exterior condition and modernized interiors. The houses were sold with protective covenants. As a group, they project a unique, continuous, and cohesive street wall that exemplifies a type of housing once common in Seattle but no longer found because of remodeling and demolition in the dense Central Area.

**U.S. Marine Hospital/U.S. Public Health Hospital/PACMED**
1200 Twelfth Avenue S.
*Bebb & Gould; John Graham Sr., 1930–32*

The former U.S. Marine Hospital forms a harmonious, intact Art Deco campus that includes the principal medical building built to form the north enclosure of a lush commons or green around which cluster two-story brick residential buildings that served as quarters for officers of the institution. Their brick and terra-cotta facades, with chamfered entrances and dormers, share the vocabulary of the dramatic hospital building, which is one of the most significant landmarks in the city, both architecturally and visually. The modernistic form of the set back skyscraper is powerfully presented through the use of horizontal bands of brick and terra-cotta for the 6-story and 13-story wings and vertical piers with recessed windows for the 16-story tower. The chevron and chamfered ornamentation is the vocabulary of jazzy contemporary design and art now referred to as Art Deco. The hospital's prominent hilltop location and the woven brick, varied colors, precise line work and banding, and fluent rhythms of its facade make this one of the most colorful and exciting buildings on the skyline. A north addition by the firm of ZGF functions as a buttress to help the original building meet seismic requirements. It is wrapped in a new brick facade that closely resembles the original. Current plans call for additional office development and parking on the north part of the site for Amazon.com, carried out by the same firm.

**Victorian Row Apartments**
1234–38 S. King Street
*Designer unknown, 1891*

See chapter 7.

**James W. Washington Jr. Home and Studio**
1816 Twenty-sixth Avenue
*E. A. Gustafson, 1918; William Bain, studio, 1965*

This 1918 Craftsman bungalow was built by E. A. Gustafson and occupied by his family until 1944. Its

interiors, including stained fir paneled walls, picture molding, built-in cabinets with beveled leaded-glass doors, and tile fireplace, are intact and represent this common building type. But the property's significance is as the home and studio, from 1945 to the present, of artist and sculptor James W. Washington Jr. His tender and often symbolic natural forms sculpted from stone have been shown throughout the world. The studio, tucked below the house on the steep eastern slope of the lot, is a two-story box equipped with steel I beams, pulleys, and floor-to-ceiling double doors to accommodate the artist's large-scale sculptural work.

# Mount Baker/Rainier Valley/Columbia City/ Rainier Beach

## Black Manufacturing Building
1130 Rainier Avenue S.
*Andrew Willatsen, 1914*

When George Black decided to build a "daylight factory" for the manufacture of his Black Bear wearing apparel, he sought out the best of efficient, modern technology and had his factory built "entirely of Washington made materials and by Washington men." Architect Andrew Willatsen's designs provided a state-of-the-art working environment, with 15,000 square feet of windows and skylights, reinforced-concrete, brick, and fire-resistant mill construction, and overhead sprinkler systems. A far cry from the "sweatshops" associated with factory work to that time, the owner's attention to the welfare of his employees extended to amenities that included a cafeteria and a roof garden. The company operated this facility until 1981. The firm of Anderson, Koch & Duaarte guided rehabilitation in 1984 for office and manufacturing space.

## Grover Cleveland High School

5511 Fifteenth Avenue S.

*F. A. Naramore, 1926–27*

In 1925, the Seattle School Board voted for construction of a six-year junior/senior high school on Maple Hill, a prominent, highly visible site on southwest Beacon Hill overlooking the Duwamish Valley. The resulting three-story block was designed in the Georgian style and executed in brick with terra-cotta trim. Each principal facade is punctuated, at its center, by a projecting pavilion featuring a triple arched entrance with brick voissoirs and terra-cotta keystones surmounted by a two-story three-part pedimented bay with Corinthian columns, richly pedimented windows, and balcony. This palace form follows the Renaissance tradition of unifying several separate building spaces and functions behind one dominating and imposing facade.

## Dunlap Elementary School

8621 Forty-eighth Avenue S.

*Floyd Naramore, 1923–24*

Dunlap was an early reinforced-concrete and brick-veneer Georgian styled building and was the first two-story elementary school designed by the school district's third architect, Floyd Naramore. Ornament was completed with cast stone in this building, and with matte-glazed terra-cotta in others. The school, one of a number funded by passage of a 1923 bond issue, incorporated new approaches to school design, including covered open air play courts, specialized staff rooms and offices, and a combination assembly-lunchroom in each school to extend its use into the community by providing public meeting space. The DLR Group has designed a new building and refurbishment of the historic structure.

## Emerson Elementary School

9709 Sixtieth Avenue S.

*James Stephen, 1909*

Emerson is one of seven brick schools designed in the Jacobean style, with terra-cotta detailing. When it was constructed, it was a twin to Greenwood Elementary School and similar to Coleman and Adams (demolished). These were the last school district buildings designed by James Stephen, whose brick model school continued to be used for many years by his successor, Edgar Blair. The elaborate curvilinear terra-cotta ornamental treatments of the central gable end were removed after 1963 and rebuilt as straight edges. But the building retains its ornate terra-cotta entrance. A 1930 addition by Floyd Naramore incorporated an impressive terra-cotta entrance with bull's-eye window above that has been salvaged and incorporated into new construction. The DLR Group has designed a new building and refurbishment of the historic structure.

## Fire Station No. Thirty-three

10235 Sixty-second Avenue S.

*Daniel R. Huntington, 1914*

One of a series of stations designed by City Architect Daniel Huntington during the transition from horse-drawn to motor equipment, Fire Station No. Thirty-three is a small wood frame building in a modified English style designed to be compatible with the surrounding residences. The wood-shingled exterior is embellished with vertical half-timbers and stucco below steeply pitched gable roofs. Multi-paned windows and second-floor bracketed window boxes originally accentuated its residential qualities. The building is now a private residence and, apart from the loss of its window boxes, has had no major alterations.

## Franklin High School

3013 S. Mount Baker Boulevard

*Edgar Blair, 1910–11; 1925*

See chapter 7.

## Krauss Residence

2812 Mount Saint Helens Place

*F. H. Perkins, 1911*

Built in 1911 for industrialist Joseph Krauss, this is an excellent example of Tudor styled residential architecture. The external form of this brick and half-timbered building is carefully composed with an informal arrangement of bays, gables, and windows. Corbels and concave brackets support overhangs, and the small divisions of upper window sash introduce a contrasting scale. The major interior spaces, including the parlor, dining room, library, and central hallway and staircase are in an excellent state of preservation. White oak and fir paneling and trim, inlaid floors, leatherlike wall coverings, woven tapestries custom designed and installed in the dining

room above the plate rail, and most of the original Art Nouveau lighting fixtures and lustre shades survive. Custom-designed colored-glass windows and transoms throughout the house are of excellent quality, particularly the large, arched stairwell window in which plant forms run freely across the borders and into the central panels. These windows and the fixtures are reputed to be the work of the Tiffany studio; they replace Belgian glass and fixtures that were ordered after the house was completed but were destroyed in the early days of the First World War en route to the United States.

### Kubota Garden
Renton Avenue S. at Fifty-fifth Avenue S.
*Fujitoro Kubota, 1929–present*

Fujitoro Kubota, a farmer in his native Japan, learned about soils in agricultural school and developed an early appreciation for the old temples and gardens of Kochi Prefecture. Moving to Seattle in 1906, he began a gardening and landscape business in 1923, gradually shifting his interest from maintenance gardening to creative landscaping and pioneering the art of Japanese gardens in Seattle. In 1929, he purchased five acres of land in what was the less developed part of the city and began a garden as a demonstration exhibit for clients. Gradually, Kubota created a rock

garden, a road system, ponds, a rose garden, a garden of lilies, and lawn areas covering over three acres. Although the garden was untended when Kubota was interned during the Second World War, he returned to pick up where he had begun. His garden has attracted visitors from all around the world and continues to provide valuable open space through the generosity of his heirs.

*Lacey V. Murrow Bridge dedication, July 2, 1940.*

### Lacey V. Murrow Bridge
West Plaza, Mount Baker Tunnel
Lake Washington; Interstate 90
*Washington State Highway Department:*
*L. Lovegren; J. Fitzgerald, 1940*

The first Lake Washington floating bridge was an engineering marvel, constituting a unique solution to the problem of spanning a 1.5-mile-wide lake with 200-foot depths and a clay bottom that would cause footing problems for conventional bridge piers. The bridge was the world's first concrete floating bridge and the longest floating bridge in the world—a combination of viaducts, trusses, and floating stationary and movable pontoons allowing for a 200-foot opening for navigation. The east portals and the Mount Baker Tunnel feature beautiful and distinctive low-relief sculptures in the style of Northwest Coast Indian art. In 1988–89, some changes were approved at the east portal to accommodate a second floating bridge. The pontoons sank during a major storm in November 1990 and the span has been largely reconstructed.

### Storey Cottages District
1706–1816 Lake Washington Boulevard
1725 and 1729 Thirty-sixth Avenue S.
*Ellsworth Storey, 1910–15*

These low-rent cottages on a 1.5-acre wooded tract in Colman Park are small-scale examples of the western stick style. The cottages are finely scaled, with excellent proportions. They exhibit the simple, direct use of local materials and skillful manipulation of site attributes that are trademarks of Ellsworth Storey's efforts to define a Northwest Regional style. The cottages are constructed with exposed framing, their 3 x 4 vertical studs supporting single-thickness tongue-and-groove fir boards that form the interior walls. Porch decks and stair railings are screened simply and effectively with vertical slatwork of alternating wide and narrow slats. A serpentine brick paved walkway with intermittent steps links one terraced set of cottages. Large firs, madronas, maples, and shrubs generously buffer and shade the site.

### Thompson Residence
3119 S. Day Street
*Designer unknown, 1897*

This 18-room house was built for a prominent Seattle attorney, Will Thompson, who was counsel for the Great Northern Railroad. One of the few extant examples of a late Victorian Queen Anne styled towered residence in Seattle, this two-story frame building with a three-story octagonal tower, incorporates machine-made bracketry, turned balusters and posts, scallop-shingled gables, and a wraparound open verandah. The residence is sited at the crest of a hill in the Atlantic–Mount Baker community and provides expansive panoramas of Lake Washington and the Cascade Mountains.

### Martha Washington School
6612 Fifty-seventh Avenue S.
*Floyd Naramore, 1920–21; 1928 (demolished)*

See appendix A.

## Montlake/Madison Park/ Madrona

### Arboretum Aqueduct
Washington Park
*Willcox & Sayward, 1910–11*

This handsome reinforced-concrete and brick footbridge conceals a sewer pipe that crosses the ravine in which Lake Washington Boulevard is located. The bridge, 180 feet long, is divided into six equal arched bays supported by pillars of reinforced concrete. The concrete sidewalls are delineated by bands of brick

infill. The practical requirements of the bridge as a conduit have been exploited aesthetically to contribute a valuable spatial element to the picturesque qualities of the Olmsted Brothers–designed parkway. W. R. B. Willcox was acquainted with the work of Louis Sullivan and Frank Lloyd Wright, and their philosophies influenced his work.

### John E. Boyer Residence
1617 Boyer Avenue E.
*W. Sankey, 1908*

The Boyer residence combines English styled half-timbering, Richardsonian stonework, Wrightian Prairie style massing, and California Craftsman style details into a highly unusual and particularly American turn-of-the-century Seattle home. The rustic, hand-hewn granite stone base pierced by arched windows is complemented by spiral patterned carved wood medallions, wide bands of casement windows, brackets and crossbeams, and broad overhanging eaves that form a rhythmic composition akin to Japanese or Craftsman style design. A series of built-up and interconnected spaces progresses from a one-story open porch to a one-story living room to a two-story central portion containing entry and dining areas below and bedrooms above. The progression of spaces culminates in the second-floor master bedroom, a massive and tapering stone tower with two broad bands of windows. The wide overhanging roofs press the house to the ground, accentuating the earth-hugging qualities of the granite base.

### Brehm Brothers Residences
219–221 Thirty-sixth Avenue E.
*Ellsworth Storey, c. 1909*

These two houses were designed by architect Ellsworth Storey for two brothers, one of whom was a builder, the other the founder of an early sausage and pickle company in the Pike Place Market. The houses reflect Storey's adaptation of native materials, compatible colors, and forms to generate an original, noneclectic regional style in his residential designs. The hallmark of Storey's work is the use of stained wood and shingles, clinker brick, river stone, and white window frames and casings. The interiors demonstrate Storey's skill in organizing spaces, maintaining graciousness with modest scale, and establishing good circulation patterns. His Craftsman-influenced woodwork and trim are reminiscent, on a more modest scale, of the work of the Greene Brothers' Pasadena residences and Frank Lloyd Wright's Prairie residences.

### Bussell Residence

1630 Thirty-sixth Avenue
*Thomas G. Bird, 1892*

Built by a real estate investor, this commodious late Victorian home was owned by E. V. Bussell from 1900 to 1928. Bussell's wealth came from a soap business and holdings in Seattle's tidelands, which many felt were worthless. In 1906, he surprised his peers by selling them to the expanding railroad network for $1.5 million. His 13-room residence, set amid landscaped lawns and affording magnificent views to Lake Washington and the Cascade Mountains, was nicknamed "the castle" by neighborhood residents. The building was faced with horizontal siding, and several varieties of scalloped shingle covered the gable ends and the circular tower. The porches and gables were decorated with scrolled brackets, turned posts, and decorative millwork. The interior was handsomely appointed with paneling, wainscoting, stained and leaded glass, and tile faced fireplaces. In 1928, new owners inspired by the Mediterranean style popularized in Rudolph Valentino's exotic films hired a contractor to turn the Victorian residence into a Spanish hacienda. Fortunately, no changes were made to the interior, which still reflects Victorian tastes. In 1994, new owners received approval to remove the stucco and restore its wooden exterior.

### Epiphany Chapel

3719 E. Denny Way
*Ellsworth Storey, 1910–11*

The Epiphany Chapel was built for the Episcopal Church to harmoniously fit into a residential neigh-

borhood. As the finest of Ellsworth Storey's three church commissions, Epiphany exhibits the trademarks of his efforts to honestly express structure and function and to provide warm, comfortable, and well scaled environments with local, inexpensive materials. The building is stylistically derived from the English Gothic but is largely devoid of the religious imagery and the stained-glass windows of more traditional houses of worship. Its bell tower and Gothic arched windows identify its function. The stucco and half-timbered sidewalls of the building rise from a clinker brick base. Cedar shakes cover the steep gabled roofs; deep overhangs protect the stucco walls but give way above the windows in order to expose them to more light. The wood structural system supporting the roof is exposed and unfinished. Both exterior and interior of the church reflect Storey's emphasis upon the interplay of light and dark, natural and painted surfaces, and his interpretation of the Arts and Crafts style.

### Forest Ridge Convent/Seattle Hebrew Academy

1617 Interlaken Drive E.
*F. H. Perkins, 1909*

Built by the Sisters of the Sacred Heart as a combination convent and boarding and day school for girls, this structure was named Forest Ridge because of its countryside location in Interlaken Park. The site was selected because it was so far removed from the "wickedness" of downtown Seattle. The convent has been an established and significant visual feature of the boulevard. Approached up sloping lawns and a curving driveway, its brick and terra-cotta facade is quite imposing. The building features a columned entrance portal, Neoclassical balustrades, ornate curved stepped false front gables, and oriel windows. The school moved to Bellevue and the Seattle Hebrew Academy moved from a Central Area location to this campus in 1973.

**Samuel Hyde Residence**
3726 E. Madison Street
*Bebb & Mendel, 1909–10*

Completed in 1910 for liquor entrepreneur Samuel Hyde, this residence and its grounds and carriage house represent one of Seattle's most distinguished Neoclassical residences. Architects Bebb & Mendel established their partnership in 1901 and gained great popularity among wealthy clients over the following 13 years of their association. This home is one of their finest collaborative efforts. The grounds are believed to have been laid out by the Olmsted Brothers who were in Seattle preparing plans for the grounds of the Alaska-Yukon-Pacific Exposition. The interior and exterior of the residence reflect a transition from the formal symmetry of Georgian, Federal, and Greek Revival residences to a more informal arrangement of spaces and forms responding to 20th-century living patterns. The primary entrance is symmetrically balanced and imposing, with a Corinthian columned portico. An Ionic columned porte cochere provides the vehicular approach along the west side. At the east rear of the residence, a brick-walled terrace is detailed with terra-cotta swags and freestanding urns. Rooms and halls are richly finished in hardwood paneling and trim and include a variety of Tiffany-styled fixtures. The music/reception chamber features Renaissance styled window casings and a frescoed ceiling. The dining room, paneled in Siberian oak, features an exceptional oil on canvas mural depicting a pastoral landscape believed to be the Lake Washington shoreline. A Tiffany-styled stained-glass window on the stair landing interprets the view of Lake Washington and the Cascades from the Hyde residence. The building now houses the Russian Consulate.

**Lake Washington Bicycle Path**
Interlaken Boulevard E.
*Office of George F. Cotterill, 1897*

Between 1894 and 1904, the City of Seattle, the Queen City Bicycle Club, and a private corporation constructed over 50 miles of bicycle paths in response to the remarkable popularity of this vehicle for transportation and recreation purposes. During that period, there were 40 bicycle dealers, four race-tracks, and a weekly cycling column in the newspaper. Seattle was in the forefront among West Coast cities in using the bicycle for basic transportation and became nationally renowned for its development of a network of recreational paths and related functions, including restaurants, restrooms, and clubhouses, designed specifically for bicyclists. None of the early shops or facilities are left, and streets, freeways, and parking lots cover the sites of early tracks and paths. The only remaining evidence of this early bicycle era is this beautiful curving stretch of boulevard between Del Mar Drive E. and 24th Avenue E., now called Interlaken Boulevard.

**Montlake Bridge**
Ship Canal at Twenty-fourth Avenue E.
*Carl Gould, Blaine & Associates, 1924–25*

Designed to complement the Gothic styled academic buildings on the adjoining University of Washington campus, this handsome eclectic bridge spans the Montlake Cut. It is a double leaf trunion bascule bridge similar in its structural components to several other canal bridges in Seattle. The bridge's two octagonal Gothic control towers are modeled in concrete, granite, and brick infill embellished with terra-cotta arched buttresses and spandrels and with colored glass windows and copper cupolas. Gothic styled lighting fixtures, also in copper, are placed at intervals along the span. These damaged and unused fixtures were restored and relit in 1989. While Carl Gould is credited with the Gothic design, other well-known Seattle architects—A. H. Albertson, Edgar Blair, and Harlan Thomas—were brought in as advisors.

## Montlake Cut
Portage Bay Ship Canal
*Army Corps of Engineers, 1917*

As early as 1854, pioneers had envisioned Seattle's maritime future as being so splendid that it would quickly outgrow Elliott Bay and require the building of a canal to open up Lakes Union and Washington to accommodate oceangoing ships. In the 1880s and 1890s, a canal was proposed south of the business district to cut through Beacon Hill and Mount Baker. The present site was finally selected by the Army Corps of Engineers and constructed with local bonds. Following completion of the Ballard locks and the dredging of Salmon and Shilshole Bays, the Lake Washington Ship Canal was developed in 1917. Because of the ability of Harbor Island to handle most cargo and oceangoing vessels, the canal has served primarily for pleasure craft since its completion. The Montlake Cut is an earthen cut joining Lake Union to Lake Washington and was planned to provide a navigable waterway for major vessels in a channel 100 feet wide and 30 feet deep. The top of the concrete revetments and the embankments on either side provide pedestrian trails and viewing points.

## Raymond Residence
702 Thirty-fifth Avenue
*Joseph Coté, 1912*

Built for Dr. Alfred Raymond (1860–1919), a leading physician and chief of brain surgery at Seattle General Hospital, this stately Georgian brick residence served for many years as the home of the British Consulate General. The exceptionally fine proportions of its rooms and their careful detailing are the work of an outstanding local architect whose talents resulted in a number of exquisite mansions and townhouses for Seattle's well-to-do. Of particular note are raised plaster ceilings in the Tudor style, a barrel-vaulted library ceiling, red and green marble fireplaces, crystal chandeliers and wall brackets, and an impressive main entry paneled in mahogany with a curving staircase

## Ellsworth Storey Residences
260 and 270 Dorffel Drive E.
*Ellsworth Storey, 1903–5*

Illinois born and educated, architect Ellsworth Storey built these homes for himself and for his par-

ents. Strongly influenced by Swiss chalets and by the prairie style of Frank Lloyd Wright, Storey's houses were prototypes for Northwest Regional style designs in residential architecture. They utilize natural and locally available materials (beach rock and cedar shingle) and appropriate roofs (pitched with wide overhanging eaves) to fit the hillside topography. The interior woodwork, particularly that of the stair halls, is reminiscent of the English Arts and Crafts designer C. F. A. Voysey. Window fenestration and the white trim contrasting with the dark-stained cedar shingles are characteristic of Storey's work. The two homes are connected by a glassed-in corridor. Although the larger residence is almost twice the size of the smaller one, it relates positively to its neighbor.

## UNIVERSITY DISTRICT/WEDGWOOD/ RAVENNA/LAKE CITY

### Blessed Sacrament Catholic Church
5041 Ninth Avenue N.E.
*Beezer Brothers, 1909–11; 1922–25*

An excellent local example of Gothic religious architecture, this red-brick edifice is detailed with cut-sandstone and cast-stone ornament in the English Gothic tradition. The exterior form honestly reflects a 200-foot-long interior nave and chancel, flanking side aisles, a crossing, and transepts. The interior was never completed as intended for lack of funds. Its exposed concrete piers, brick wall surfaces, and exposed steel trusses reveal the structural elements that the intended plaster cladding, Gothic ornament, and wood beam veneers would have hidden. A dramatic 206-foot-high tower would have been complemented by a twin tower had the church been completed as designed. The single south tower is framed at its corners by heavy, stepped-back buttresses. The bell chamber is exposed through twin

lancets at each of the tower's four faces. Rising from the bell tower is an octagonal spire of copper plates laid in a herringbone pattern. Because of the church's location atop a knoll surrounded by residences, the church and its surroundings evoke images of Chartres and other medieval cathedral towns.

### Bryant Elementary School
3311 N.E. Sixtieth Street
*Floyd Naramore, 1926; 1931*

Bryant was one of a number of flat-roofed, reinforced-concrete and brick veneer Georgian styled buildings designed by the school district's third architect, Floyd Naramore. The quoins, cornice, and entrance bay were completed with matte-glazed terra-cotta. The school, one of a number funded by passage of a 1923 bond issue, incorporated new approaches to school design, including covered open air play courts, specialized staff rooms and offices, and a combination assembly-lunchroom in each school to extend its use into the community by providing public meeting space. It was the first in the district designed to accommodate the "semidepartmental," or "platoon," system, which offered students above the third grade classes focusing on specific subjects taught by specialists. This required rooms devoted to library-reading, music, fine and industrial arts, sewing, cooking, and physical education. The firm BLR-B is currently designing additions behind the existing building.

### Cowen Park Bridge
15th Avenue N.E. at Sixtieth Street
*Clark Eldridge, Bridge Engineer, 1936*

Replacing two wooden trestle bridges—one for trolleys and the other for pedestrians—this open spandrel reinforced-concrete arched bridge springs from abutments and rises to a height of nearly 60 feet above the old Ravenna Creek bed. The arch, with its vertical pier abutments and deck supporting members, embodies the successful marriage of engineering and aesthetics. Fluting on the piers and columns emphasizes the verticality and apparent lightness of the structure. At the portals and over the piers, ziggurat-like projections embellish 12 foot tall attenuated Art Deco light standards. This bridge is the finest of a number of bridges constructed under the Works Progress Administration and demonstrates an awareness of and concern for the functional expressiveness of reinforced concrete.

### Eckstein Junior High School
3003 N.E. Seventy-fifth Street
*Mallis, DeHart, Hopkins, 1949–50*

Nathan Eckstein represents a unique combination of modernistic, Art Deco, and International School styling that is highly reminiscent of housing developments, schools, and other public buildings designed and built in Holland by architects of the Dutch Expressionist School, notably de Klerk, J. J. Oud, and Wilhelm Dudok between 1923 and 1933.

The massing of major elements, including gymnasium, heating plant, and chimney; the use of curving elements as foils and pauses in the lengthy horizontal bands that form classroom masses; the extensive use of glass block and corner windows; corner entrances; polished aluminum detailing, especially in the stepped-back trim along the curvilinear sidewalls of the auditorium–all combine to generate an outstanding, well-conceived school complex.

### Jolly Roger Roadhouse
8721 Lake City Way N.E.
*Designer unknown, 1929 (burned)*

See appendix A.

### Ramsing Residence
540 N.E. Eightieth Street
*Designer unknown, 1908*

This one and a half story gabled and dormered frame residence represents Seattle's most extensive use of decorative machine cut shingles. They cover nearly every surface of this simple Victorian home. Fish scale and fancy sawn shingles surface the walls, gables, barge boards, and eaves. With the exception of a 1937 porch modification and window sash replacements, this house retains its original turn-of-the-century floor plan and facade treatment.

### Twentieth Avenue N.E. Bridge
Ravenna Park at Twentieth Avenue N.E.
*Frank Melvin Johnson, 1913–14*

The Ravenna Park bridge is an outstanding example of a three pin arch steel bridge. The design was chosen for its pleasing appearance, economy of construction, and flexibility of the structure under stress in spanning the deep ravine of Ravenna Park, a site that posed problems because of the sandy soil of the embankments. The design took into consideration

the fine vegetation of the park and the footpaths that were partway up the sides of the ravine. It accommodated the growing demand for automobile passage with a well-cambered deck. The bridge handrails are of steel pipe placed atop a balustrade of steel cross and vertical braces. Handsome cast metal lighting fixtures and round arched concrete balusters at either end of the bridge provide a refreshing pedestrian experience, particularly so since its closure to automobiles some years ago.

### University Heights Elementary School
5031 University Way N.E.
*Bebb & Mendel, 1902; James Stephen, 1907–8*

Designed by the prestigious local firm of Bebb & Mendel, this two-story, hip-roofed, frame schoolhouse is symmetrical in plan, with a central pavilion and two identical projecting pavilions. Its modified classical appearance features a gable treatment reminiscent of the Mission Revival style or a borrowing of the crow's rest gables popular in Dutch and northern European design. The school had been planned for an original enrollment of 200; by the early 1920s, it was the largest grade school in Seattle, its two wings of 1908 complemented by seven portable units on the grounds to accommodate 1,506 children. In terms of progressive education, the school contributed greatly to the planning and implementation of new programs, including individualized instruction. The building is leased to the community by the Seattle School District and is seriously in need of repair.

### University Methodist Episcopal Church
4142 Brooklyn Avenue N.E.
*George W. Bullard, 1906–7*

See chapter 7.

### University Unitarian Church/University Presbyterian Church Chapel
4555 Sixteenth Avenue N.E.
*Ellsworth Storey, 1915–16 (altered)*

This building, now occupied by the Presbyterian Church, is an excellent and sensitive interpretation of a late medieval English country chapel adapted to a local denomination's specific needs. Its qualities are enhanced by landscaped grounds, including mature elm trees and hedgerows and a lych-gate. Closely resembling Ellsworth Storey's Epiphany Chapel of 1910–11, this single-story rectangular building has projecting gabled wings and a smaller gabled entrance porch. The materials used were brick at the ground level and stucco with some half-timbering and dark stained shingles above. With the exception of a Gothic arched window at the center of the north gable, most of the casement windows are of diamond paned leaded glass. Storey's concern for detail shows itself in the fine gable braces supported by brackets and the entrance porch bargeboards with pierced triangular motifs. The chapel's romantic east facade is reminiscent, in a more modest way, of Bernard Maybeck's Berkeley work. The interior of the chapel is small and intimate, with piers and arches faced in gray cast plaster and dark wood wainscoting.

## WALLINGFORD/FREMONT/GREEN LAKE/BALLARD/LOYAL HEIGHTS

### B. F. Day School
3921 Linden Avenue N.
*J. Parkinson, 1891–92; J. Stephen, 1900; E. Blair, 1916*

B. F. Day is the oldest continuously operating public school in the city. In 1891, B. F. and Frances Day donated a portion of their 160-acre farm as the site for a Fremont school building, provided that the school district erect a brick building "to cost no less than $25,000." Parkinson, Seattle School Architect at the time, designed a two-story 8-room schoolhouse organized within a series of bays defined by structural pilasters. In 1900, a nearly identical addition to the north by James Stephen followed Parkinson's design and produced a central Roman arched entrance recessed between two wings. This H-shaped form was added to again in 1916 to provide two north and south pavilions, whose brick and detailing complement the earlier building in form, scale, and

symmetrical positioning. The school underwent a major rehabilitation in 1989–90 overseen by BJSS Group in Olympia, Washington.

### Drake Residence
6414 Twenty-second Avenue N.W.
*Designer unknown, 1900*

This modest Victorian cottage is a rare local example of a dog trot plan—a form developed in the Deep South. The symmetrical building has a central portal located in a recess between two matching four-window angled bays, the whole being covered by a hipped roof. Originally, the central hall extended from the entrance through the house to the rear door. About 1910, a wing was added to the rear of the house, somewhat changing this configuration. The cottage uses typical framing elements, moldings, and siding, as well as modest machine-produced brackets.

### Fire Station No. Eighteen
5427 Russell Avenue N.W.
*Bebb & Mendel, 1910–11*

Designed by two of the area's most prolific residential architects, this brick firehouse was originally built for horse-drawn equipment. Its modified Germanic style, replete with characteristic stepped gable or crow's rests, as they are sometimes referred to, reputedly responded to the large number of northern European and Scandinavian residents in the Ballard community. Originally, the firehouse had a substantial central bell tower with paired brackets and mock balconies on all four sides. In order to free the ground floor from interior columns, the second floor of this building had a unique structural system; loads for the floor were carried by metal columns suspended from specially designed roof trusses. The design firm of Makers refurbished this early Historic Seattle project for restaurant use in 1976.

### Fremont Bridge
Fremont Avenue N. over Lake Washington Ship Canal
*F. A. Rapp, Bridge Engineer; D. R. Huntington, pier design, 1917*

When the Lake Washington Ship Canal was constructed, making possible the passage of oceangoing ships into Lakes Union and Washington, the creek from Lake Union into Salmon Bay was greatly enlarged and the timber trestle bridges that had served traffic from Seattle to northern communities were replaced by the Fremont Bridge. It was one of three draw span bridges built between 1917 and 1919 and employing technology developed in Chicago in 1898. Ballard, University, and Fremont Bridges are bascule bridges with counterweight balancing and cantilevered "leaves." The mechanisms and counterweight pits are housed in two concrete piers, each with towers. Of the three bridges, the Fremont is closer to the water by 15 feet and, consequently, has the distinction of having opened and closed its double leaf gates more often than any other Seattle drawbridge. The Fremont community attaches great value to the bridge as an identifiable and historically significant landmark. Bright orange was selected by the Fremont Community Council to distinguish their bridge from other bridges throughout the city, but it faded quickly, and the bridge is now painted blue with orange accents.

### Fremont Car Barn/Red Hook Ale Brewery

3400 Phinney Avenue N.
*Designer unknown, 1905*

This building was the first major streetcar service facility built "north of Seattle" and represented a new era in service and streetcar dependability. On April 13, 1941, the era ended with the last running streetcar, No. 706, pulling into the Fremont Car Barn. Access to Fremont was greatly increased by streetcar service from downtown and lines that connected Fremont to Ballard, Phinney Ridge, and Green Lake. The trolley barn was constructed to lubricate, repair, and clean streetcars and as a dispatch office for conductors and administration. To accomplish its functions and store up to six tracks for indoor major repairs, the brick building is 170 feet long from north to south by 160 feet wide on its north elevation. The south elevation is only 66 feet wide. It is divided into a major hall on the east and smaller halls on the west. The heavy timber post construction has been modified with steel support columns and beams, its roof monitor and wood cornice removed, the south opening sealed, and a new facade installed. However its facade still exhibits ornamental stepped brick corbeling, external pilasters, miniature sheet-metal cupolas at its four principal corners, and original wood windows. The main hall is now a brewery.

### Fremont Hotel

3421–29 Fremont Avenue N.
*Designer unknown, 1900*

The Fremont Hotel is of frame construction but has a curving two-story facade of rusticated cast stone that is complemented by similar facades on the opposite side of the five cornered intersection which defines the commercial and social center of Fremont. Prior to the turn of the century, Fremont was a separate town, governed by its own mayor and city council. The hotels and commercial ventures provided lodging and services for workers in a local lumber mill and in the barns and maintenance shops of the Seattle streetcar lines that were located nearby. The Fremont Hotel had the infamous distinction of being a principal gambling center for residents of Seattle; that part of the building's less respectable past can be found in extant secret gambling rooms.

### German Congregational Church

1763 N.W. Sixty-second Street
*Designer unknown, 1894*

Built in 1894 as the German Church, this is one of Seattle's last surviving examples of the vernacular frame church, a form common in small communities during the latter part of the 19th century but all but disappeared from major metropolitan areas. Its recognizable form consists of a frame meeting hall given religious meaning with the addition of a square based bell tower and several Gothic arched windows and doors. The building is simply clad in shiplap siding with decorative shingle in the gables and at the midsection of the tower.

### Green Lake Public School

2400 N. Sixty-fifth Street
*James Stephen, 1901–2; 1907 (demolished)*

See appendix A.

### House of the Good Shepherd/
### Good Shepherd Center

4649 Sunnyside Avenue N.
*Breitung & Buchinger, 1906–7*

The sisters of Good Shepherd arrived in Seattle in 1890 at the invitation of the bishop of Nisqually. They took care of orphans and young girls who had been involved in social or personal misbehavior.

Having progressively outgrown two Seattle houses, a fundraising campaign resulted in the purchase of a large tract of land in the Wallingford section of Seattle and construction of a handsome, up-to-date facility for the sisters and their charges. The main building has masonry exterior walls and interior cast iron columns and beams. It was built in the Italianate style; a rusticated brick masonry ground floor and brick upper floor are embellished with Corinthian capital pilasters and an elaborate bracketed cornice. A statue of the Good Shepherd is placed in a niche over the main entrance portal, and a two story chapel located in the central bay is defined by its handsome stained-glass windows. In the 1970s, a cupola atop the building was destroyed by fire and has not been replaced. The grounds, originally consisting of orchards, vegetable gardens, a poultry house, and root cellars, provided solitude, security, and recreational opportunities for the sisters and the young women under their care. The City of Seattle purchased the property in 1976 and transferred the buildings to Historic Seattle Preservation and Development Authority. The building has been undergoing renovation and upgrades that will be completed in 2002. Good Shepherd Center is currently providing office and studio space for the Meridian School, Seattle Tilth, the Wallingford Senior Center, and other community groups. The Meridian Playground is maintained by the Department of Parks and Recreation and open to the public for a variety of recreational uses.

**Interlake Public School/Wallingford Center**
4416 Wallingford Avenue N.
*James Stephen, 1904; 1908*

See chapter 7.

**Latona Public School**
401 N.E. Forty-second Street
*James Stephen, 1906; Edgar Blair, 1917 (demolition pending)*

Latona Public School combined two individually significant school buildings that clearly illustrated the progressive development of public schools during the first two decades of the 20th century. Both buildings were essentially nonstylistic in form and composition and exemplified characteristics of economical and functional design, as well as integrity of form and materials. The 1906 frame building is a virtually unaltered representation of the standard 8-room model plan. Like John Hay and Summit Schools, it is dominated by two octagonal turreted towers at either side of the main entrance that house ventilation stacks and spiral stairs. The 1917 building, similar to Seward Public School of the same year and embellished with a central classically inspired terracotta portal, is to be demolished as part of upgrades to the 1906 building and a new building by Bassetti Architects. See chapter 2.

**Louisa Building**
5218–20 Twentieth Avenue N.W.
*Designer unknown, 1902*

The Louisa is a triangular, two-story building with brick bearing walls and interior mill construction. It is a highly visible landmark from many vantage points in the central business district of Ballard. Its architectural details and proportions are common to many buildings in the Ballard Avenue Landmark District nearby.

**Norvell Residence**
3306 N.W. Seventy-first Street
*Designer unknown, 1908*

With its wealth of ornate brackets and turrets, its gingerbread balconies and the asymmetry of its roof lines and windows, this two-story residence is a free adaptation of French and Swiss chalets. Its lively composition of horizontal and emphatically expressed wood frames is dynamic and the individual elements are fanciful to an extent rarely found in a Seattle house. Features include broad roofs and wide overhanging eaves with carved roof rafters and zigzag-patterned diagonal struts for support. The building's most notable eccentricity is a turret popping through the sloping roof and capped by a four-sided flared cupola resting partly on the roof plane and partly on brackets. The form resembles that of the old clock tower in Bern, Switzerland. An adjoining stable is designed in the same style, with elaborate bracket consoles beneath the overhanging eaves of the roof.

### Salmon Bay Bridge
Lake Washington Ship Canal
*Great Northern Railroad, 1914*

The Salmon Bay Bridge is the only railroad bridge across the Lake Washington Ship Canal. Its counterpart on the Duwamish waterway was erected two years earlier and had the distinction of being the first Strauss heel-trunnion single-leaf bascule bridge west of Chicago. Both bridges are dramatic examples of an age of development in engineering in which function and speed prevailed over aesthetics. The structural steel frame of the Salmon Bay Bridge responds in seconds in a jackknife fashion to approaching trains on the track between Magnolia and Ballard. Most of the time, the bridge folds in on itself to allow boats to navigate the canal. It provides a vital rail link in Seattle's role as a receiver and distributor of goods to and from national and foreign markets.

### Seattle Gas Light Company/Seattle Lighting Company/Seattle Gas Company/ Gas Works Park
Lake Union
*Designer unknown, 1906, 1937, 1945–47;*
*Richard Haag Associates, 1973*

Gas Works Park is an internationally recognized example of reclamation of a hazardous industrial site for public enjoyment. The Lake Station gas manufacturing plant on Lake Union was the largest private utility of its time in Seattle, operating as Seattle Lighting Company until 1930, when its name changed to Seattle Gas Company. Its primary product was gas manufactured from coal and later from oil. In addition to its manufacturing equipment, the site housed storage tanks, boiler house, pump and compressors house, offices, laboratories, and other support facilities. The City of Seattle began purchase of the abandoned gas works in 1962, completing its payments in 1972. In 1970, Richard Haag Associates began preparation of site analysis and a master

*Richard Haag at Gasworks Park.*

plan for a new park on the site in which preservation of a portion of the gas works was recommended for its "historic, esthetic, and utilitarian value." The park includes seven components: earth mound, north lawn, towers, prow, picnic lawn and shelter, play barn, and south lawn. The towers, tanks, and pipes of the gas works are reminders of the city's industrial heritage. Their scale and form, as well as their location on the north shore of the lake, make them visually compelling symbols of industrial development.

### Wallingford Fire and Police Station
1629 N. Forty-fifth Street
*Daniel Huntington, 1912–13 (altered)*

This building was one of two designed to accommodate equestrian police patrols and horse-drawn fire equipment; it is the only extant example of such a combined service facility in Seattle. The exterior form of the building, with its long sweeping roofline and use of shingles as a skin, is comparable to earlier shingle style residences popularized on the East Coast during the 1880s. It was considered to be an original American architectural innovation, particularly suitable for residences. Daniel Huntington intended the low-key residential character of this civic building to harmonize with the many Craftsman style gabled houses and bungalows in the neighborhood. Huntington's work included a number of firehouses and police stations, a steam plant, and public libraries. In his role as City Architect, he had a significant impact upon the quality of public architecture in the first decades of the 20th century. The building was rehabilitated by Arai/Jackson in 1985–86 to provide a community library and health center.

*Tall-masted sailing ship passes from Lake Union into the Ship Canal prior to completion of George Washington Memorial Bridge span.*

### George Washington Memorial Bridge
Aurora Avenue N.
*Jacobs & Ober for Washington State Highway Department, 1932*

The first major highway bridge in Seattle, this was also the first fixed-span bridge high enough above the water to allow passage of most conventional watercraft. The structural steel cantilever deck bridge has a steel superstructure supported on reinforced-concrete piers embedded in bedrock beneath Lake Union's muddy bottom. The roadway deck extends 1,450 feet, with a 1,200-foot north approach and a 500-foot south approach of steel and concrete for a total length of 3,150 feet. At highwater, clearance at the center of its elliptical main arch is 135 feet. The bridge demonstrates a unified design of all its elements, including the cantilevered arches, roadway, piers, and approaches. Its dramatic location serves as a monumental portal bridging Lake Union to the westerly portion of the ship canal.

## West Seattle/Georgetown/ South Park

### Admiral Theater
2343 California Avenue S.W.
*B. Marcus Priteca, 1941–42*

The nautically inspired Admiral Theater is the last surviving of a number of important theaters in West Seattle. It is also a rare remaining example of the neighborhood theater work of one of the nation's leading theater designers, B. Marcus Priteca, with interior decoration by the famed Los Angeles deco-rator A. B. Heinsbergen. Priteca's vaudeville and motion picture palaces for Alexander Pantages put him in great demand, and he did work for the Orpheum Corp. and for Warner Brothers. In addition to the Admiral, his work for the John Danz–owned Sterling Recreation Organization included the Magnolia, the Granada, the Majestic/Bay, the Neptune, and the Uptown. Its design, a remodel and addition to the Portola Theater, reflected contemporary taste for the Streamlined Moderne, a perfect choice considering the maritime heritage of the city and the founding of Seattle at Alki Point. Heinsbergen's mural of the landing of Captain Vancouver, a compass surrounded by signs of the zodiac, and undersea motifs with seagulls and shell borders carried the theme. While numerous alterations have occurred over time and it is now a multiplex, the essential nautical moderne character remains.

### Baker/Satterlee Residence
4866 Beach Drive S.W.
*Designer unknown, c. 1906*

This residence is an unaltered variation of a common early-20th-century Seattle residential type often referred to as the Classic Box. Classic boxes were middle- and upper-middle-class residences often built from pattern book designs. In Seattle, many of these can be traced to publications prepared by Fred L. Fehren and V. W. Voorhees, who termed them Spanish Colonial, probably because of the wide overhangs and generous enclosed porches. They are typically characterized by their boxy massing, hipped roof forms, and symmetrical street facades, often featuring projecting corner window bays and central hipped dormers. The first-floor porches and entrance locations vary considerably to accommodate narrow rectangular lots. The symmetrical layout and external composition of the west facade of the shingled Baker house consisted of a full front verandah with scrolled brackets and second story square corner bays and was made possible by its generous site. The tiered effect created by receding volumes and rooflines at the west facade is unique in this case, and sets the house apart from its numerous classic box relatives on Seattle's north Capitol Hill. Furthermore, the landscape elements and siting contribute to its character. The house is set back from the street and overlooks a gently sloping lawn with a fishpond in the foreground and Puget Sound beyond.

## Concord Elementary School

723 S. Concord Street
*Edgar Blair, 1913*

Concord Elementary School was designed in the Colonial Revival style by the school district's second staff architect, Edgar Blair. It is identical to McGilvra and McDonald schools, which are three-story, nine-room model schools—"fireproof" buildings constructed from steel, brick, and heavy timber. The rectangular entrance portal is framed with molded terra-cotta with an ornamental keystone. The school is situated on a knoll and enjoys a position of high visibility in the South Park community. Refurbishment of the historic building and a new building adjoining it are being designed by Tsang Partnership.

## Duwamish Railroad Bridge

Duwamish Waterway south of Spokane Street
*H. E. Steven, 1912*

The role of the railroads in developing the commercial and industrial resources of Seattle has been significant. This Strauss heel-trunnion single-leaf bascule bridge, nicknamed a "jackknife bridge," was one of the first four of its kind in the country and the only one of its type west of Chicago. It shortened the 5 to 6 minute opening time of earlier drawbridges to a mere 20 seconds and its mechanism was so delicate that one man could operate it by pulling a wire rope. Nevertheless, the bridge was generally operated by a 25-horsepower engine that set in motion its extension or retraction. Like a huge mechanical monster, it tucks its head deep into its chest to allow passage to navigation and stretches out its tail to permit trains to pass through its skeletal body. The "head" of the monster is a 500-ton reinforced-concrete weight counterbalancing the steel movable-span Warren truss.

## Fauntleroy Community Church

9260 California Avenue S.W.
*Original designer unknown, 1914–17; Stuart & Durham, 1950; 1957*

Affectionately referred to as "the little brown church in the wildwood" during its early years, the Fauntleroy Community Church is an important institutional landmark in West Seattle, significant socially and culturally as an expression of community initiative and cooperation. Its origins date from informal services in 1906 and the raising of a rustic

wood chapel in 1908 on a donated lot with lumber provided by the Colman family. The same "barn-raising" spirit was again present in 1914 and 1917 when a gymnasium and bell tower were added. Of these original structures, only the board and batten walled gymnasium, with its angle braced gables, remains on the site. The new church (1950) and an education and social wing (1957) are designed using pitched roofs, vertical board and batten siding and fieldstone; the new tower is of fieldstone with a wooden belfry and pointed spire. The choice of materials and design elements reflect and complement the rustic character of the older building, and the complex generally responds sensitively to its beautiful wooded hillside, with a large window that opens the interior up to the forest.

## Fir Lodge/Alki Homestead Restaurant

2727 Sixty-first Avenue S.W.
*Fred L. Fehren, 1903–4*

This rustic log building with broad hipped roof and hipped dormers was part of a turn-of-the-century estate for William and Gladys Bernard. Its rough-hewn exterior was carried into the interior in varnished log walls, log beams, and tongue-in-groove ceilings. The style represents a nostalgic look back at a time when Seattle was just starting to shed its pioneer rusticity for up-to-date urbanity. It reflects the philosophy of the American Arts and Crafts movement, in which the use of local and natural materials, simplicity of plan and interior, and respect for the natural environment were key values. Bernard established a soap manufacturing business in the city and his wife devoted her long life to children's charities. The building was sold to the Seattle Auto and Driving Club in 1907, an organization of owners and enthusiasts of the newfangled horseless carriage. It is now a popular restaurant that transports its patrons back to a simpler past.

## Gatewood Elementary School

4320 S.W. Myrtle Street
*Edgar Blair, 1910; Floyd Naramore, 1922*

Modeled loosely after English Jacobean manor houses of the 17th century, Blair's 1910 brick and terra-cotta trimmed building is symmetric, stately, and a distinguished landmark in this southwest Seattle community. The 1922 addition uses similar materials to visually tie the two sections together. The school is named for real estate developer Carlisle Gatewood, who came to Seattle in 1900 and platted large areas of Gatewood Hill to the east of the school, including Gatewood Gardens and Gatewood Acre Tracts. He was also the financial backer of the streetcar line that served the school. Refurbishment of the historic building and a new building were designed by BJSS of Olympia, Washington.

## Georgetown City Hall
6202 Thirteenth Avenue S.
*V. W. Voorhees, 1909–10*

Prior to its annexation to Seattle in 1910, the separate municipality of Georgetown built a substantial city hall and fire station that was the focus of all municipal services, including the police court, jail, treasurer, engineer, mayor's office and City Council chamber. The first building in Georgetown to have both hot and cold running water, the city hall is two stories tall, its exterior facade primarily clad in clinker brick with buff-colored brick quoins and entablature. A clock tower with steeple similar to an earlier one was reconstructed during the building's refurbishing for a community center and dental clinic. The building's presence is a reminder of the community's past independence from Seattle. With urban industrialization of the area, the once thriving residential community of Georgetown has been all but obliterated and its integrity as a separate town lost with the notable exception of the city hall and several adjoining structures.

## Georgetown Steam Plant
Ellis Avenue S. at S. Warsaw Street
*Frank B. Gilbreth, 1906*

Built by the Seattle Electric Company, the largest streetcar and utility in the city, the Georgetown Steam Plant was the earliest reinforced-concrete power plant in Washington. Its vertical Curtis steam turbine generator was, at the time, the most significant advancement in the history of industrial technology, hastening the way for mass production of electric power for home and industry. The Georgetown plant supplied peak-load capacity in periods of heavy use. In 1912, it became part of a larger power network and was used for emergencies until 1964. With advancements in power production, its once innovative turbines became obsolete, but because of its minor role in power production, it was not mod-

ernized or dismantled. Consequently, it is the only power plant in the country that still contains examples of the world's first large-scale steam turbine. The plant is a National Historic Mechanical Engineering Landmark and is listed in the National Register. A local group plans to open it as a museum and interpretive center for industry and technology.

## Hainsworth Residence
2657 Thirty-seventh Avenue S.W.
*Graham & Myers, 1907*

William Hainsworth, industrialist and real estate developer, came to Seattle in 1889 and settled in an underdeveloped area of what is now West Seattle. He commissioned architects John Graham Sr. and David Myers to design a house in the style of a timbered English manor house. In its asymmetric form, the application of nearly continuous window bands in its bays, its multiple dormers and gables, an overhanging bracketed second floor, and its use of stucco with half-timbering, the three-story home successfully evokes the spirit of Elizabethan England— something that many Seattle architects attempted to do but few achieved. The house was surrounded by formal gardens, tennis courts, ponds, a summerhouse, and a playhouse for the children, making it a most impressive estate in this developing residential neighborhood. The grounds were subdivided and

the original outbuildings torn down to make way for small brick English style houses in the 1930s. Nevertheless, the main house—sited to take full advantage of unobstructed views of the city, harbor, and mountains—is substantially intact.

### Hiawatha Playfield
2700 California Avenue S.W.
*Olmsted Brothers, 1911*

This playfield represented a radical new direction that marked changing attitudes toward the physical and mental health benefits to children of supervised recreation. In 1903, the Olmsted Brothers provided a plan for the acquisition of a broad system of parkways and parks for Seattle. In 1907, the city annexed five outlying districts, including the town of West Seattle, and commissioned the Olmsteds to prepare a supplemental report. The 1908 report included definitions of various types of parks and playgrounds and reported on Eastern United States activities in the field of the "new recreation." The landscape firm recommended location of playfields adjacent to schools so that teachers could direct playground activities and supervise organized sports programs. The report gave top priority to a playground site in West Seattle. A focal point of the new playfield was to be a Recreation Center or Field House that includ-

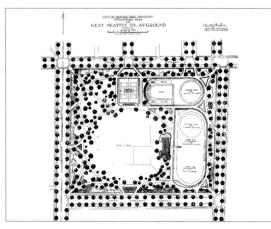

ed club rooms and a large social room. The Olmsted firm designed the playfield and the Recreation Center was dedicated in 1911 (this building was remodeled substantially in 1948–49 and is not designated). Although landscape elements are substantially as they were originally, changes have occurred to accommodate changing forms of recreation. Nevertheless, Hiawatha Playfield placed Seattle in a class with eastern cities like Philadelphia, Cincinnati, and Chicago—the leading exponents of this type of building for indoor recreation.

### Log House Museum Building
3003 Sixty-first Avenue S.W.
*Fred L. Fehren, 1903–4*

See chapter 7.

### Schmitz Park Bridge
Admiral Way at S.W. Stevens Street
*C. H. Eldridge, City Bridge Engineer, 1935*

While other Works Progress Administration bridges were spandrel arches spanning deep ravines, the height and width of the valley through Schmitz Park dictated a more conservative approach. Experiments in hollow concrete girder construction were undertaken in Europe in the 19th century, but applications in the United States did not occur until the 1930s. This process allowed for lightness and economy of materials while providing structural strength. The longest span built using this innovative technique was the Henderson Bay Bridge in Pierce County, Washington. The Schmitz Park Bridge, at 175 feet, was the second longest of its type at the time of construction and encouraged the use of hollow concrete forms extensively in subsequent highway bridges. This flattened-arch single span features Art Deco detailing, including zigzag moldings between support posts and stepped back surfaces below the deck that accentuate the shape of the arch.

### Seattle Brewing & Malt Co. Building
Rainier Cold Storage & Ice
6000–6004 Airport Way S.
*Herman Steinman; Carl Siebrand, 1900–1914*

This collection of contiguous masonry structures is an excellent, intact example of turn-of-the-century industrial architecture. It was one of the largest breweries in the West when it was completed in 1903 and with further additions became the sixth-largest brewery in the world and the largest industrial establishment in the state. The brew house was completed in 1901; the malt house in 1903; the general office building at the end of 1905; the bottling works in 1906. The architectural treatments of the buildings range from Romanesque Revival to the Italian Renaissance and French Baroque. The general office building was originally designed to frame a piazza with pool and courtyard. The brew house wall framed the north and east sides of the piazza, and the office building framed the south side. Part of the brew house that framed the east side is missing now.

*West Seattle High School near completion, November, 1917.*

## West Seattle High School
4075 S.W. Stevens Street
*Edgar Blair, 1917; 1924*

Architecturally, the West Seattle High School demonstrates a rational and expressive approach to the functional needs of high school students. The two story building is E-shaped in plan, with a low-pitched tile roof. It consists of a central pavilion flanked by classroom wings and by a gymnasium and auditorium. The building is handsomely executed in buff brick and cream colored terra-cotta in a modified Romanesque style. It displays excellent and varied brickwork, combined with lunettes, brick panels, colored, glazed tile, and terra-cotta colonettes, bracketry, and panels. Major refurbishment of the historic building and additional space constructed behind it, to the south, are being designed by Bassetti Architects.

## OBJECTS

### *Arthur Foss* Tugboat
Central waterfront/Lake Union
*Oregon Railway and Navigation Company, 1889*

Launched in Portland, Oregon, in 1889 as the steam tug *Wallowa*, this wood-hulled vessel served on the

Columbia River before joining a fleet of ships headed for the Alaska goldfields. In the ensuing decades, the boat logged thousands of miles between Alaska and Puget Sound ports, towing sailing ships engaged in lumber and wheat trade. In 1930, the tug was sold to the Foss Launch and Tug Company and renamed *Arthur Foss*. In 1934, its steam engine was replaced by diesel. That year the tug starred in the MGM motion picture *Tugboat Annie*. Donated to Northwest Seaport in 1970, the tug awaits a home on south Lake Union with other vintage ships.

### Brill Trolley No. 798
METRO Trolley Barn
*J. G. Brill Company, Philadelphia, 1940*

This trackless trolley represents the conversion of Seattle's track trolley system to a more efficient and flexible overhead electric trolley system. Trolley No. 798 is one of a fleet of 100 such trolleys ordered by the city and constructed by a local firm, Pacific Car and Foundry of Renton (PACCAR), based upon a prototype built in Philadelphia. In addition to the importance of these new pieces of equipment in upgrading and improving a transit system that had been overtaxed by an influx of workers and the military prior to the advent of World War II, their construction by a local firm represented the city's efforts to counteract Seattle's Depression era economy by encouraging local manufacture. Trolley No. 798 is the last operational survivor of this type of vehicle in the city. Its mohair upholstery, Art Deco period graphics, and streamlined form were carefully replicated during major rehabilitation of the vehicle in the late 1970s. It is one of a fleet of historic trolleys and motor coaches designated by King County Council.

**Clocks**
**Various locations**
Mayer Company, Howard Company, 1900–1930

The design and commercial use of timepieces within freestanding cast-iron cases appears to be a particularly American horological development of the mid-19th century. Although major manufacturers were located in the Northeast, an important West Coast supplier was the Mayer Company of Seattle (1897). In this city, street clocks reached their peak of popularity during the first two decades of the 20th century, becoming prominent advertising for jewelry and retail stores. Their numbers led some observers to refer to Seattle as the "city of clocks." The heaviest concentration of these clocks was found near the intersection of Pike Street and Fourth Avenue, the jewelry district for many years. Although recently the number of street clocks has dwindled, there are ten working clocks protected by city ordinance. They range from simple, two-faced, round-headed clocks with fluted columns and square pedestals to four-faced clocks with ornate crests, replete with coach lamps.

Benton's Jewelers, c. 1911, 3216 N.E. Forty-fifth Street

Ben Bridge Jewelers, c. 1929, 409 Pike Street

Carroll's Jewelers, c. 1913, 1427 Fourth Avenue

Century Square, c. 1903, 1529 Fourth Avenue

Lake Union Cafe, c. 1925, 3119 Eastlake Avenue E.

Greenwood Jewelers, c. 1914, 129 N. Eighty-fifth Street

Hong Kong and Shanghai Bank, c. 1910,
    Second Avenue near Columbia Street

Myers Music, c. 1906, 1206 First Avenue

Earl Layman Clock, c. 1905, 300 First Avenue S.

E. J. Towle Co., c. 1910, 406 Dexter Avenue N.


**Fireboat *Duwamish***
NOAA Lake Washington
*McAllaster & Bennett, 1909*

The fireboat *Duwamish* was designed, built, and operated during the period when large-pumping-capacity fireboats were needed to protect the large wooden warehouses, wharves, and docks loaded with high-value cargo on the central waterfront. Designed by a firm of local naval architects, consulting engineers, and marine surveyors and built locally by the Richmond Beach Shipbuilding Company, the steam-powered steel-hulled boat had its greatest challenge in 1914 when the Grand Trunk Pacific Dock, the largest wooden structure of its kind on the Pacific Coast, burned out of control. The fireboat prevented nearby piers from being destroyed. The boat was retired from service in 1985 and is currently owned by the Shipping and Railway Heritage Trust and awaiting repairs. It is listed on the National Register as well.


**Infanta/M.V. *Thea Foss***
Lake Union
*Leslie Edward Geary, 1930*

Local yacht designer Geary prepared plans for this 120-foot motor yacht for John Barrymore, famed Shakespearean actor and screen star, as a present to his bride, actress Delores Costello. At her suggestion, he named the boat *Infanta* to honor their expected first-born daughter. Built at Craig Shipbuilding Company of Long Beach, California, it was an outstanding work by its designer, constructed of riveted steel plate and built of the finest materials available for its important owner, at the considerable cost of $225,000. Interiors included a dining saloon connected to the galley belowdecks with a dumbwaiter, a "smoking room," originally furnished with a fireplace, sideboard, bookcases, and gun and fishing lockers, the main saloon, which originally contained a piano, bookcases, and a large settee, and handsomely outfitted staterooms. While these interiors have been altered, they still contain wood-paneled walls and trim and some original lighting and fixtures that characterize this gracious period of pleasure yachting. In 1950, the yacht was purchased by locally founded Foss Launch & Tug Company, which restored it for a private corporate yacht. In 1987, it was acquired by Totem Resources Corporation.


**M.V. *Malibu***
Lake Union
*Leslie Edward Geary, 1926*

The *Malibu* was built for Mrs. Kay Rindge and her daughter, Mrs. Rhoda Adamson, owners of the Malibu Potteries in southern California. The 100-foot motor yacht was the last major collaboration between two of Seattle's maritime industry leaders, the designer Leslie Edward Geary and the boatbuilder Norman J. Blanchard, whose boat works was located on Lake Union. It was constructed of Douglas fir, Alaska yellow cedar, and Port Orford cedar, with teak and bronze trim. A 1973 refitting raised the wheelhouse, replaced the twin masts with a single mast forward of the stack, and added low metal bulwarks to the bow. Interiors were also altered at that time. Totem Resources, the current owners, have restored the vessel within this 1973 reconfiguration.

**W.T. *Preston* Snagboat**
Anacortes, Washington
*U.S. Army Corps of Engineers, 1915; 1940 (moved)*

See appendix A.

**Lightship *Relief/Swiftsure***
Ship Canal/Lake Union
*U.S. Department of Commerce and Labor, 1904*

The steel hulled lightship *Relief* is the oldest steam-driven lightship on the Pacific Coast. Built in Camden, New Jersey, in 1904 and christened the *San Francisco,* it was fueled by coal but was built with masts and rigged for sails to be used if it drifted off station. The original lamps were whale oil burning, and their three beacons could be seen from two to three miles away. Lamps were changed to kerosene and finally to electricity in 1920, increasing visibility to 18 miles. Operated by the U.S. Department of Commerce and Labor, the agency that had jurisdiction over lighthouses and ships, the *San Francisco* served at the entrance to San Francisco Bay. In 1939, the ship came under the Coast Guard, had its name changed, and assumed duty as a relief ship for lightships serving the Columbia River Bar until 1960. The *Relief*—now renamed the *Swiftsure*—is also listed on the National Historic Register. Along with other vintage Northwest ships, it awaits a permanent wharfside home as part of a proposed maritime museum.

**S.S. *San Mateo***
Fraser River, British Columbia
*Southern Pacific; Golden Gate Ferries, 1922 (moved)*

See appendix A.

*Virginia V*
Lake Union
*Matthew Anderson, 1922*

Built in Maplewood, Washington, as a mail boat, the *Virginia V* is one of a large number of Puget Sound commercial ships collectively called "the Mosquito

Fleet." This boat is one of the last survivors. Its original owners were the West Pass Transport Company, which operated the *Virginia V* from Seattle to Tacoma via the West Pass of Vashon Island. It delivered groceries and mail and carried passengers an average of 125,000 miles per year. In 1939, it was withdrawn from the Seattle-Tacoma route, having served over 8 million passengers. It is now a private excursion boat listed on the National Historic Register. At 125 feet long and 24 feet broad, it has a distinctive straight vertical bow and glass-windowed main and deck levels. The *Virginia V* is powered by a triple expansion reciprocating steam engine of 400 horsepower. It is currently undergoing a $3.5 million renovation that includes a new boiler and a rebuilt engine.

**Schooner *Wawona***
Lake Union
*Hans Bendixen, 1897*

The *Wawona* is a three-masted baldheaded schooner of 468 tons built as a lumber schooner with a capacity for 630,000 linear feet. Its 156-foot-long and 36-foot-wide wood hull was constructed on Humboldt Bay in California in 1897 and was powered only by sail. The schooner operated exclusively in the Pacific Coast trade until 1914, when it was purchased by a fisheries company in Anacortes and became the "highliner" of the Bering Sea cod-fishing fleet. Used as a barge during World War II, it passed through a variety of owners and is currently under restoration as part of a maritime museum complex. The *Wawona* is the last surviving 19th-century sailing vessel of its type on Puget Sound and is an irreplaceable resource. Unfortunately, while the hull is sound, millions of dollars will be needed to make the extensive repairs and reconstruction above the water line.

*Entrance to the Interurban Building (Smith Tower Annex),*
*John Parkinson, 1889. The Pioneer Building is reflected in glass.*

102

# Chapter Four

# HISTORIC DISTRICTS: CONTROLLED CHANGE

Seattle is a city composed of neighborhoods, each with its own distinct heritage. Many older neighborhoods originated as independent towns accessible to Seattle by water, trolley lines, and the interurban rail system prior to and shortly after the turn of the century. Ballard, Columbia City, Georgetown, and other incorporated communities were eventually annexed to Seattle. They have attempted to maintain their individual identities despite the encroachment of industry, multifamily housing, traffic arterials, and automobile-related business. Of the many late-19th- and early-20th-century towns that existed within the physical entity that is now collectively called Seattle, Ballard and Columbia City have had particular success in retaining the architectural harmony of building forms and continuity of streetscape that offer the resident and visitor the opportunity to experience the character of late-19th- and early-20th-century Northwest milltown life.

Recognizing their assets as historic resources, the City of Seattle has established these neighborhoods

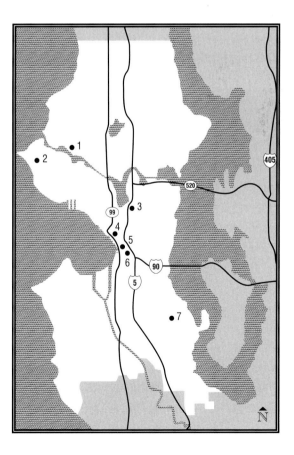

*Right, Historic Districts: 1. Ballard Avenue, 2. Fort Lawton,*
*3. Harvard /Belmont, 4. Pike Place Market, 5. Pioneer Square,*
*6. International Disrict, 7. Columbia City*

as historic districts. They are two of seven such districts established by ordinance. Other protected areas are Pioneer Square, Pike Place Market, International District, Harvard/Belmont, and Fort Lawton. The intent of designating historic districts is not to freeze these neighborhoods in time or to stifle development but rather to direct upgrading and new development in a sensitive way that recognizes and respects the value of the height, scale, materials, and palette of the existing buildings and the integrity of the pedestrian-oriented streets.

Apart from the city's efforts to create awareness of the value of these neighborhoods, in 1975 architects and University of Washington professors Victor Steinbrueck and Folke Nyberg began a landmark inventory of urban resources with the help of Historic Seattle Preservation and Development Authority and grants from the City of Seattle and the National Endowment for the Arts. Using neighborhood volunteers, they developed *A Visual Inventory of Buildings and Urban Design Resources for Seattle, Washington.* The publication and accompanying maps describe neighorhood history, common building types, significant buildings, landscapes, streetscapes, and view corridors for nearly a dozen major city neighborhoods. Although not accurate in all its details, this study did reveal that we should not take our neighborhoods for granted. Each one contains valuable built resources worthy of protection.

## PIONEER SQUARE PRESERVATION DISTRICT

The brick and stone buildings of Pioneer Square compose one of the largest and most intact groupings of late-19th-century commercial buildings left in a major American city. It was Seattle's first historic district, and the restoration and rehabilitation of its buildings served as the inspiration for the Seattle Landmarks Preservation Ordinance and for the formation of other historic districts within the city. Located at the south end of the Central Business District, Pioneer Square was built on the fortunes of the lumber mills, the railroad, maritime trade, and Yukon gold. Long neglected and left to decay as businesses moved northward and eastward, the district today bustles with a variety of activities. Its shops, offices, residences, galleries, restaurants, and parks reflect over 35 years of attention and support from the city, private investors, and the community.

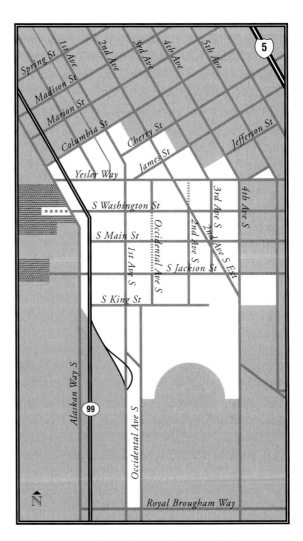

Besides the favorable conditions of its deepwater harbor, there was little else to recommend Seattle as a site for a city. A stretch of tide flats and steep cliffs challenged anyone interested in building even the smallest settlement. No overland routes existed to link the area to the East and Midwest, and the formidable terrain promised to make future development of such routes difficult. Undaunted, the settlers began the slow process of carving a village out of the surrounding wilderness. The level land along the waterfront was an important attraction for the village's earliest lumber industries. Logs were harvested from the forested slopes east of Front Street (now First Avenue) and skidded downhill along Mill Street (now Yesler Way) for processing and shipment at the water's edge. Henry Yesler's steam sawmill, the first in the territory, became the nucleus of the town. All business activity clustered around it and along the relatively flat area defined by Commercial Street (now First Avenue S.).

Hotels and stores were built for a growing popu-

*View of Pioneer Square in 1931 shows continuous rows of two- to four-story masonry commercial buildings between Occidental Avenue S. and the waterfront. The buildings in center foreground are now the site of Occidental Mall.*

lation; nearly all were built of wood. In 1889, a fire destroyed 25 square blocks—virtually the entire commercial district. Because the fire caught Seattle in the midst of a growth cycle that was both expanding and diversifying the city's economy, it proved more of a boon than a major setback. The sensational story of the fire, combined with glowing booster reports of the city's fervor to rebuild, attracted thousands of new settlers. It also brought a number of talented architects from other parts of the country who joined with resident architects and builders to design hotels, offices, and commercial buildings that would accommodate the population and activity of a city of 100,000 people—several times the size of the city left behind in the ashes.

After the 1889 fire, a city ordinance mandated that buildings be constructed of fire-resistant timbers, masonry, and stone. In the remarkably short period of two years, reconstruction was nearly complete, and Seattle could boast an up-to-date downtown business district in the latest architectural styles, frequently drawing upon Richardsonian Romanesque commercial buildings as models. Buildings were generally of three to five floors; their red-brick

*Rendering of Elmer Fisher's Pioneer Building.*

*Labor Day parade passes in front of the pergola at Pioneer Place in 1912.*

facades were usually quite restrained in their ornamentation. Sidewalls were left blank in anticipation of the next adjacent structure, as each parcel was filled in. Despite their various facade treatments, individual buildings fit harmoniously with their neighbors on the street. In part, this could be accounted for by the large number of buildings designed by a relatively small number of architects. Prominent among them were Elmer Fisher, Saunders & Houghton, John Parkinson, and William Boone. Fisher alone was reputed to have designed nearly 50 buildings in the city in a period of 18 months.

The 1897–98 Klondike Gold Rush inspired another decade of substantial growth and strengthened the commercial district with its requirements for outfitters, hotels and rooming houses, and related trades. But by the turn of the century, plans were being initiated to accomplish massive regrading of hills north and east of Pioneer Square. A newer, more "modern" financial, retail, and entertainment district developed along Second and Third Avenues. As businesses moved uptown prior to World War I, Pioneer Square became a warehousing district and a haven for low-income, transient laborers. After World War II, derelict buildings fell victim to new seismic and fire codes adopted by the city. Nearly 15,000 housing units were lost citywide in the ensuing decades. In this Skid Road area, old buildings were torn down and replaced with parking lots. Cornices and decorative features were removed from many of the

remaining structures as protection against accidents (particularly following the 1949 earthquake). Upper floors were declared unsafe for human occupancy and left to decay. Ironically, the inattention and neglect of those years protected the majority of buildings in Pioneer Square until a more enlightened attitude toward the contribution of older buildings to community vitality began to surface in the 1960s.

In 1963, a small group of architects and developers—among them Ralph Anderson and Alan Black—recognized the aesthetic and potential commercial value of the Square's buildings. Their efforts to renovate and lease several properties, including the Globe and Union Trust Buildings, attracted a great deal of public attention. Larger projects, on the scale of the Pioneer Building and the Grand Central Hotel, further encouraged business interest in the area.

With the support of the mayor, city agencies, and the community, Pioneer Square became the city's first historic district in May 1970. The original boundaries of the district were contained within a 20-square-block area extending from Cherry Street to S. Jackson Street and from Alaskan Way to Third Avenue. In 1973, a Special Review District encompassing a larger area was formed to protect Pioneer Square from traffic impacts and development pressures that were anticipated with completion of the King County domed stadium. The expanded Preservation District was a 40-block area extending as far east as Fourth Avenue S. and north from S. King Street to Columbia Street. The district consisted of a pedestrian-oriented core north of King Street and a buffer zone oriented toward light manufacturing extending around the site of the stadium. In 1987, the boundaries were expanded again to the southwest, based upon an expanded survey and inventory of historic buildings. These warehouse and manufacturing buildings between the railroad tracks and Alaskan Way S. to Royal Brougham Way are intact structures that are historically and functionally related to the historic district and reflect the development of industry, railroad transportation, and commerce.

The district's goal is to preserve its historic integrity and architectural identity and ensure sensitive restoration of existing buildings while seeking economically viable new uses for those buildings that are currently underutilized and derelict. To that end, guidelines have been developed to encourage responsible repair and maintenance, to reinforce the design integrity of facades, and to encourage ground-level

*The Union Trust is one of several buildings on Occidental Avenue S. newly refurbished in the 1960s. The planting strip predates the pedestrian malling of the street.*

uses that promote an active pedestrian environment. Limiting through traffic in certain areas of the district, creating small cobblestone- and brick-paved parks and tree-lined walks, and establishing office and residential uses above street level in former hotels and warehouses are methods by which these goals have been achieved. Height and bulk limits have been placed on new construction. Owners, tenants, or developers wishing to change an existing building exterior must abide by regulations governing the materials, colors, shape, and lighting of signs; the awnings, canopies, and ornamental features applied to the facades; and the location and configuration of parking and automobile access. These guidelines do not discourage development in the district; rather, they reinforce and strengthen its existing identity and enhance its 19th-century character while also stimulating business, a variety of uses, and increased activity.

Since 1970, Pioneer Square has been the site of many successful restoration and adaptive reuse projects. Senator Warren Magnuson's efforts resulted in significant federal grants to Seattle. Pivotal early projects were made possible by substantial private investment and by public/private partnerships. As a result, the area now boasts a strong mix of market-rate residential units, shops, and office spaces. Accompanying new development have been public improvements to streets, sidewalks, and parks.

Tax incentives allowed the private sector to help implement public purposes—preservation, housing, employment, and neighborhood revitalization—while strengthening the fiscal base of the community. In the Pioneer Square Preservation District, an average of 42,000 square feet of space was rehabilitated annually between 1970 and 1976. Refurbished office, apartment, and retail space nearly quadrupled after the enactment of the Tax Reform Act of 1976. This act was the first use of the Internal Revenue Code to provide incentives for rehabilitation and to actively discourage demolition. A 1978 Revenue Act added a provision allowing a special 10 percent tax credit for expenses incurred in rehabilitating eligible structures. Public improvements to streets, sidewalks, and parks accompanied restoration of buildings.

The rapid pace of redevelopment in the early 1980s was encouraged by the Economic Recovery Tax Act of 1981, which provided investment tax credits and depreciation allowances for developers of National Register properties, and by the allocation of Urban Development Action Grant loan funds and Section 312 Housing loan funds. In Pioneer Square, the Economic Recovery Tax Act had stimulated rehabilitation of 18 buildings by the end of 1984 involving private investments in excess of $100 million. According to a study by Historic Seattle Preservation and Development Authority, the adaptive use of these previously empty buildings generated 88 apartments and 1.2 million square feet of commercial space. In addition to the economic benefits of creating 1600 permanent, private-sector jobs and 1,100 construction jobs, over $3.6 million was paid in state sales taxes on construction and annual real estate taxes increased approximately $1 million per year. All of these benefits were stimulated by $15 million in investment tax credits allowed under the Tax Reform Act.

An often overlooked provision of the 1976 Tax Reform Act, the donation of conservation easements on developable property, continues to provide developers with major tax deductions amounting to the difference between the fair market value of the property before and after the restrictions of the easement. The development group for the Arctic Club and Alaska Buildings made a charitable contribution in perpetuity of the facade of each building and of the development rights relating to each building to the State Office of Archaeology and Historic Preservation prior to restoration and rehabilitation.

Construction in Pike Place Market, along First Avenue, and in Pioneer Square in the 1970s and 1980s focused attention upon the design of infill buildings within a historic district. The erection of the eight-story Olympic Block to replace a gaping hole at the pivotal corner of First Avenue and Yesler Way (resulting from the collapse of the Olympic Building in 1973) stimulated debate over the new building's scale, facade materials, and design. Should new construction attempt to replicate the old designs of adjacent buildings or can a new facade, using contemporary materials and design, fit comfortably and nonintrusively in the older context? Two designs were rejected before a compromise was reached. Design review provided a valuable learning experience in citizen interest and participation in the design and development process.

This first renaissance of Pioneer Square came to a halt with changes in federal tax legislation in 1986 that changed the method by which benefits were provided to developers of historic properties. Coupled with a downturn in the economy in the late 1980s and new construction that drew business out of older buildings into high-rises in the Central Business District that were offering bargain leases and incentives, bankruptcies became commonplace. One of the positive trade-offs for the city was its ability to purchase the Alaska, Arctic Club, and Dexter Horton Buildings at bargain basement prices.

The development of the Special Tax Valuation program partially countered the loss of incentives on the federal level. Among the beneficiaries were the St. Charles Hotel, refurbished for offices, the Our Home Hotel, turned into condominiums, and the State Hotel and the Delmar. In 1993, the run-down Pioneer Square Hotel was rehabilitated to become the first tourist hotel in the district. In the 1990s, housing has been an important focus in the district. The Florentine, a condominium project in a redeveloped warehouse building on First Avenue S., extended retail south of S. Jackson Street for the first time. Recent developments, including the Lofts on Third Avenue S. and the planned Palmer Court even further south, should bring more round-the-clock activity to the area.

A building boom has recently occurred in the southeast section of the district—some might call it a second renaissance—that includes new construction of King Street Center, restoration of King Street Station and Union Station, new office buildings over the former Union Station tracks (now a new garage), and proposals for a new hotel that will carry construction into the millennium. The real estate portfolio of the late Sam Israel, one of the city's largest landholders, has been turned into a major redevelopment program by Samis Foundation. In Pioneer Square, historic properties will be upgraded for a variety of commercial and retail uses. They include the Smith Tower and adjoining Florence and Collins Buildings, Corona Hotel and Butler Hotel (garage) on Second Avenue, Terry Denny Building on First Avenue S., and U.S. Rubber Building on S. Jackson and Third Avenue S. While there is no question that these buildings need care and upgrading, such changes as removal of the upper-floor facade of the Butler Hotel and proposed and initiated changes to historic interiors in the Smith Tower to create "A" class office space have been controversial issues for both the Pioneer Square Board and Seattle Landmarks Preservation Board.

The impact of new football and baseball stadiums and demolition of the Kingdome have been the focus of many business owners, residents, and civic groups. They are monitoring these projects and trying to work together to read through the plethora of construction documents, studies, urban design schemes, and traffic studies to ascertain their compatibility with the district and its goals. It has been a very difficult process, with compromises on many sides.

Pioneer Square has been and continues to be a diverse community. Today, it has its share of shelters and missions; artist studios, artist live/work spaces, and art galleries; taverns, sports bars, nightclubs, and restaurants; condominium and rental housing; and retail, antique, and souvenir shops. With that kind of diversity, there are bound to be differing opinions, and those on land use are particularly challenging. It is impossible to speak with one voice that reflects a balance of needs and addresses residents, economic development pressures, congestion, and traffic. Four community groups tackle such issues: Pioneer Square Community Council, Pioneer Square Business Improvement Area, Pioneer Square Neighborhood Planning Committee, and Pioneer Square Community Development Organization.

While the development climate in the late 1990s echoes that of the early 1980s, is it a renaissance or merely the beginning of a decline in the appreciation of traditional values and of the character of the historic neighborhood? Will all the upgrades simply lead to higher cost leases and rents that will force marginal art galleries, restaurants, and other businesses and low-cost rental residents and artists out? Will it have the effect that is occurring now in places like Old Pasadena, where national chains are moving in to the retail outlets emptied by individual businesses and turning the look of the historic district into a shopping mall? Or will the district do as it has done several times in the past—accommodate

change gracefully, retaining its dignified backdrop for new generations of users?

Several outstanding restoration, renovation, and adaptive reuse projects that have contributed to the current healthy character of Pioneer Square are described below.

*The Grand Central Hotel is derelict in the early 1970s.*

### Grand Central on the Park
216 First Avenue S.

Initially named the Squire Latimer Block and designed by Comstock & Troetsche in 1889–90 to house offices, this keystone structure in Pioneer Square functioned as the Grand Central Hotel during the Klondike Gold Rush and thereafter. By the 1930s, this and surrounding buildings had decayed in reputation and physical condition. The building was bought in 1971 by developers Richard White and Alan Black and architect Ralph Anderson, renamed Grand Central on the Park, and returned to its original use as an office building. The new owners gave it needed modern amenities and altered it only slightly to allow for more public use of its street level. The exterior was cleaned and store windows were changed to provide consistency throughout the facade. A handsome iron grille embellishes the gateway to a shopping arcade that connects First Avenue with Occidental Park. This city-financed open space was designed by the landscape firm of Jones & Jones to replace a parking lot. Its boulevarded cobblestone plaza, benches, fountain, contemporary bandstand, and glassed-in dining pavilion provided a variety of public amenities where none existed. Some were successful and some failed. But to many people, the successful restoration of the Grand Central on the Park was seen as the catalyst that spurred major redevelopment of the area.

*Left: The first-floor shopping arcade connects First Avenue with Occidental Mall. Above: Ivy-covered Grand Central faces onto Occidental Mall.*

## Pioneer Building
600 First Avenue

Located on the site of pioneer Henry Yesler's home, Elmer Fisher's Pioneer Building was constructed in two stages between 1889 and 1891 and is Seattle's most flamboyant and original interpretation of Richardsonian Romanesque commercial style design. Until 1974, five of the building's six floors had been empty for over 25 years. Despite the loss of its central tower and the accumulation of nearly a century of grime, the neglect had preserved the building facade and interiors. In 1973, the Theta Corporation hired architect Ralph Anderson to rehabilitate the building. Although the structure was reasonably sound, roof leaks had seriously damaged the northwest corner of the building, requiring internal bracing and new supporting columns. The roof was completely redone, rotting floors and joists were replaced, the skylights were rebuilt, and the sheet metal cornice was completely reconstructed. The original hydraulic elevator shaft, turned into vaults for tenant use when the city's first electric elevators were installed, was used to conceal the building's new heating, ventilating, and air-conditioning systems. The two open-cage elevators were adjusted to

*Sixth-floor offices in neglected and decaying condition, 1968.*

accommodate safety glass enclosures to meet fire codes.

Other work on the building to meet fire and seismic code requirements included installation of a sprinkler system, fire stairs, and a safety glass smoke relief panel in the skylights, tying back of parapet walls, reinforcing floors, and using metal tie rods to connect exterior walls to floors. Facade cleaning,

*Pioneer Building after rehabilitation.*

*The larger of two dramatic interior courts provide light to inner offices.*

patching, and repainting, terra-cotta repair, window replacement, new storefronts, and stripping and refinishing of doors, wainscoting, and staircase balusters turned the derelict building into the city's premier example of restoration. The success of the Pioneer Building stimulated rehabilitation projects in neighboring blocks of Pioneer Square.

*Pergola prior to restoration, 1970.*

## Pioneer Place Pergola
First Avenue and Yesler Way

For residents and visitors alike, the symbol of the renaissance of Pioneer Square has been the graceful glass and metal pergola, or waiting shelter, at First Avenue and Yesler Way. Designed by Julian Everett, it was constructed in 1909 at the transportation hub of the city—where the James Street, Yesler Way, and First Avenue streetcars met. The ornate Beaux Arts structure also marked the entrance to what has been called the "Queen Mary of johns," which certainly was in its time one of the most up-to-date and richly appointed underground public comfort stations in the country. These two public amenities were installed to impress visitors to the 1909 Alaska-

*Elevator lobby, Alaska Building.*

*The restored pergola with James Wehn's Chief Seattle fountain in foreground.*

Yukon-Pacific Exposition. After World War II, the rest rooms were closed and the pergola fell into disrepair. The metalwork rusted and the damaged glass was replaced by a sheet metal roof.

In 1973, funded by a $150,000 donation by the founder of United Parcel Service (first established in 1907 in Pioneer Square) and $100,000 from the City of Seattle, the pergola and the park in which it stands were restored under the supervision of the firm of Jones & Jones. Using original cast-iron benches and lampposts as models, pine and mahogany patterns were made for new castings. The ornate patterns of the hollow core metal lamps serv-

ing as vents for the underground rest rooms were meticulously duplicated using original blueprints as guides. The park also includes a replacement totem pole and a fountain and bust of Chief Seattle by Northwest sculptor James Wehn. The rest rooms, however, remain closed and inaccessible.

## Alaska Building
618 Second Avenue

This handsome brick- and terra-cotta trimmed structure was designed by Eames & Young of St. Louis with local associates Saunders & Lawton for a consortium of stockholders of the Scandinavian American Bank and J. C. Marmaduke, a Missouri developer. Constructed in 1904, it was Seattle's first skyscraper, its steel-frame construction being, at that time, a marvelous innovation. The Hoge Building (1909–11) and the Smith Tower (1910–14) joined it to establish lower Second Avenue as the city's new financial and commercial center. In addition to providing office space, the building was the home of the Alaska Club and featured a ballroom on the penthouse (14th) floor.

The Alaska Building had been reasonably well maintained, although periodic remodeling and modification of its interior spaces had occurred when, in

*Alaska Building.*

*Mutual Life Building.*

1982, it was renovated by Carma Developers and Foster/Marshall in a $12.2 million project to provide 124,000 square feet of net rentable office space. Necessary work included exterior masonry cleaning and repair, installation of air-conditioning, ventilating, and plumbing systems, upgrading of lobbies, installation of new elevators, renovation of common areas, including elevator lobbies, corridors, and entry fronts, and placement of new ceilings and fixtures. The architectural firm of Stickney & Murphy took particular care in cleaning and repairing marble walls, ceilings, and archways in the principal lobby, cleaning and repairing original brass hardware and ornaments, and providing contemporary lighting fixtures and torchères that would highlight the lobby's dignified marble walls.

**Mutual Life Building**
605 First Avenue

Built on the site of Henry Yesler's cookhouse, and the original site of the First National Bank of Seattle, the Mutual Life Building is one of the keystone structures of the Pioneer Square Preservation District. The

*New torchères dramatically illuminate the restored wood-paneled entrance foyer.*

first floor and basement were built in 1890 by Henry Yesler and designed by Seattle's preeminent architect, Elmer Fisher. In 1897, five additional floors were added to the building by the new owner, the Mutual Life Insurance Company; they were designed by James Blackwell, who also designed the 1904 rear addition and the 1916 storefront and basement alterations. When Historic Seattle Preservation and Development Authority acquired the building in 1982, it had been vacant and virtually without maintenance for almost 15 years.

In 1983, Historic Seattle entered into a long-term lease with the Emerald Fund for the purpose of restoration. Due to the building's deteriorated condition, its size, and its inefficient floor plan, a public/private partnership was formed to ensure the economic feasibility of rehabilitation. Designs by the firm of Olson Walker called for a $3.6 million rehabilitation and reconstruction to provide 11,000 square feet of retail space and five floors of 7,000 square feet of office space. Work was completed in 1984 with the help of investment tax credits and an Urban Development Action Grant loan. Mutual Life Associates currently leases the building from Historic Seattle.

*A new stairway recedes upward to top-floor skylight in refurbished Heritage Building.*

## Heritage Building
111 S. Jackson Street

This classic sandstone and brick structure, built in 1904, was renovated by the Heritage Group in 1982 at a cost of $3.5 million to provide deluxe office and retail space. The completed building now houses the

NBBJ Group—appropriately, the rehabilitation architects for this project. To passersby, the restored facades belie the extensive transformation carried out within the 65,000-square-foot interior to accommodate a 235-person staff. Except for the discreet addition of a new entry vestibule, solar-tinted windowpanes, a skylight, and a rooftop greenhouse, the turn-of-the-century sandstone exterior is virtually intact. Inside, the warehouse has been turned into flexible open-planned space on either side of a dramatic five-story skylit staircase that bridges the two office halves and provides a compelling focal point. Shallow balconies reinforce the visual connection of the central stairwell to adjoining spaces.

*A rendering of Court in the Square shows the two warehouse buildings bridged by a glass atrium.*

## Court in the Square
401 Second Avenue S.

The DKB Corporation rehabilitation of two adjacent early-20th-century brick commercial buildings for office space provided the architectural firm of Anderson Koch Duarte the opportunity to design a dramatic glass-enclosed grand lobby court and a vaulted canopy that provides an elegant and airy entrance between the two buildings. The seven-story Goldsmith Building of 1906 and its northern neighbor, the five-story North Coast Building of 1900, have been completely rehabilitated into modern professional office space featuring exposed beams and high ceilings. New windows, French doors opening onto wrought-iron railed balconies overlooking the lobby court, and penthouses with private garden terraces are features that give Court in the Square a sense of community. The translucent sloping roof of the lobby court is designed to open during summer months to allow for fresh-air circulation.

*A newly constructed glass-walled facade opens up formerly dark office space to light. The alley has been developed into an attractive promenade with reflecting pool.*

*Offices with French doors and balconies face onto the all-weather courtyard.*

## Merrill Place

First Avenue S. between Jackson and King Streets

This ambitious whole-block development consists of the renovation of three significant First Avenue commercial buildings and a 1909 Jackson Street warehouse, erection of a new parking facility, and construction of a central plaza. Owned by the R. D. Merrill Company, the project was developed by the Heritage Group Ltd. with two architectural firms, Olson Walker and NBBJ Group, jointly collaborating on renovation and new construction.

Originally serving as warehouse and commercial space, each of the four buildings has a dignified architectural quality. The Hambach Building, a seven-story structure, was designed by Saunders & Lawton and constructed in 1913. Its renovation features first-floor retail and offices. The Seller Building, in the center of the block, was designed by A. Warren Gould in 1906 and now provides ground floor retail and six floors of office space. Its alley facade has

been replaced by a dramatic aluminum and green glass stepped-back curtain wall that rises a full seven floors and faces a reflecting pool in the central plaza. The architects saw the glass wall as an opportunity to provide brighter, more pleasant work environments for office tenants in the building, the floors of which tended to be dark and somewhat dreary. The five-story Pacific Marine Schwabacher Building was designed by the distinguished firm of Bebb & Mendel in 1905. Its red-brick facade is delineated with cast terra-cotta ornament inspired by Louis Sullivan designs. The Schwabacher Building now provides refurbished retail space, offices on the next two floors, and residential units on the top two floors. The fourth structure, designed by Bebb & Gould, initially provided a handsome, state-of-the-art performing hall for the Empty Space Theater. This outstanding recycling of an entire block of buildings into a lively inner-city neighborhood was accomplished at a cost of approximately $30 million.

# PIKE PLACE MARKET HISTORIC DISTRICT

The Pike Place Market serves as a vital cultural and economic center in the heart of downtown Seattle. It began as a street market in 1907 intended to provide the rapidly growing city with a good source of fresh, locally grown produce at reasonable prices with higher incomes for area farmers, who could sell directly to consumers rather than going through brokers and middlemen. The market was an instant success. Meat, fish, and restaurant merchants soon joined the farmers and rapid expansion proceeded. Major portions of the main market building were completed by the end of the first year. The Economy Market, Corner Market, Sanitary Market, and lower levels of the main building were built within the next ten years. Hotels were concentrated in the market area to house visiting seamen, farmers, and local residents. Over the years, many food-related shops and small independent businesses were established to expand the original concept of a produce center.

During World War II, the market began to deteriorate, partly because the internment of Japanese Americans resulted in a great loss of market farmers. In the 1950s and 1960s, the advent of shopping centers and grocery chains, the increasing popularity of frozen foods, and suburban expansion dispersed many of the shoppers who had traditionally relied upon the market for their daily needs.

In 1963, a comprehensive redevelopment and highway plan for downtown included recommendations to modernize the market area with new office towers and parking structures. The threat of its dem-

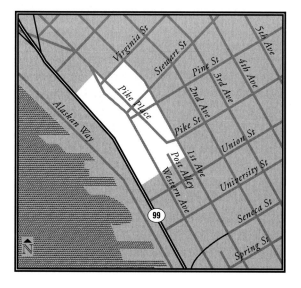

olition aroused a citizen protest by Allied Arts of Seattle, which formed a subcommittee that later became known as Friends of the Market. Led by architect and preservationist Victor Steinbrueck and others, this organization advocated preserving the market—both its buildings and its unique character. To do so, the group was forced to sponsor a public initiative, which passed overwhelmingly in 1971. In order to ensure the protection of the market from unsympathetic modernization efforts that would alter its unique qualities, the Keep the Market Initiative included specific provisions for the creation and regulation of an historic district. The Urban Renewal plan was revised accordingly.

In late 1971, the Pike Place Market Historic District was formally established by city ordinance. Its initial boundaries were specified as a seven-acre area from Virginia Street to Pike Street and from Western Avenue to First Avenue. However, these boundaries were subsequently expanded westward in 1984 and 1991. The district includes buildings that serve the market commercial purposes, as well as approximately 400 residential units. The Market Historical Commission, composed of residents, merchants, property owners, architects, and representatives of civic organizations, was established to review use and design applications. The commission guidelines recognize that uses are as important in the market as are the buildings themselves. Specific guidelines address farmer-grown and fresh-produce businesses and other small owner-operated businesses serving local clientele, priority market uses, mix of business types, the design of individual business spaces and displays, including signage, and pedestrian orientation of the shops and public access. Additional guidelines, like those for other historic districts, address issues of height, scale, materials, and colors appropriate within the district boundaries. They also follow the standards set by the U.S. Secretary of the Interior.

Federal grants were secured with the help of Senator Warren Magnuson, and under the leadership of George Rolfe, the first Pike Place Market Preservation and Development Authority (PPMPDA) director, work began. Between 1972 and 1978, the market underwent a meticulous rehabilitation of its older buildings and upgrading of facilities, as well as the sensitive design of infill housing and commercial buildings in keeping with the utilitarian character of the original market structures, most of which were constructed prior to 1916. The Pike Place Project strengthened and reinforced the lively and diverse

*Pike Place bustles with activity, c. 1915.*

nature of downtown Seattle and reestablished a permanent residential community, as well as food and flower stalls, groceries, specialty shops, and restaurants.

The PPMPDA, a public nonprofit corporation, was established in 1973. It serves as property manager for most of the market district. However, several buildings remain in private ownership. During the extensive 10-year restoration and redevelopment effort, approximately $50 million in public funds and $100 million in private funds were channeled into the market to reinforce the district as a living, shopping, and meeting place for people of all income levels, social and ethnic backgrounds, and cultural tastes. Using a variety of funding mechanisms, the buildings were brought up to fire and safety codes, stalls and shops were improved, and housing appealing to all income levels was developed. (There are currently 100 farmers, 150 craftspeople, and 250 commercial tenants within the district boundaries.) The project

*The Public Market Center sign is a familiar beacon visible for many blocks along Pike Street.*

received nationwide recognition, including a 1985 American Institute of Architects Honor Award to the late George Bartholick, supervising architect for the rehabilitation of the core of the market.

Several changes have occurred in the market since then. In 1986, Market Park was added to the district

*The Corner Market Building at First Avenue and Pike Street.*

*Workers repair and repaint the central market arcade.*

and then renamed Victor Steinbrueck Park in honor of the park's designer and Market champion. In the late 1980s, the plans to construct the Heritage House and PDA garage (along with a skybridge connecting the project to the main market buildings) were the impetus for an additional expansion of the district boundaries. This expansion allowed the Market Historical Commission to regulate new construction along the west side of Western Avenue, including the Desimone parking lot, which is the last undeveloped parcel within the urban renewal area.

Because the market is so intensely used by local shoppers and tourists, it requires continuous maintenance and repair. Major changes to the market since its initial rehabilitation include covering of the previously open Desimone Bridge area; installing a tile floor underwritten by contributors; constructing an entrance information kiosk; in-kind replacing of deteriorated windows; and installing a new awning system that functions both to enclose the North Arcade during cold weather and to provide cover into Pike Place Market for farm sales tables that are set up during the warmer months. Currently, a small interpretive facility is being constructed (with financial support from the Market Foundation) adjacent to Heritage House on Western Avenue. A commemorative mural that will honor Japanese American farmers is being installed within the Main Arcade.

During the 1990s, the market has been the subject of front-page headlines for a number of reasons. The Urban Group, a New York investment firm that purchased investment tax credits to several rehabilitated market buildings, challenged the PPMPDA over ownership. No sooner was that threat addressed with a major cash infusion from the state legislature

than proposed changes to rules governing the use of day stall space angered craft day stall users and provoked the first strike in recent market history. The issue was raised as the PPMPDA attempted to revise a 1983 agreement that regulates day stall uses within the market and is intended to retain a balance of farmers and craftspeople. The reality of the market is that preserving uses has and continues to generate controversy. Nevertheless, it has been the market's strength that, for over 90 years, it has adapted to both merchant and shopper needs while retaining its unique character.

The three projects below are indicative of the variety of building types and uses that have been preserved to make the market a successful inner-city neighborhood.

### Sanitary Market
1514 Pike Place; 1531 First Avenue

Reputedly named the Sanitary Market because it was the first building in the market to prohibit horses from entering, the original four-story structure of 1910 was reconstructed as a two-story building with rooftop parking after a fire gutted the upper floors in 1941. The 1981 rehabilitation by the firm of Bassetti/Norton/Metler sought to restore the two demolished levels for housing above stalls and shops at the Pike Place and First Avenue levels. Housing reflects the diversity of market tenants and includes subsidized and middle-income accommodations ranging from studio and one-bedroom to two-bedroom townhouse units. Eight of the units were funded with a Section 8 rent supplement provided through the U.S. Department of Housing and Urban Development.

*Sanitary Market, with additional floors, after restoration, 1981.*

### Stewart House
1902–10 Pike Place; 80–82 Stewart Street

Originally built for George and Harriet Bremer as a workingman's hotel in 1902, this one- and two-story wood frame lodging house was provided with a brick retail addition in 1911. It provided short-term low-cost single-room housing for Seattle's growing population of seamen, longshoremen, and waterfront workers. Each room had a gas burner and sink, and communal bathroom facilities were located on each floor. Following the opening of Pike Place Market in 1907, farmers often took advantage of the cheap accommodations at the Stewart House. In continuous use until 1977, the building was closed for fire code violations and its demolition was close at hand. Citizen support for restoring it and maintaining its important low cost housing function finally succeeded, and architect Ibsen Nelsen was put in charge of a complete rehabilitation of the original wooden structure and design of a new four story addition with red brick veneer. The deterioration of the wooden building required extensive foundation work and the nearly complete reconstruction of the principal

facades. The interior now provides 39 single rooms, each containing a small sink-stove-refrigerator unit, and men's and women's bath facilities on each floor. The original lobby, with its captain's chairs looking out on Stewart Street, was restored for use as a communal lounge. The new portion of the building, constructed on Pike Place to the west of the original Stewart House, provides 48 subsidized studio and one-bedroom apartments and 13 retail spaces.

*Seattle Garden Center with additional level for offices set back from Pike Place.*

### Seattle Garden Center
1600 Pike Place

To architect Arne Bystrom, the Seattle Garden Center represented a time, a style, a history, and a presence that no new structure could capture. One of several small and deteriorating retail buildings adjacent to the main Pike Place Market buildings, the Garden Center was considered for demolition when Bystrom and two partner merchants purchased the two level structure from the city. While restoring the original building for a garden center and kitchenware shop in 1979, Bystrom added a third level for his office that is set back from Pike Place to provide a terrace above the Garden Center.

The style of the addition complements the Art Deco embellishments added to the 1902 building in 1931; these included zigzag coping and fluted columns. Metal sash windows, layered wood moldings, glass wall partitions, and hand designed wood furnishings and cabinets express Bystrom's appreciation for the works of the Arts and Crafts movement and Japanese architecture, as well as a respect for the characteristic Art Deco motifs that were a part of the modified turn-of-the-century facades. With its pink walls, green trim, and roof trellises, the Seattle Garden Center is a pleasant survivor within the Pike Place Market Historic District.

# International Special Review District

The International Special Review District has been home to Japanese, Chinese, Filipino, and other Asian groups since the turn of the century—a place to live, to work, to eat, to socialize, and to celebrate. A part of the downtown, and yet distinct and apart from it, this neighborhood provides housing and community services to a diverse ethnic population. It consists of a largely harmonious grouping of early-20th-century commercial and hotel buildings that collectively form a dense, cohesive, and self-sufficient community for Seattle's Asian ethnic groups. In Washington State, only Seattle developed an extensively organized Chinatown that attracted Asians residing elsewhere in the state who wanted to enjoy the linguistic and cultural opportunities of a larger community. Despite continuing efforts by outside forces to uproot the population, demolish its buildings, divide it with freeways and arterials, and insensitively upgrade and remodel its original facilities, the International District continues to provide a viable and lively inner city environment that retains its ethnic identity. In large part, its integrity has been saved by and enhanced under Special Review District supervision.

Seattle's first Chinese residents were brought to

*King County attracted a large Japanese labor force. Japanese Village, Kerriston, Washington.*

the Northwest in the 1860s to provide cheap labor to build the railroads, work in lumber mills, process fish, and provide domestic service. Several merchant and manufacturing shops were established, as well as boardinghouses that provided immigrants with shelter and some sense of community. These buildings were located adjacent to Henry Yesler's mill and eventually developed along Second, Occidental, and Third between Yesler Way and S. Washington Streets.

During the 1880s, the 400 Chinese living in the Puget Sound area met with forceful hostilities when a nationwide depression caused the total shutdown of hundreds of factories and mines. The completion of the Northern Pacific and Canadian Pacific Railroads threw thousands of white and Chinese laborers out of work, swelling the labor market in the Northwest. The frustrated anger caused by widespread unemployment was directed at the Chinese population, nearly all of whom were deported after riots in 1886. Japanese immigrants soon arrived in Seattle to fill the vacancies left by the Chinese, taking over their dwellings and jobs as farmhands, domestic servants, launderers, and shop owners.

The few Chinese merchants who remained in Seattle after the 1886 riots continued to contract Chinese labor in the face of resentment. Chinese were recruited to rebuild and expand the Yesler sawmill operation in 1888, to construct the Seattle, Lake Shore, and Eastern Railroad, begun in 1887, and to work in salmon canneries. After the fire of 1889, the Chinese built or leased buildings on both sides of lower Washington Street, and Chinatown developed with a mix of eating establishments and merchant shops. Family associations, or tongs, served as the key social and economic institutions for immigrant families. The influx of single male laborers

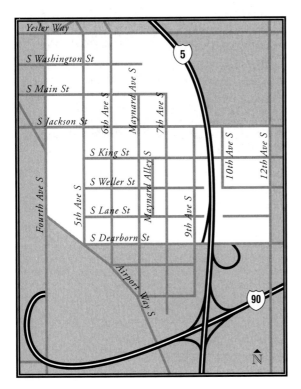

*The regrading of S. Jackson Street (left) and S. King Street (center) seen from Fifth Avenue S. In widening S. Jackson, the building on far left lost its turreted corner tower. Academy of the Holy Names (1883–84) is at center. The frame buildings that would become the Far East Building are at left, on the north side of S. Jackson Street.*

resulted in crowded conditions in the restricted confines of S. Washington Street.

Immediately after the regrading of S. King Street, begun in 1907 as part of the Jackson Street regrade project, a Chinese investment group led by prominent community leader Goon Dip built a series of buildings on the south side of King Street from Eighth Avenue S. to Maynard Avenue S. that was the catalyst for the development of a new Chinatown. Chinese Consulate offices were founded and schools were built.

Adjacent to Chinatown, Japanese Americans formed a substantial community extending from Second to Twelfth Avenues between Yesler Way and S. Jackson Street called Nihon Machi or Japantown. Its commercial center was at S. Main Street and Sixth Avenue S.

Throughout Chinatown and Japantown, dozens of inexpensive hotels served single men working in the maritime, timber, and coal mining trades, seasonal laborers in the region's farms and the Alaskan canneries, and families who worked in the district's shops and restaurants. Robert Kovalenko, a local architect who has renovated a number of single room

*A hotel entrance incorporates Chinese roof tiles and sculpted cap and shield to make its Western architecture more approachable to Asian residents.*

occupancy hotels in the district, points out, "Whole families would live here. Kids would play in halls, the doors would be open—like living in a house. Landlords made it affordable. A lot of the people who owned these buildings brought workers over from China and rented to their employees. It's still happening."

The continuing existence of the International District has been tested time and again. The intern-

*Family association meeting rooms with balconies to the street add visual interest to typical brick buildings.*

*With its distinctive porch, tile roof, and uplifted corners, the Chinese Benevolent Association has been a community resource since its construction.*

*The Nippon Kan was community center and performance space for the Japanese community. Its restored offices and auditorium continue to serve these functions for a broader audience.*

ment of Japanese families during World War II forced an exodus that destroyed the vital community on S. Main Street. After the war, opportunities for education, housing, and work outside the district drew younger generations, leaving the historic neighborhood to a largely single male and senior low-income population.

Stricter building and fire codes also resulted in the closure or demolition of many transient hotels and threatened the architectural integrity of the area. After a disastrous hotel fire in the 1970s, tighter city fire codes required upgrades of the old hotels. Many owners could not afford to install sprinkler systems or meet other code requirements. They had to close them, which hastened neglect and decay.

The construction of Interstate 5 in the 1960s had physically divided the area and eliminated businesses, homes, and churches. But it was the completion of the King County domed stadium in 1975 and the perceived impact of traffic and parking on this fragile neighborhood that stimulated grassroots support for the formation of a historic district under city regulation to protect its physical and cultural integrity. A Special Review District was approved in 1973 governing a large multiblock area from Dearborn Street north to Yesler Way and from Fourth Avenue S. to Twelfth Avenue S. The District Board composed of mayoral appointees and elected community members reviews applications for conditional uses, special exceptions, variances, planned unit developments,

amendments to the zoning maps, and Certificates of Approval for changes to existing buildings and use of properties, and for compatible design.

The historic core was listed on the National Register of Historic Places in 1987 to safeguard the urban mix of commercial buildings, hotels, and theaters that evolved to serve this multicultural community. The district's buildings offer a unique opportunity to experience the manner in which people of Asian cultures build and shape the physical aspects of their community within the context of an American city. Although its masonry and terra-cotta faced buildings are typical of early 20th century commercial districts, the community's ethnic traditions are expressed in the decoration and use of these buildings by their owners and occupants.

The most obvious visual manifestation of the district's oriental cultural background consists of the many signs written in Chinese and Japanese calligraphy to denote the location of prominent family associations and businesses and to advertise local sales and public events. Other building features unique to the International District are the many balconies on the upper stories of brick buildings. Belonging to private families or clubs, the balconies follow a southern Chinese tradition of providing cool and pleasant outdoor living space overlooking the street activity below. The ground-level shops that face onto mid-street alleys are also carryovers reflecting Far Eastern roots. The intent of the district regulations is to protect these features and to encourage new development to complement them and to encourage pedestrian activity.

Housing improvements have come slowly to the district. Change of use from hotel to residential triggers compliance with a host of city codes. It takes a great deal of money to do redevelopment. In the 1980s matching funds were available from the federal government at low interest rates through a number of innovative programs, including Forward Thrust and Block Grants. A significant tax credit program provided incentives to developers who rehabilitated historic properties. One early project was the renovation of the Evergreen Apartments (Tokiwa Hotel, 1916) by architects Arai/Jackson for the developer Toda, Chin & Arai, completed in 1981. During this period, several market rate (nonsubsidized) housing projects in the International District were completed, including the Far East Building by architects Kovalenko Hale for Wai C. Eng and the Freedman Building (1910) by architects Arai/Jackson for Min & Etai Yamaguchi, both completed in 1984.

In the leaner 1990s, there has been little incentive for developers of market rate or for-profit housing that could bring young professionals into the district. It is more difficult to put together financing packages without the help of low-interest rates and investment tax credits. Consequently, most of the recent and current projects are designed for low-income, subsidized housing sponsored by nonprofit housing groups.

Another stumbling block to redevelopment lies in family ownership of the properties themselves. Robert Kovalenko gives as an example, "When a father dies, he leaves the building to all the siblings. Or the building may have been owned from the beginning by a number of people. It's not uncommon to have some buildings with 20 or more owners."

Some housing projects completed since 1990 have included the Rex Hotel, renovated by architect Joey Ing for Wa Sang Foundation and completed in 1995; the Ohio Hotel (1909) renovated by developer Paul Chow and completed in 1991; the Bush

Hotel (1915) renovated by architects Kubota Kato & Tonkin Hoyne Lokan, Inc., for the Seattle Chinatown IDPDA; and the Eastern Hotel (1911) by architect David Dow, renovated by Kovalenko/Hale for Interim Community Development Association.

The district is home to 1,700 people, a high percentage of whom are seniors. And although a number of buildings have been renovated, a lot more remains to be done. There are still about six vacant buildings, and the same number, although occupied, need major rehabilitation. Several are by important local architects, such as John Graham Sr. and Andrew Willatsen.

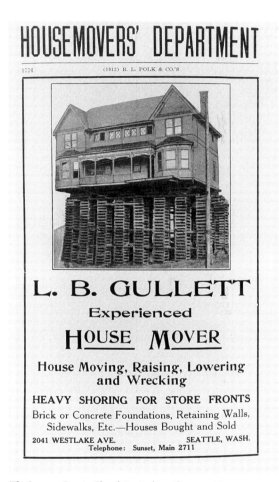

The Japanese Baptist Church is raised on pilings awaiting a new ground floor in this advertisement promoting a local moving company.

### Far East Building
640 S. Jackson Street

The renovation of the Far East Building in 1984 was an early and visible project ushering in new housing. The building is a phenomenon of the regrading of Seattle's hillsides—a hybrid that combines two-cen-

*Architect Kovalenko chose facade materials and colors to distinguish the apartments from ground-floor retail.*

tury-old frame buildings with a c. 1909 brick and post and beam retail building. The gabled structure served as the Japanese Baptist Church; its neighbor was a workingman's hotel or apartment building. It and the church building were joined to provide 40 rooms and 7 retail storefronts after the regrading. Known as the Leyte Hotel, the structure stood vacant for approximately 20 years and faced severe structural failure, dry rot, and general deterioration from lack of maintenance by the time of its refurbishment.

Developer Wai C. Eng and architects Robert Kovalenko and Robert Hale planned the rehabilitation. The building was gutted, and the second and third floors were redesigned to provide 14 one- and two-bedroom market rate apartments. Bedrooms with decks were added to the attic space of the gable roof. Colors were selected to relate to those used in the district, and iron balcony railings utilized Chinese lattice patterns to reflect the balconies facing onto streets that are a feature of older buildings in the area.

## NP Hotel
306 Sixth Avenue S.

Despite its name, the NP Hotel was not affiliated with the Northern Pacific Railroad. Designed by architect John Graham Sr., this masonry and heavy-timber building was Japanese operated from its beginning in 1914 until 1953. By that time, it no longer catered to the same well-heeled Asian guests who were picked up at the waterfront by the hotel limousine. Closed since the 1970s, it was sold to Interim Community Development Association, the agency responsible for the present renovation, completed in 1994.

Interim worked with Robert Kovalenko and Robert Hale. The project included historically accurate rehabilitation of both exterior and interior. Most

*Prior to renovation, the NP Hotel was a grime-covered brick building with rusting or missing sheet metal cornices and signage.*

*The cleaned building sports repaired and reconstructed sheet metal cornices, canopy, and signage.*

of the building's single rooms were reconfigured into studios, one-, and two-bedroom units, with top floor units providing skylit lofts. The second floor retains its historic configuration as single rooms with bathrooms down the hall. Wherever feasible, original doors and transoms were reused. In 1995, the project received the State Historic Preservation Officer's Award and an Award of Merit from the Washington Trust for Historic Preservation.

# Ballard Avenue Landmark District

Settled in the late 1880s, primarily by immigrants from Scandinavia, the town of Ballard grew up around its shingle mills and a lucrative fishing industry. Ballard Avenue was the first business district. Its banks, hotels, and shops served the town until that role was assumed by nearby Market Street. The Ballard Avenue Landmark District buildings provide a unique view of small-town development from the 1890s through the 1940s.

Although settlers had arrived in the Ballard area as early as the 1850s, it was in the 1880s that directed development began to occur. In 1887, Captain William Ballard formed the West Coast Improvement Company. He sought to develop 720 acres on the north shore of Salmon Bay known as Gilman Park. Upland lots were platted for commercial and residential use and larger waterfront parcels were designated for industrial uses. With its easy access to the waters of Salmon Bay and Puget Sound, the area quickly attracted settlers and laborers in the lumbering and fishing industries. Stimson Mill, the first of fifteen lumber and shingle mills, was operating there by 1888. The mills supplied most of the heavy timber for the rebuilding of Seattle after the Great Fire of 1889. Attracted by the area's similarity to their homelands, immigrants from Norway, Finland, Sweden, and Denmark arrived. They filled the need for fishermen and boatbuilders. In 1890, a rail link with Seat-

tle made the area more accessible for the exchange of goods and services. The town of Ballard was incorporated in 1890, with a population of 1200.

By 1895, Ballard was home to the world's largest shingle industry, employing some 570 men. By 1904, the town's 20 mills had reached a daily output of three million shingles and the fishing fleet was rapidly becoming a major industry, joined by iron foundries, shipyards, forges, pipe works, and boiler works. Rapid development was not achieved without cost. The shortage of water (Seattle refused to share its Cedar River supply), as well as sewage and school funding problems eventually led to the town's consent to annex to Seattle in 1907. At that time, Ballard was the seventh-largest city in Washington, with a population of 10,000. Ballard Avenue was the commercial center. Major banks, stores, and hotels shared the street with trolleys and the Interurban rail line.

The development of Ballard was furthered by the completion of the Hiram M. Chittenden Locks and the Lake Washington Ship Canal in 1916. The new waterway linked Puget Sound with a vast inland harbor composed of Salmon Bay, Lake Union, and Lake Washington. This expanded harbor increased Seattle's well earned reputation for superior navigational facilities.

While Ballard Avenue continued to serve as the principal business street, by 1930 development had inched toward its intersection with Market Street. Lower Ballard Avenue remained industrial, combined with some stores and hotels. From World War II on, light industrial uses occupied most of Ballard Avenue. The neglect of this area as Market Street became the official "Main Street" of the community effectively arrested its development from the 1940s until the late 1970s. The fact that hardly any

*Bolcom Mill in Ballard, 1910.*

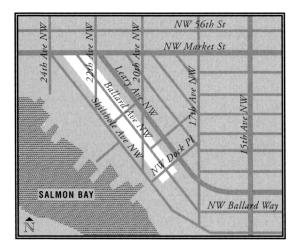

*Twentieth Avenue W. looking north, 1910.*

improvements or modernization occurred during that time left the street and its buildings in a historically intact state reflecting their early functions.

The restoration of the North Star Hotel was the pivotal project spurring revitalization of the street in the 1970s. As the first such project in the area, the hotel drew attention to the potential for similar work on Ballard Avenue. A local business association was formed, an inventory of buildings was completed by the city at their request, and in 1975, Ballard Avenue was considered for landmark designation. The ordinance creating a district specified a four-block area from Dock Street north to Market Street. It created a District Review Board consisting of property owners, businesses, an architect, and a historian who are responsible for reviewing proposed projects under an established set of guidelines.

The Ballard Avenue Landmark District possesses distinct characteristics typical of turn-of-the-century "Main Street" architecture. Most buildings were built between 1890 and 1930. A few wood frame buildings remain among the more prevalent unreinforced masonry buildings. Later buildings of reinforced concrete complete the streetscape. Buildings were commonly three stories or fewer, with storefronts at street level and apartments and hotels on the upper floors. The district's locally cut granite curbs

*Ballard City Hall, 1902.*

are virtually intact and, in some locations, still contain hitching rings. District guidelines address the scale of new developments, the types of materials to be used that are consistent with existing building facades, the encouragement of mixed uses, sensitive treatment of architectural features, the relationship of buildings to open public areas, landscaping, signage, and general maintenance.

Since its district status was achieved, a combination of public programs and private investment has upgraded the avenue. The formation of a Local Improvement District (LID), along with Community Development Block Grant, Economic Development Administration, and 1% for Art funds, has resulted in the repaving of key intersections in brick, resurfacing of sidewalks, street tree planting, and new light fixtures. Redevelopment of individual buildings, such as the Cors and Wegener and Flatiron Buildings, has been accomplished with a strong sense of community pride.

Compared to the flood of business activity and building projects recently occurring in Pioneer Square, Pike Place Market, and the International District, the pace is considerably slower along Ballard Avenue. Interest has been shown in several buildings, and a major new residential development is being proposed adjacent to Ballard Avenue that will front it as well. Consequently, it is subject to design review. There is also evidence of a strong arts community developing, and a number of new businesses and cafes have recently increased street life and encouraged residents and visitors to explore the streets and experience the area's small-town appeal.

## Columbia City Landmark District

Columbia City was one of several independent mill towns settled in the late 1880s. Located in the Rainier Valley seven miles southeast of downtown Seattle, its growth was primarily influenced by good rail access and its proximity to Lake Washington. The lumber mills are gone and the railroad tracks have been removed, but Columbia City still retains evidence of its heritage as a self-contained turn-of-the-century community.

Until 1890, Columbia City was a sparsely populated town established for the purpose of processing lumber and providing shingles and wood products for Seattle, particularly in the reconstruction of the city after the Great Fire of 1889. In 1891, the estab-

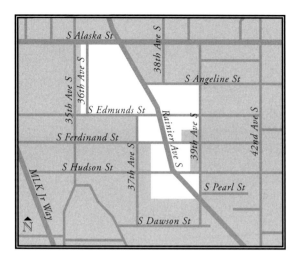

*Real estate promotion in Columbia City, 1908.*

*Columbia Hotel, Rainier Avenue S., at S. Ferdinand Street.*

*Columbia City early in the century. Rainier Avenue S. is the main arterial.*

*Carnegie Library, Columbia City.*

lishment of the Rainier Avenue Electric Railway (later the Seattle, Renton, and Southern Railway) along Rainier Avenue from Seattle to Columbia City provided the vital transportation link for getting these products to market and allowed finished goods to reach Columbia City in return. Incorporated in 1893, Columbia City developed a thriving business district along Rainier Avenue to provide a centralized market place and entertainment center for new resi-

dents of this and the surrounding communities of Atlantic City and Brighton. The arrival of the railway was a boon to the development of land owned by C. D. Hillman. Lots were sold quickly, and wood frame residences were built on the side streets off Rainier Avenue. In the ensuing years, prior to and after the town's annexation to Seattle in 1907, some notable public buildings were erected to serve the community: Columbia Elementary School, a Carnegie Library, Fifth Church of Christ Scientist, and a Baptist Church. Columbia Park, known as the "Village Green," was dedicated for public use.

As the forests around Columbia City disappeared, the business establishment made plans to drain nearby Wetmore Slough and make the town into a seaport as part of the Lake Washington Ship Canal development. However, the port never developed and the slough was filled by 1920. Residents and businesses continued to settle in Columbia City through the 1930s, although by the 1940s the district had stabilized and little new development occurred. A supermarket, bank, and series of storefronts were built in the late 1950s.

Renewed interest in Columbia City began in the mid-1970s with the formation of a number of community organizations that focused on finding ways to revitalize the neglected area. During the process of establishing a long range plan, the Columbia City District Association requested that the city survey the area and consider landmark designation. In 1978, the Landmarks Preservation Board established and Seattle City Council designated a historic district extending from S. Alaska Street to S. Hudson Street centering on either side of Rainier Avenue S. It includes more than 40 commercial and residential buildings, plus Columbia Park and a Carnegie branch of the Seattle Public Library. An Application Review Committee advisory to the Landmarks Preservation Board was established to review and comment on proposed projects within the district.

The Columbia City Landmark District represents typical turn-of-the-century American domestic, commercial, and civic architecture. Most buildings along Rainier Avenue were built prior to 1925 and are brick or wood faced. Generally, they are three stories or fewer with continuous storefronts on the street level and offices, meeting rooms, or housekeeping rooms above. This particular mix of commercial and residential uses give the street a strong pedestrian orientation.

The guidelines recognize these characteristics and seek to stimulate harmonious development with existing commercial, residential, and public buildings. Specific guidelines address the character, proportion, and scale of buildings; specific types of building materials consistent with the brick- and wood-clad structures; the special relationships among buildings and public areas; the nature of signage, lighting, street furniture and accessories. A Local Improvement District (LID), funded by public programs and private investment, utilized these guidelines in establishing design elements that resulted in inlaid brick sidewalks, benches, traffic improvements, underground wiring, street trees, and pedestrian signals—all of which encouraged pedestrian activity and new business along the arterial that had brought the railroad and prosperity to Columbia City nearly a century ago. Perhaps the greatest commitment of money and energy went toward conversion of the former Fifth Church of Christ Scientist into a community center.

While other neighborhood commercial centers, such as Belltown, Fremont, Green Lake, Madrona, and Pike/Pine, shed their shoddy character with the input of new owners and residents, Columbia City continued to lag behind. Long-time businesses shut down and marginal businesses came and went. The neighborhood is home to Caucasians, Asians, African Americans, and Latinos, and the low-income levels of Rainier Valley residents is complemented by the high-income families who live a few blocks east on the bluffs and shore of Lake Washington.

In recent years, change has been more rapid. One of the most visible signs of positive change was the 1997 conversion of Fifth Church of Christ Scientist into the Rainier Valley Cultural Center. The new facility, operated by SEED (South East Effective Development), a nonprofit community revitalization group, provides Columbia City with performance, educational, and community meeting facilities. It is the headquarters of the Rainier Valley Historical Society. The venerable building on the Village Green was repaired and painted, ramps and walkways were provided for barrier-free access, and the interior was refurbished.

Several Seattle-based chain restaurants and cafes have opened along the main street, joining new restaurants and a tea room. SEED has renovated eight apartments in the Columbia Hotel. With each project comes new signage, window and door replacement, and paint colors that go through design review in Columbia City and approval by the Seattle Landmarks Preservation Board. These small incremental changes are enlivening Rainier Avenue while they return buildings closer to their original appearance.

Columbia City is also a National Register District. In 1998, evaluation by consultants as part of a study of areas that would be impacted by the development of a rapid-transit route determined that the National Register District boundaries were eligible for expansion to include additional historic residential properties.

## HARVARD/BELMONT LANDMARK DISTRICT

The Harvard/Belmont Landmark District on the west slope of Capitol Hill developed as a prestigious neighborhood of gracious homes and large estates, some with spectacular views. In the early part of this century, many of Seattle's wealthy and influential families built fine residences and established important cultural institutions here. With continued main-

*Fisher Flour Mill monies built side-by-side English half-timbered homes for both father and son.*

*Famed New York architect Charles Platt designed a handsome Greek Revival home and formal gardens for R. D. Merrill.*

tenance and a fairly stable population, the buildings in the district retain the gentrified setting and privacy valued in single-family residential neighborhoods. Equally attractive early communities of this kind, such as those on First Hill and lower Queen Anne Hill, have been encroached upon by hospitals, apartment and condominium blocks, and commercial developments oriented to the automobile that have altered their historic integrity and harmonious appearance. By contrast, the Harvard/Belmont District is surprisingly well preserved. Its combination of urban and almost pastoral qualities—the tree-lined streets, several open vistas, and wood ravines to the northwest—along with some outstanding residential architecture, make for an area of exceptional character that is still very much an inner-city neighborhood

accessible to downtown, schools, churches, and a lively shopping district.

Much of what is known today as the Capitol Hill community was developed by realtor J. A. Moore, whose name is borne by a hotel and theater building at Second Avenue and Virginia Street that he had constructed in 1907 in anticipation of visitors to the 1909 Alaska-Yukon-Pacific Exposition. Moore opened the area north of Howell Street to homeowners in 1901, naming it after Capitol Hill in Denver, Colorado. The area had enormous advantages as a residential district: closeness to the Central Business District and spectacular views. As a result, many magnificent homes were built on this section of the hill, primarily from 1905 until 1930.

The East Park Addition that encompasses much of the Harvard/Belmont District differed from its neighboring plats. In addition to applying the traditional grid system of platting, its planners laid out a number of irregularly shaped streets that generally followed the natural land contours. Space was also set aside for parks, fountains, and other community facilities. Choice lots were soon the sites of Tudor, Federal, and Georgian styled mansions for the city's influential leaders of commerce and industry, as well as simpler family homes in various eclectic styles. These houses joined a number of more modest late-19th-century Victorian residences.

Architects of nationwide influence, such as Charles Platt, and others of regional significance, such as Carl Gould, Arthur Loveless, and Joseph Coté, were responsible for elegant residences and commercial buildings. By 1910, the district was

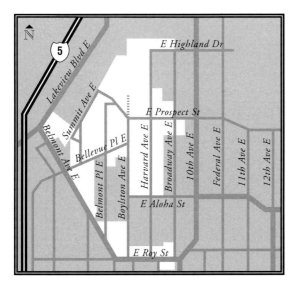

*Arthur Loveless designed this English styled apartment and retail building with a restful interior courtyard in 1931 on Broadway E. and E. Roy Street.*

home to Samuel Hill and H. C. Henry (railroads), C. H. Bacon, J. H. Bloedel, and R. D. Merrill (lumber), C. J. Smith (banking), O. W. Fisher (flour mills), and John Eddy (shipbuilding). Queen Marie of Romania, her children Prince Nicholas and Princess Ileana, Marshal Joffre of France, and Grand Duchess Marie of Russia were among the many distinguished foreign guests to the district.

Distinctive apartment complexes were built in the 1920s. The English Tudor, French Norman, and Mediterranean styled buildings were complementary to neighboring private homes in size and detailing. In particular, the apartments built by Fred Anhalt provided innovative plans, a high level of craftsmanship, underground parking facilities, and beautifully planted and carefully maintained courtyards.

The 1920s also brought the development of cultural institutions. The Cornish Institute, a modified Spanish styled building, was constructed with funds raised by prominent members of Seattle society. Begun by Nellie Cornish seven years earlier as a music school, it grew to include art, drama, and painting. The school became an appreciated leader in the cultural life of the city. The Woman's Century Club (now the Harvard Exit Theater), built nearby

*Oak Manor, 730 Belmont E., was one of Fred Anhalt's finest apartment homes.*

*Ibsen Nelsen's design for townhouses adjoining the R. D. Merrill residence used a traditional vocabulary of brick and cast stone, pitched roofs, and window bays.*

several years later, provided a three story brick building with two auditoriums that served as meeting and performance space for the female establishment in Seattle. In more recent years, some modern residences have been built on empty lots. Their discreet character and judicious use of screening have generally enabled them to blend into the area. Other undeveloped lots have become small parks, further enhancing the visual aesthetics of the neighborhood.

To recognize, preserve, and protect the significant assets of the Harvard/Belmont area, local residents initiated the process by which their neighborhood became a landmark district in 1980. The boundaries are specified as a 14-block irregularly shaped area encompassing over 80 residential and institutional buildings and four open spaces. Preservation in the district appropriately extends beyond the individual buildings to encompass the streets, landscaping, walled drives, retaining walls, signs, street furniture, lighting standards, and accessories, as well as visual focal points and views into and out of the district. Consequently, the district's Development and

Design Review Guidelines emphasize preservation of views through building heights, landscaping, and conformity to land contours; open spaces surrounding buildings; consistency of materials for buildings and retaining walls; compatibility of architectural styles; maintenance of landscaping for appearance and privacy; location of parking so that it is screened or at the rear of the building; and small and subdued signs compatible with the structure.

Designation provides protection against the loss of any buildings that have been evaluated as architecturally or historically significant or those that, though of lesser importance, are key features in forming a cohesive and consistent streetscape. It also provides protection for landscape, street trees, and street features which individually or collectively contribute to the overall character or image of the district. Landmark recognition gives the neighborhood residents more control over their district's stability. It ensures through regulation of demolition, alteration, and new construction that the elements that give the neighborhood its specific character will always be protected.

## Fort Lawton

Seattle and King County's enduring U.S. Army garrison post, Fort Lawton, resulted from active lobbying by local groups to establish a military reservation in order to boost the local economy. As part of this effort, Magnolia Bluff property owners donated over 700 acres of prime land to the U.S. government. Originally named Camp Lewis in 1895, the fort was developed over the next two decades following site plans prepared by the Olmsted Brothers.

The fort was carefully planned to relate to the topography, vegetation, and vistas of this spectacular hilltop site overlooking Puget Sound and the Olympic Peninsula. The core of 24 buildings at Fort Lawton were handsome examples of simplified Greek Revival architecture, constructed with Chuckanut sandstone foundations, lapped cedar siding, Philadelphia slate roofing, hardwood floors, and pressed metal ceilings. The turn-of-the-century officers' quarters, barracks, post exchange, and gymnasium were grouped around a distinctive oval parade ground. Trolley cars from downtown brought Seattle residents here to participate in parades, ceremonies, and concerts in the parklike environment.

The facilities served as a peacekeeping fort, a training post, and the second-largest point of embarkation for troops on the West Coast during World War II. Listed on the National Register, the fort was turned over to the City of Seattle in the early 1970s under an

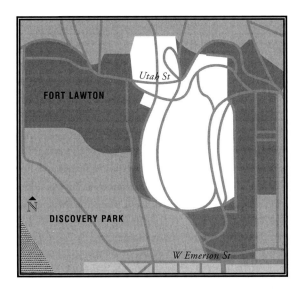

agreement that the buildings would be preserved. It became the object of controversial debates and public hearings over its future use as part of Discovery Park that pitted the Department of Parks and Recreation, whose interest was in creating a passive open space park and razing the historic buildings, against the city's Landmarks Preservation Board and historic preservation advocates, who insisted on preservation of all the buildings as significant to the history of the city, region, and nation. Ultimately, a compromise was reached in which the officers' row residences were retained, although seven supporting buildings were demolished. The remaining buildings were mothballed and are not to be used.

*Fort Lawton oval parade ground and officers' quarters, c. 1909.*

*The grandeur of the Neely mansion is evident even in decay.*

# Chapter Five

# THE HISTORIC PRESERVATION MOVEMENT IN KING COUNTY

The King County Landmarks and Heritage Program combines traditional and innovative historic preservation practices in the most comprehensive heritage program in Washington State. In 1998 alone, the Landmarks and Heritage Commission served as the landmarks board for 10 suburban cities, in addition to its work in unincorporated King County. In this same year it administered approximately $800,000 in grant funds and provided a wide range of technical assistance and training services to over 150 organizations and agencies throughout King County.

King County is a complex region in which to work. It encompasses 2,200 square miles and is home to 1.6 million residents. It is the tenth most populous county in the United States and, as of 1999, has 39 cities within its borders. Its geography is varied, stretching from the islands of Puget Sound to the crest of the Cascade Mountains. Within this region the challenges facing historic preservationists are multifaceted, ranging from preservation of archaeological sites to conservation of small-town historic commercial cores. The agricultural buildings and landscapes of the county are threatened by development. His-

toric vessels that sailed and steamed through the waters of Puget Sound and serviced its earliest communities are decaying. Much has been accomplished but a great deal remains to be done.

## DEVELOPING A LANDMARKS PROGRAM

King County's preservation program was the outgrowth of several important trends and factors, but two catalysts stand out as being particularly significant. The first of these is the National Historic Preservation Act of 1966, which spurred the development of federal, state, and municipal preservation programs; and the second is the United States Bicentennial of 1976, which mobilized people across the country to get involved in heritage activities. Together, these initiatives contributed to a new public history ethic in the region to preserve the wealth of historic and cultural resources in place—as part of the environment, as part of communities—and to organize and mobilize the citizenry to get the job done. These initiatives were the primary factors in the growth of heritage organizations in King County and were the determining factors in the establishment of King County's Office of Historic Preservation in 1978 (now the Landmarks and Heritage Program).

During its preparations for the Bicentennial, the King County Arts Commission established a Historical Committee, and Commissioners Dottie Harper, Elaine Griffin, and Pat Brunton were instrumental in getting the Landmarks and Heritage Program under way. King County funds were appropriated to make small grants for heritage programs. From these grants came a number of historic site guides, history books, and museum exhibits. In that same year, the Arts Commission hired Art Skolnik as Historical Coordinator to work with historical organizations and to plan for historic preservation in the county. Concurrently, representatives from a number of different heritage groups began to meet and discuss common interests. Working with the county's historical coordinator these activists organized a working group that incorporated as the Association of King County Historical Organizations (AKCHO) in July 1977. During this period the county launched the first phase of its Historic Resource Inventory project, which surveyed and documented 540 properties with the assistance of AKCHO members.

In 1976, the county amended its Comprehensive Plan to include provisions to guide land use decisions involving historic sites. In 1978, with assistance from the AKCHO, the county organized an Office of Historic Preservation and appointed Jake Thomas the first Historic Preservation Officer.

King County recognized early on that economic incentives play an important role in encouraging private investment in historic building preservation and restoration. Shortly after establishing the Office of Historic Preservation, the county authorized Federal Housing and Community Development Block Grant funds for historic building restoration. Providing incentives to property owners would become increasingly important after the county passed its Landmarks Ordinance. Although the authority to designate landmarks without property owner consent and to regulate changes to historic properties is a key feature of the ordinance, incentives would prove critical to the success of the program.

In 1979, AKCHO representatives once again worked with the county, this time to establish the Museum Assistance Program, unique in the region, which continues to administer grant funds and provide technical assistance to many area heritage groups. The Community History newsletter, issued

*Pacific Coal Company, Newcastle, 1909.*

*Tribal workers in the Snoqualmie hop fields, now Meadowbrook farm. Hops was one of the county's traditional early crops.*

since 1983 by the Landmarks and Heritage Program, was a direct outgrowth of the AKCHO minutes and newsletter. Charles Payton has served as the coordinator and support for these allied organizations and compiles and edits the newsletter.

As the county's historic preservation program gained momentum, AKCHO members turned their attention to developing a mechanism for protecting significant historic resources. In 1980, the King County Council adopted Ordinance 4828, which established the King County Landmarks Commission to designate resources of historic or architectural significance as landmarks and to regulate their restoration, alteration, and demolition. The commission's authority, however, extended only to unincorporated King County.

The ordinance outlined objective criteria against which all landmark nominations are to be reviewed for eligibility and also stipulated that the commission adopt design standards to guide its deliberations. One of the most important elements of the ordinance is the provision that designation does not require the consent of the property owner, reflecting the belief that landmarks are a community resource, protected and preserved for the benefit of all.

Criteria established by the county generally conform to those used by the National Register, the state, and the city of Seattle to determine landmark status (see criteria in appendices B and C). The key differences are the age factor—the city designates properties 25 years old or older, whereas the county recognizes properties 40 years old or older—and the provision in the county criteria for designation of archaeological sites that yield important prehistorical or historical information.

An object, improvement, site, or district may also be designated a Community Landmark if it is valuable for its prominence, age, siting, or scale but does not meet the more stringent criteria for designation as a King County Landmark. Community Landmarks are identifiable visual features of a neighborhood or area and contribute to the neighborhood's or area's distinctive quality or identity. In Seattle, this urban design character is one of the criteria in evaluations for landmark status and is given equal weight to other criteria.

By 1981, nine Landmarks Commission members had been appointed, the majority initially recruited from AKCHO member groups. The first chair of the commission was also AKCHO's first president, Phyllis Keller. The first King County landmarks were designated in 1982. In King County work focused on protecting individual buildings and ensembles of buildings. And unlike the dense urban environment of Seattle, King County preservationists faced the unique challenges of protecting predominantly rural resource types. The early designations tended to focus on properties of obvious aesthetic, architectural, or historical significance. The historic contributions of women and ethnic groups and the simple vernacular forms of architecture which predominate in unincorporated King County, particularly properties associated with the county's agricultural history, were often not addressed.

In an effort to better identify, evaluate, and protect heritage resources throughout the county, the Office of Historic Preservation undertook the preparation of King County's Heritage Resource Protection Plan in 1983. Modeled after a program developed by the U.S. Department of the Interior, its purpose was (1) to develop a process for efficient coordination among agencies that deal with issues affecting historic resources and (2) to establish a framework for rational, consistent decision making in the management of historic resources.

The approach used to develop the plan included dividing cultural resources into 14 groups based upon King County history: (1) Agricultural; (2) Commercial/Professional/Office; (3) Defense/Fortified/Military; (4) Educational/Intellectual; (5) Entertainment/Recreational/Cultural; (6) Funerary; (7) Governmental/Public; (8) Health Care; (9) Industrial/Engineering; (10) Landscape/Open Space; (11) Religious; (12) Residential/Domestic; (13) Social; and (14) Transportation. The study identified characteristics that define and give meaning to each resource group and established a context for evaluating King County vernacular buildings and rural landscape. Completed in 1985, the plan provided a comprehensive framework for future designation of properties in King County. Also in 1985, the county revised its Comprehensive Plan by adding a chapter called "Heritage Sites" that articulated eight historic preservation policies.

Since 1982, the county has designated nearly 70 individual landmarks and four historic districts. Nevertheless, this represents only a small percentage of those buildings and sites that are potentially eligible for recognition and protection. Furthermore, the rate of development in King County has far outpaced the abilities of the Office of Cultural Resources. By the end of 1979, King County had identified over 900 historic sites, ranging from log houses to dairy farms to steamboats. They stretch across the landscape from Skykomish to Vashon and Enumclaw to Shoreline. But rapid population growth and expansion of industry and commerce into rural landscapes has taken its toll. In less than 20 years, in some of the county planning areas, more than 40 percent of these important sites and properties have been lost.

## EXPANDING THE SCOPE

The focus of the King County program has evolved considerably over the last ten years under the leadership of Historic Preservation Officer Julie Koler. While individual landmarks are still designated, much more attention is paid to historic districts and downtown revitalization. Concerns about broad community appearance and landscape/townscape conservation issues are at the forefront. And archaeological site identification and protection is a top priority. Better understanding of the broad cultural attitudes which underlie preservation and recognition of the critical role which education plays in engaging the public in the business of preservation are important underpinnings of the program's growth.

Expansion of the program has also grown out of changing concepts of what is historic and what should be preserved. More and more people recognize that historic preservation is central to our quality of life and has more to do with the present and the future than with the past. Increasingly, historic preservation is rooted in the need for interconnectedness and continuity in our local communities. This awareness was stimulated and strengthened by the structure of the King County program and its close ties with the larger heritage community through the AKCHO network.

King County formally recognized the changing nature of historic preservation and its role in enhancing quality of life for county residents when it revised Ordinance 4898 in 1992. Among the revisions was changing the name of the Landmarks Commission to the Landmarks and Heritage Commission to reflect its role in providing funds and technical assistance for a broad range of heritage organizations and activities.

*Cedar Mountain, 1889, was one of many towns in the county that existed solely to house workers in the local timber industry.*

The ordinance was also revised to clarify and strengthen the commission's authority to protect landmark properties from demolition and moving. These revisions were inspired by the loss of two significant buildings in the Burton Historic District on Vashon Island. Burton is typical of the many small "crossroads" communities that once dotted the rural landscape of King County. As gathering places for residents of outlying areas, these communities historically consisted of a general store/post office, perhaps a cafe, church, livery stable or garage, a few residences, and often a warehouse, grain elevator or other storage or shipping facility for goods. Typically, these crossroads communities were clustered around transportation nodes such as the intersection of two or more roads or the intersection of a road with a river or railroad crossing.

In King County today only a handful of these communities remain sufficiently intact to convey their historic origins. Burton was one of them. The community's significance was documented in 1985 for inclusion in the county's Historic Resource Inventory as a historic district; however, it was not designated as a King County Landmark District until 1990. The landmark designation was triggered by property owners' requests to relocate two historic houses from the center of the district to outside the district boundaries. In their place the owners pro-

posed to construct an inn. The houses were modest, vernacular buildings which had not been significantly altered since their construction in the early years of this century. As individual buildings, neither one was eligible for landmark designation but their location at the center of the district provided a critical anchor for the area's overall visual integrity.

The Landmarks Commission acted quickly to designate the district and to work with the property owners to explore adaptive reuse of the houses for innkeeping purposes; however, a number of forces converged which eventually thwarted these efforts. The property owners, already well along in their planning for the inn, were not amenable to revising their plans to incorporate the historic buildings. Their sentiments were supported by some of the adjacent property owners, who were surprised by the swiftness with which the commission designated their buildings as part of the district and were wary of the implications of designation for their own properties.

Following a long and contentious review of the Certificate of Appropriateness application to move the buildings, the commission denied the request, in large part because the property owners failed to provide convincing evidence that removal of the buildings was necessary in order to establish an inn on the site. The property owners appealed the decision to

*The Boeing Airplane Company "red barn" at its original site near the Duwamish River, 1917.*

the King County Council, the council overturned the commission's denial of the application, and the buildings were subsequently removed from the district. Following the loss of these houses, the commission removed Burton from Historic District designation, citing irrevocable loss of historic fabric and overall visual integrity.

The Burton Historic District might still be intact today if not for an important missing piece in the commission's arsenal of regulatory tools. Although the ordinance gave the commission authority to deny relocation of landmark buildings, and even provided for evaluation of the economic impact on the property owner of approval or denial of such a request, it failed in two critical areas. It did not require that the owner prove a condition of unreasonable economic return, and in doing so take into consideration all available economic incentives and other possible alternatives to moving the buildings. Nor did it spell out the information that is required of the property owner to support a claim of unreasonable economic return. Had these provisions been in place at the time, the commission would have had a much stronger legal basis on which to deny the request.

King County's commitment to historic preservation and the heritage community was further articulated in the Comprehensive Plan, which was revised in 1992. The new "Cultural Resources" chapter of the plan significantly expands the original "Heritage Sites as Open Space" chapter to protect and enhance the King County cultural environment and regional cultural systems. It includes policies to preserve significant historic resources and to guide King County in creating and sustaining heritage facilities and services. The chapter focuses on the need for partnerships and collaboration with other jurisdictions, organizations, and individuals.

To ensure that all county residents have access to the tools of preservation, in 1994 the Landmarks and Heritage Program developed what is now called the Historic Preservation Interlocal Agreement Program. As of 1999, 10 cities in the county participate in this program and several more are interested in joining. In order to participate, a city must adopt a landmarks ordinance modeled after the county's and then enter into an interlocal agreement with the county for provision of designation and regulatory services. All municipally designated landmarks within the cities are eligible for participation in the county's incentive programs.

As the legislative and legal underpinnings for historic preservation have been strengthened by the county, so too has its commitment to funding historic preservation activities. Several factors have contributed to this. During the 1980s, federal cutbacks in funding for domestic programs decreased dollars available to the preservation community. In King County, the Community Block Grant moneys that had been used for restoration projects were eliminated for that purpose in 1989. This, combined with rapid loss of historic resources due to suburban growth, led to a special initiative by the Landmarks Commission in 1989 to establish stronger local support and to build an incentive package which would encourage people to restore and preserve their buildings.

## PROVIDING INCENTIVES

Today, King County has an array of incentive programs ranging from low-interest loans to special tax programs which encourage property owners, nonprofit organizations, and local governments to preserve their historic properties.

### Tax Programs

The controls imposed by landmark designation are balanced by a generous program of incentives. Two of these programs, Special Valuation and Current Use Taxation, rely on the local property tax system to create preservation incentives. The Special Valuation program, enacted by the state in 1985 and implemented in King County in 1989, subtracts eligible costs associated with the restoration of historic properties from the owner's property taxes for up to 10 years. The primary benefit of the program is that during the 10-year special valuation period, property taxes do not reflect the value of improvements made to the property. The Landmarks and Heritage Commission acts as the review board for projects in King County. The typical restoration project in the county is generally much smaller than the large commercial rehabilitation projects that have benefited from this program in the city of Seattle.

A program of broad appeal in King County has been the Current Use Taxation program. Under this program, property owners may be eligible for some tax relief if their land contains one or more cultural or natural resources, such as designated landmarks, archaeological sites, forest or farmland, recreation areas, watersheds, or scenic view corridors. Implemented in 1992, the program works to preserve open space on private property by establishing a "current use taxation" property tax assessment that is lower than the "highest and best use" assessment which would otherwise prevail. The reduction in taxable value ranges from 50 percent to 90 percent for the portion of the property in "current use." Landmarks qualify for a 50 percent reduction in the taxable value of the land portion of the assessment. City of Seattle landmarks and properties listed on the National Register of Historic Places are also eligible to participate in this program.

The Tax Reform Act of 1986 permits owners of buildings listed in the National Register of Historic Places to take a 20 percent income tax credit on the cost of rehabilitating these buildings for industrial, commercial, or rental residential purposes. Many King County landmarks are eligible for listing in the National Register. An owner investing in rehabilitation of a registered historic property will have credit against federal taxes. The Preservation Assistance Division of the National Park Service monitors this program.

### Low-Interest Loan Program

Revolving loan funds have long been an important preservation tool, largely because of the limited funds available to most preservation organizations and because these programs leverage a tremendous amount of private-sector support. A revolving loan fund is a pool of money that is loaned out, often at

significantly reduced interest rates, and as the loan is paid off, the funds return to the pool to be loaned out again. Most preservation loan funds are used to purchase endangered properties either directly or by means of loans to other parties.

King County launched its revolving fund in 1992 when the King County Council appropriated $500,000 for that purpose. Unlike many preservation loan funds, the King County program is used for restoration and rehabilitation purposes rather than to purchase endangered properties. The Landmarks and Heritage Program works cooperatively with two private banks to administer the program: residential loans are available through Washington Mutual Bank for owner-occupied landmark properties; and loans for commercial properties are available through Valley Community Bank in Duvall. Interest rates for both programs are generally three to four points below the current market rate.

Only property owners of King County landmarks and landmarks located in participating "interlocal" cities are eligible to apply at this time. However, it is a goal of the Landmarks and Heritage Commission to increase the principal available in the fund and to expand the pool of eligible properties to city of Seattle landmarks and those listed on the National Register of Historic Places. Use of the fund may also be expanded to include purchase of endangered properties.

### Grant Programs

King County has supported landmark restoration and rehabilitation projects through direct grants-in-aid for many years. Relatively small investments of public dollars have leveraged millions of private dollars and returned scores of deteriorated historic buildings to new life.

King County's Hotel Motel Tax revenue funded grant programs have become significant sources for the support of landmark restoration and historic preservation projects in Seattle and King County. Of particular note is the Cultural Facilities Grant Program, which supports landmark projects, although its uses are currently restricted to a particular category of properties. For the first two years of the program, funds could be used to purchase, restore, or rehabilitate any designated King County landmark. However, in 1992 state legislators restricted the pool of eligible applicants. Eligible properties now must be used predominantly as cultural facilities.

Through the Cultural Facilities Grant Program,

*Vital transportation links in early King County, such as the Kenaskat Station of the Northern Pacific Railroad, have disappeared.*

landmark properties throughout King County have been restored and adaptively reused, including the Enumclaw Masonic Hall, the Blue Heron Art Center/Vashon Odd Fellows Hall, the Dougherty House in Duvall, the Snoqualmie Railroad Depot, the Neely Mansion and its Japanese American bathhouse, the Issaquah Railroad Depot, and the Renton Fire Station.

King County has also invested millions of dollars in the restoration and adaptive reuse of a number of city of Seattle landmarks that are also cultural facilities, including the Good Shepherd Center, the *Virginia V,* the schooner *Wawona,* the Georgetown Steam Plant, the Dearborn House, the Rainier Valley Cultural Center, ACT Theater, the Seattle Asian Art Museum, the Log House Museum, and the Pike Place Market.

The Cultural Facilities Grant Program has supported the acquisition, construction, and rehabilitation of museums and other heritage facilities, as well as equipment, fixtures and other fixed assets, including storage fixtures, environmental controls and lighting systems.

Recognizing that the Cultural Facilities Grant Program is limited in breadth, the King County Council from time to time makes special grant moneys available to support landmark restoration, stabilization, and rehabilitation. In 1993, the council made a special appropriation of $100,000 to stabilize four endangered landmarks in rural communities. In 1995, $500,000 was awarded to 30 landmark projects. Grant awards ranged from $2,920 for facade stabilization of the Colvos Store on Vashon Island to $67,000 for restoration of the administration building at Camp Waskowitz, a Civilian Conservation Corps Camp located in North Bend.

From its inception, the Landmarks and Heritage Program has nurtured the belief that historic preservation is about more than saving buildings. It is also about saving the stories of the past and making that history come alive in museums and through education programs and interpretive materials. Since 1990, the Landmarks and Heritage Program has helped heritage groups of all types reach a broader audience and deepen understanding and appreciation of the past. The Special Projects Grant Program has helped fund a variety of heritage activities ranging from historic resource surveys in the cities to the publication of major new histories to the development of long-term exhibits. It is also a major funder of exhibits, videos, and tour guides that feature landmarks and historic sites in Seattle and King County. Finally, the Cultural Education Grant Program has brought heritage organizations and specialists into classrooms across the county to develop educational resources that allow students to better understand our past and to cultivate a sense of place. It is, perhaps, the region's greatest source of support for historic preservation education programs that interpret the built environment as well as archaeological heritage.

### Technical Assistance

Owners of designated King County landmarks and landmarks located in participating cities are eligible to receive a range of technical assistance services from the Landmarks and Heritage Program. Primary among these are consultations with members of the Design Review Committee, who review and approve all changes to designated features of significance of landmark properties. The committee comprises architects and preservation specialists, who share their technical and practical information. In addition, the office maintains information on both preservation issues and local history and publishes the monthly newsletter Community History, which keeps readers informed of issues and changes in the historic preservation field on a statewide level.

Although King County has made significant advances in the last 20 years in the preservation funding arena, much work remains to be done. Among the immediate goals are establishment of an annual dedicated revenue source for landmark restoration and archaeological site preservation, and significant expansion of the loan fund. The county is also actively exploring opportunities for expanding the private sector's role in supporting preservation.

## CHALLENGES

The greatest threat to the county's historic resources is the rapid pace of suburban development, which is destroying archaeological sites and historic agricultural communities and landscapes and sending property values skyrocketing. Continued efforts in integrating preservation into local land use planning, developing local political support for preservation, and finding new funding sources are critical if preservation is to succeed in this environment.

Many smaller communities around the county, such as Fall City and Preston, and cities such as Kirkland and Shoreline are reeling under the impact of new and proposed development. Destruction of significant historic buildings and incompatible infill development in these areas have disrupted the ambiance of once peaceful communities. Developers are constructing new buildings to the full extent permitted under land use laws. The county and its partner cities must look carefully at existing land use controls in older areas to ensure that zoning densities, height allowances, and floor area ratios do not encourage destruction of the historic environment. Building codes must also be systematically examined to reduce conflict with preservation goals. Much work remains to be done in the field of archaeology as well. Current laws are inadequate to protect these non-renewable resources.

One Eastside city that has responded to the challenges of growth is Kirkland. The Kirkland Historic Commission was founded in 1976 and changed its name in 1992 to the Kirkland Heritage Society to reflect the broader objectives of its members. Some of the organization's goals include: recording and collecting historical data for eventual establishment of an archive and museum; locating, designating, and protecting historic sites and structures; creating and promoting legislation for such preservation; and encouraging private-sector acquisition of endangered sites. In 1994, Bob Burke and Barbara Loomis took the lead in preparing a preservation report to educate and provide adequate resources to the city council, the growth management commission, planning commission, and city staff in updating the Land Use Policies Plan. The report included an overview of Kirkland history, identified historic resources based upon 1992 and 1994 surveys, and suggested a historic preservation plan element and implementation strategies.

Despite its small membership (about 100), the Society has increased public awareness of heritage in the community with programs in oral history, a curriculum for elementary schools, historic interpretive markers, and monthly lectures. Downtown property and business owners have recently organized a Main Street program modeled after the program initiated by the National Trust for Historic Preservation. Their most visible effort in 1999 was the successful move of the Greek Revival style Christian Science Church (1922)—the last historic church building in the city—from a site scheduled for condominium development to safe ground at the the corner of Central Way and Market Street.

The King County Landmarks and Heritage Commission's work to maintain its existing programs and to develop a regional preservation program requires maintaining and developing local political support for preservation. The successes to date are the result of working closely with AKCHO and with King County elected officials to ensure that preservation interests are on the table at all times. Now efforts must be directed to the suburban cities where elected officials and staff are facing preservation issues for the first time. Successful partnerships with the cities must be based on strong local leadership, which requires a clear understanding of the importance of preservation to their communities and a clear vision of what preservation can and cannot do for their communities.

A successful regional preservation program requires adequate staffing and broad volunteer assistance. It also requires that preservationists be represented on the many boards and commissions that do not have preservation as their primary function, such as planning commissions and urban design boards. It is only through the political process that preservationists will make preservation a priority of local government.

With broadened political support, King County's preservation community can continue to expand funding opportunities, but, in the competition for scarce public dollars, this will require even greater innovation and accountability. Accessibility to historic properties must be expanded to a broader public, and education must be at the forefront of this effort. Improved funding for preservation will require that new and stronger networks be established between local governments, preservationists, nonprofit organizations, and the private funding community.

Preservation of rural agricultural resources is one of the most challenging issues confronting King County. As historic farming practices die out, or as new farming technologies render buildings obsolete, the impetus to retain the historic buildings is gone. Nowhere is this more evident than in the dairy communities of the Snoqualmie Valley and the Enumclaw Plateau. Here, the once prominent dairy industry has all but disappeared, and the picturesque barns, outbuildings, and landscapes are being lost at a rapid rate.

**New Approaches**

Historic preservation has been democratized in King County. The Landmarks and Heritage Commission no longer focuses only on individual buildings or districts. Today the commission is concerned with preserving entire landscapes, roadways, and communities. But the tools for this work are inadequate. A new vocabulary is required.

To address this expanded view of what is worthy of being preserved, the commission is exploring several new approaches, one of which is the conservation district. Unlike traditional historic districts, conservation districts are not limited to areas of obvious architectural value or certifiable historic significance, nor are they constrained by specific age requirements. They are designed to protect areas whose character or value is found in the relationships among topography, vegetation, architecture, open space, and other appurtenant features, regardless of age. These areas have a distinct local identity worthy of preserving, but they may not have architecture as a primary focus. History as a criterion of significance may not be applicable. As communities and rural areas throughout King County are threatened by rapid growth, conservation districts may be an important new mechanism for protecting special qualities that would otherwise be lost.

The evolution of King County's Landmarks and Heritage Program must also include ongoing refinement of the existing regulatory framework. At this writing, the commission is reviewing a Certificate of Appropriateness for demolition of the Elliott Farm, the last intact example of an early-20th-century dairy farm in the Maple Valley area. The farm is sited on a knoll above the Cedar River just east of the city of Renton. Highly visible to travelers on the adjacent Maple Valley Highway, the farm is cherished by residents of the area and passersby alike.

The farm was purchased in 1995 by a developer who subsequently constructed housing units on land adjacent to the farm and who now wants to demolish the farm buildings to construct additional units. The owner's argument for demolition is that the buildings have deteriorated beyond the point of reasonable restoration. Not convinced, the commission hired its own experts to assess the situation and their findings support adaptive reuse of the buildings as a viable alternative to demolition. But the commission's hands are tied. Although it can deny the demolition request, the ordinance does not contain minimum maintenance or antineglect requirements,

*The various outbuildings and barns of Elliott Farm could be razed for housing.*

thereby leaving the owner free to effectively demolish the farm by not maintaining it.

In response to the Elliott Farm controversy, the Landmarks and Heritage Commission is considering revising the ordinance to include minimum maintenance or antineglect (or affirmative maintenance) requirements. Minimum maintenance provisions typically stipulate that buildings be maintained in accordance with local building and housing codes, while antineglect requirements often go a step further by specifying a list of defects that must be repaired on a continuing basis. While provisions such as these raise a number of questions, such as how inspections of landmarks for defects are to be made and who pays for the necessary repairs, they are a necessary part of the commission's tool kit if preservation is to succeed.

At the same time the commission refines its approach to preservation of the built environment, it is creating a comprehensive archaeological resource protection program. In 1999, working in partnership with the King County Transportation Division,

the commission will begin a countywide planning process to identify, document, and protect the rapidly disappearing archaeological resources located throughout the county.

As it explores new tools to get the job done, the King County Landmarks and Heritage Program is also exploring new strategies and organizational structures for funding historic preservation. A goal of the commission in the millennium is to educate those individuals and entities who control wealth about the value of historic preservation. Foundations, corporations, and local endowments have the potential to support preservation activities at a much higher level than is now the case. Other local governments must also be encouraged to step up to the funding plate. Perhaps the time has also come for the formation of a broad-based regional preservation agency that can actively leverage public dollars through private and corporate grants and provide a cohesive, articulate voice for historic preservation and heritage in this region.

*The Erick Gustave Sanders house in Auburn (1912) is an excellent example of Craftsman style residential design.*

# Chapter Six

# DESIGNATED LANDMARKS IN KING COUNTY

The King County Landmark and Heritage Commission designates landmarks in unincorporated King County and in cities where the commission serves as the city's Landmarks Commission through interlocal agreements. The following landmark descriptions are grouped geographically in the following order:

- Vashon Island
- Seattle and Mercer Island
- Northwestern King County
- Lake Sammamish Area
- Snoqualmie Valley
- Northeastern King County
- Southeastern King County
- Southwestern King County

Since, for the most part, King County landmarks encompass agricultural, rural, and vernacular town forms, few architects were involved in their construction. The listings below do not generally include architects' names, except in those cases where they are known. The builders were frequently the original owners and occupants of the property, assisted by community carpenters, stonemasons, and tradespeople. In the case of agricultural properties, the homes, barns, and outbuildings were built at various times; the text makes some effort to explain the evolution of these properties. Dating rural buildings is also less precise than it is for architect-designed buildings in cities, where municipal records, newspaper and periodical articles, and permits exist. Sometimes the date is only in the recollections of current or former owners to whom information has been passed on.

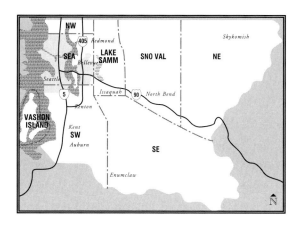

# Vashon Island

### Burton Masonic Hall
23927 Vashon Highway S.W., Vashon
*Howard C. Stone, 1894*

The Burton Masonic Hall, built in 1894, is a prominent structure in the Vashon community of Burton. Constructed by carpenter/builder Howard C. Stone, the building has a prominent front gable roof and a shed roof porch across the front that offers views of the harbor. The lodge was originally constructed by the Woodmen of the World. The Mark P. Waterman Lodge No. 177 of the Free and Accepted Masons acquired the building in 1925. The first floor has long housed commercial uses, with the upstairs reserved for lodge meetings and social gatherings.

### Colvos Store
123rd Avenue S.W. and Cove Road
*Trones & Parker, 1923*

The Colvos Store opened in 1923 and immediately became a focal point for the Scandinavian community of Colvos on the west side of Vashon Island. The small, one-story country store, with its false front or boomtown facade, had a board sidewalk to keep customers out of the mud and a gas pump—the only one on the west side of the island. Both these features remain today. Built by the partnership of John Trones and Gustaf Parker, the store had several different owners and is now a residence.

### Dockton General Store and Post Office
25908 Ninty-ninth Avenue S.W., Dockton
Maury Island
*Designer unknown, 1908, 1922*

Located in the community of Dockton on the southwestern part of Maury Island, the general store

and post office building is the only well-preserved example of an early-20th-century commercial building on Maury Island, Like country stores on neighboring Vashon Island, the Dockton General Store was built close to the water in order to serve customers who traveled by boat. As the automobile brought greater mobility to rural residents, many small stores lost business as their former customers traveled to more regional stores and markets. The owners of the Dockton store defied this trend by offering automobile repair service and selling gasoline, thus ensuring that their customers with cars still visited the Dockton store. The store was restored in the early 1990s for use as office space.

### Harrington-Beall Greenhouse Company Historic District
18515–18606 Beall Road S.W., Vashon
*Harrington; Beal families, c.1885–1989*

This 23-acre district, located several miles southeast of Vashon's business center, is significant for its association with the development and growth of the horticultural industry in King County from 1888 to 1989, and for its contribution to the cultivation and preservation of orchids and roses. The complex was a prominent Vashon Island commercial operation and employer since the establishment of the greenhouse company in 1888. In the plant's 101 years of business, the company became the largest grower of roses in the nation and an orchid establishment of international renown. The Vashon plant closed in the 1970s when operations were moved to Bogotá, Colombia. The district contains 59 greenhouses representing 100 years of the evolution of greenhouse technology and the power plant used to generate the heat for the greenhouses. The homes of Harrington and Beall family members, including the 1885 Hilen Harrington Log House, an 1892 Queen Anne style house built by the Harrington family, and the c. 1898 Beall Family Home, are also within the district.

### Marjesira Inn
25134 Vashon Highway S.W., Vashon
*Ira and Jessie Case, 1906*

Ira and Jessie Case began building the Marjesira Inn in 1906 on a steep bluff overlooking Quartermaster Harbor in the Vashon summer community of Magnolia Beach, just south of Burton. With the help of a local carpenter, they constructed the four-story shingle-clad building with extensive porches expanding the living space outside. The wharf in front of Marjesira was the point of entry for the Magnolia Beach community, and the inn provided lodging, the post office, and a small store where Jessie's fresh baked bread was a great attraction. Ira Case made many contributions to the development of Vashon Island. He published a series of island newspapers, served in the state legislature and worked for the development of the island's roads and ferry service.

### Thomas and Etta McNair House
22915 107th Avenue S.W., Burton
*Thomas McNair, c. 1890*

In 1884, Thomas and Etta McNair began living on and improving their land claim near Burton on Vashon Island. Every Monday, Thomas McNair commuted to Tacoma by rowboat. He would spend the week in the city while Etta worked on their farm. Like many other early settlers, the McNairs lived in a log house while starting out. In about 1890, Thomas built a substantial two-story wood-frame house that reflects the influence of the Queen Anne style in its asymmetrical elevations, ornate gable-end ornamentation, and elegant porch. Thomas also constructed a number of other Burton area structures, including the Quartermaster School.

### Mukai Agricultural Complex
18005–18017 107th Avenue S.W., Vashon
*Denichiro Mukai, 1910*

The Mukai family played an important role in pioneering technologies that changed the nature of the strawberry industry. Denichiro (B.D.) Mukai immigrated to San Francisco from Japan in 1885 and came to Seattle in 1906. After learning about Vashon strawberries while working at a wholesale business in Seattle, Mukai moved to Vashon Island with his wife

Sato Nakanishi in 1910 to start their own strawberry growing business. Sales of the perishable berries was limited to local markets. In 1924, the Mukais, joined in their work by son Masa, set up the first processing plant on the island. Using an innovative process to prepare the berries for freezing, the Mukais were then able to sell to distant wholesale markets at more competitive prices. Kuni Mukai, whom B.D. married following Sato's death, designed the garden that surrounds the family house. It combines traditional Japanese gardening principles and plants with Western suburban garden features such as lawns. Her tea parties, held when the cherry blossoms bloomed, were memorable social events in the community. The Mukai home, Japanese garden, and strawberry-packing plant stand today as reminders of the family's contributions to the industry. Restoration work is under way on the garden, and the packing plant has been adapted for reuse as artists' studios and shops.

### Captain Thomas Phillips House
11312 S.W. 232nd Street, Vashon
*Captain Thomas Phillips, 1925*

Captain Phillips played an important role in the history of Puget Sound's "Mosquito Fleet" of steamboats (so called because they swarmed the inland waters and were considered pests by larger oceangoing vessels). The fleet carried passengers, supplies, mail, and freight among settlements along the coastline from Olympia to Port Townsend in an era when boats provided the only reliable transportation between isolated waterfront communities. Phillips, who started his seafaring career at age 14, was captain of well-known steamers, including the George E. Starr, Vashon, Dove, and ferry Kitsap, and worked on a number of others. Most of his work related in some way to Vashon Island, his home. His modest one-story Craftsman house sits on a large flat lot west of Burton on Vashon Island.

### Schwartz-Bell House
20233 Eighty-first Avenue S.W., Vashon
*B. Schwartz, 1930*

The Schwartz family settled in the Vashon community of Ellisport in 1930 in hopes that the fresh air would be better for their children's health than the coal smog in the city. During the Great Depression, many Puget Sound area families built homes with designs that required few construction skills and made use of materials that could be obtained at little or no cost—and often from the home site itself. The Schwartz-Bell house, a one-story pole-frame log building sheathed in cedar log slabs, is an example of this type of Depression era home.

## Smith-Baldwin House
11408 Cedarhurst Road, Vashon
*Harlan Thomas, 1912*

The Smith-Baldwin house, located on a low bank waterfront lot on the northwest end of Vashon Island, was designed in 1912 by noted Seattle architect Harlan Thomas for Elizabeth N. Smith. The house, known as the "Rose Cottage," is built in the Georgian Revival style. Expansive multipaned windows, beveled siding, the truncated hip roof, the prominent oversize porch, and Thomas's use of patterned brick and roses on pergolas and trellises all combine to create a house sited and scaled to complement its natural setting. In 1908, Smith's daughter, Dr. Belle Baldwin, and her husband Albert, moved to the property. Among the first wave of women to be awarded medical degrees, Dr. Baldwin graduated from the University of Michigan in 1888. She maintained a practice in Seattle and lived at Rose Cottage until 1942. The house is now part of the Vashon Park District's 13.5-acre Fern Cove Preserve. A gambrel roofed carriage house has been restored for use as an interpretive center.

## Hilmar and Selma Steen House
10924 S.W. Cove Road, Vashon
*Designer unknown, 1911*

The Steen House, built in 1911 for Norwegian immigrant Hilmar Steen and his wife, Selma, is one of the outstanding examples of Craftsman style architecture in rural King County. The large two-story house features a spacious inset porch, as well as corner bay windows with beveled glass in the upper sash, a clinker brick foundation and river rock bases for the porch piers. The remarkably unaltered interior of the house is trimmed with dark-stained fir. An elaborate art glass window lights the stair hall. When the house was built, Hilmar and his brothers were operating a lumber mill with a log pond and a short spur logging road on the logged-off property. The mill supplied the house with electricity, making it one of the earliest electrified houses on the island.

## Vashon Hardware Store
17601 Ninty-ninth Avenue S.W., Vashon
*Designer unknown, 1890; 1935*

Located on a prominent corner at the main intersection in Vashon Center, the hardware store has served Vashon residents for many years. Constructed in 1890, the building housed the first store on the island. In 1935, owner George McCormick hired A. C. Harrington to build an addition for the store. At the same time, the storefront was updated with a new Streamlined Moderne look and stylized 1930s signage. The store interior retains its high ceilings, wood floors and original display counters and continues to provide island residents with hardware and garden supplies.

## Vashon Odd Fellows Hall/Blue Heron Art Center
19500 Ninty-ninth Avenue S.W., Vashon
*Francis Sherman, 1912*

Francis Sherman constructed the Odd Fellows Hall in 1912 with labor and materials donated by members of the Lodge. The building, which faces onto Vashon Highway, features a welcoming full-width front porch. In 1927, the lodge expanded the hall by adding single-story wings. The original, gable-roofed portion of the hall constitutes the center section of the present building. In conjunction with the women's chapter of the International Order of Odd Fellows (Rebekah Lodge No. 277), the Odd Fellows hosted holiday celebrations, social events, and theatrical performances. Vashon Allied Arts now operates the building as the busy Blue Heron Art Center.

# SEATTLE AND MERCER ISLAND

## County-City Building/King County Courthouse
516 Third Avenue, Seattle
*A. Warren Gould, 1914–17; Henry Bittman and J. L. McCauley, 1929–31*

The King County Courthouse is a dignified example of early-20th-century civic architecture in the Beaux Arts style. Prominent local architect A. Warren Gould guided the first phase of construction. Gould's original plan for a 23-story towered edifice was scaled down considerably to five stories. In 1931,

architects Henry Bittman and J. L. McCauley completed the second phase, which called for six additional stories and brought the courthouse to its current height. A major remodeling in the 1960s that was intended to capture the spirit of urban renewal and cosmetically disguise the building's true age destroyed many original features of the elegant marble-clad lobbies, windows, and entrance portals. Until 1962, the courthouse accommodated the offices of King County and Seattle government and was known as the County-City Building. Today the building houses offices of the County Executive, County Council, and county court system.

### Luther Burbank School Historic District
Luther Burbank Park, 2040 Eighty-fourth Avenue S.E., Mercer Island
*Designer unknown, 1904; Floyd Naramore, 1929*

In 1890, Major Newell started the Boys and Girls Aid Association, a school facility for indigent children in Seattle. The school moved to the northeast end of Mercer Island in 1904 and was operated by the Seattle School District as the Mercer Island Parental School. The school expanded to include an administration building, additional classrooms, dormitory, activity buildings, hospital, laundry, and farm with a large dairy barn. The school was converted into an all-boys facility in 1928 to provide a group residential environment and training in practical living skills. The school, renamed to honor botanist Luther Burbank, operated until 1956. School structures remaining on the site today include a 1929 brick dormitory designed by Floyd Naramore in the French Provincial style. They currently serve as the King County Parks Department Administra-

tion Building, a steam plant, and the foundation of a large dairy barn.

## NORTHWESTERN KING COUNTY

### William E. Boeing House
The Highlands, Shoreline
*Charles Bebb, 1914*

William Boeing is best known as founder of the Boeing Airplane Company, which he began as Pacific Aero Products in 1916. Before his pioneering work in aviation, Boeing pursued a successful career in the timber industry. In 1909, Boeing purchased several lots in The Highlands, a new exclusive residential community located on a wooded bluff overlooking Puget Sound north of Seattle. Boeing's expansive Mediterranean Revival residence was designed by Charles Bebb and completed in 1914. Boeing lived in the house until 1954, when he donated the estate to Children's Orthopedic Hospital and moved to his country estate near Fall City. It remains a private residence.

### Crawford Store
2411 N.W. 195th Place, Shoreline
*John Holloway, 1922*

The Crawford Store is the last intact retail building in the historic Richmond Beach business district. John Holloway, an early resident of Richmond Beach, built the two story wooden structure in 1922. The building, with a large covered front porch, faces the road which once led to the railroad depot. Langford and Eva Crawford were the first in a long line of people who operated the store and lived in the apartment above it.

**Charles and Elvera Thomsen Residence**
7332 N.E. Simonds Road, Kenmore
*Alban Shay, 1927*

Also known as Wildcliffe Farm, this elegant country home built in the French Provincial style sits on the south bank of the Sammamish River. The house was designed by Alban A. Shay and built for Charles and Elvera Thomsen. Thomsen, a successful businessman who founded the Centennial Mill Company and later acquired the Pacific Biscuit Company, retired in 1937 and turned his hobby of growing blueberries into a lucrative venture. After planting 27,000 blueberry bushes on the property's river bottomland, Thomsen built a cannery and shipped as many as forty tons of blueberries annually under the Wildcliffe Farm label. The interior of the house features a gracious hall, elaborate paneled woodwork, and ornate period tilework in the baths.

## LAKE SAMMAMISH AREA

### Archaeological Site 45-KI-22

In 1993, King County Landmarks and Heritage Commission designated the county's first landmark archaeological site. Located in the Bear Creek Planning Area, the site contains several middens—piles of discarded shells and fire-cracked rock which suggest the site was a source of freshwater mussels and other food resources. It is a rare example of a freshwater shell midden. To protect the valuable information that the site contains in its undisturbed state, owners are required to seek the approval of the Landmarks and Heritage Commission and the State Office of Archaeology and Historic Preservation before doing any excavation work in the vicinity.

### James W. and Anna Herr Clise Residence
Marymoor Park
6046 Lake Sammamish Parkway N.E., Redmond
*Max Umbrecht, 1907*

Willowmoor, the country estate of James and Anna Herr Clise, stands at the entrance to King County's Marymoor Park near Redmond. The original part of the Tudor Revival house was designed by Max Umbrecht and was built as a hunting lodge. It was later expanded for use as a permanent family residence. The estate eventually grew to 28 buildings on 350 acres. The boathouses, Dutch windmill, dovecote kennels, roaming peacocks, barns, and greenhouses became an area attraction. James Clise experimented with innovative agricultural practices for which he won regional and national awards and set records. Anna Clise played an active role in civic life, most notably as a founder of Children's Orthopedic Hospital and benefactor of the Seattle Conservatory. Today the house, windmill, staff library building, and one historic barn remain on the site. The Marymoor Museum of Eastside History is located in the house.

### Gunnar T. and Anna Olson House
20015 N.E. Fiftieth Street, Redmond
*Gunnar and Anna Olson, 1912*

This single-story farmhouse constructed in Happy Valley east of Redmond by Gunnar and Anna Olson is a fine example of a pattern book Craftsman bungalow. In addition to the house, the 3.5-acre property also includes a garage, cement milk house and barn. In the early 1900s, settlers, including the Olsons, cleared the heavily wooded valley and established small subsistence farms. From the old valley road, which runs parallel to SR 202 on the south side of the valley, one can still see small farmhouses with surrounding pastures and small barns as well as the historic Grange hall.

### Red Brick/James Mattson Road
196th Avenue N.E. between
Union Hill Road and Redmond–Fall City Road,
Redmond vicinity
*Designer unknown, 1865; 1913*

The Mattson Road contains the longest stretch of exposed historic red brick highway in King County. In 1901, the northern route between Seattle and Snoqualmie Pass, first developed as a road in 1865, was realigned to create what is now 196 Avenue N.E. in order to eliminate a long, difficult grade. The dirt and gravel road was often impassable, and with the growing popularity of automobile travel local resident James Mattson and his neighbors pressed the county to pave the road to provide an all-weather surface. In 1913, the road was paved with red bricks manufactured in Renton. In the late 1910s, the road became part of the Yellowstone Trail. This was a well-signed and promoted transcontinental route developed by automobile promoters to encourage and direct early automobile travelers in the age before state or federal highway networks were created. In 1989, the King County Department of Public Works restored the brick surface, which had deteriorated severely.

### Issaquah Sportsmen's Club
23600 S.E. Evans Street, Issaquah
*City of Issaquah, 1937*

Since its construction in 1937, the clubhouse has housed the Issaquah Sportsmen's Club, which was founded in 1920 as a recreation, social, and habitat conservation association. The city of Issaquah built the clubhouse through the support of the Works Progress Administration (WPA). To increase employment during the Great Depression, the WPA provided federal funds to hire workers for local projects. The city provided equipment and materials. The use of inexpensive locally available lumber in the clubhouse's construction is reflected in the vertical half-log construction and the use of peeled logs to support the eaves and porch roof and to trim window and door openings. A prominent gable roofed porch dominates the facade, and solid wooden shutters protect the windows when the building is not occupied.

## SNOQUALMIE VALLEY

### Dougherty Farmstead
N.E. Cherry Valley Road, Duvall
*Designer unknown, 1888*

Built in 1888 when Washington was still a territory, the Dougherty House has been at its present location since 1909. The house originally stood closer to the Snoqualmie River, in the town of Cherry Valley. In 1909, when the railroad line was extended through the Snoqualmie Valley, the town's structures were moved up the hill and the town of Cherry Valley was renamed Duvall. Outbuildings, including a bunkhouse (1909), garage (1919), milk cooler (1918), and milk shed (1940), were added to the farm as the

Tolt River, a hipped roof with dormers, and diamond pane windows.

Doughertys developed their dairy operation. The house, which retains many of its original interior and exterior features, is now owned by the city of Duvall and is undergoing restoration by the Duvall Historical Society, which will use it as an interpretive center.

### Commercial Hotel
31933 W. Rutherford Street, Carnation
*Designer unknown, 1913*

Small hotels played an important role in the economic and social development of King County's rural communities by providing temporary housing for newly arrived workers drawn by opportunities in booming logging and agriculture operations. Constructed in 1913, just after the town's incorporation and the arrival of the railroads, the two-story Commercial Hotel provided lodging and a community gathering place in its restaurant. The hotel's streetfront commercial space was demolished during the Depression, and the hotel rooms were converted to apartments.

### Entwistle House
32021 Entwistle Street, Carnation
*David Entwistle, 1912*

The David and Martha Entwistle House was built in 1912 during a time of tremendous growth in the community of Tolt, now known as Carnation. Arrival of the Great Northern Railroad in 1910 and the Chicago, Milwaukee & Puget Sound Railroad in 1911 triggered the rapid development of the area's agricultural and logging industries. David Entwistle was the son of early Tolt pioneers James and Sarah Entwistle. The Entwistle house, built in the Craftsman style, has a recessed full-width front porch supported on piers built of river rock from the nearby

### Odd Fellows/Eagles Lodge and Hall
3940 Tolt Avenue, Carnation
*Designer unknown, 1895*

The original Odd Fellows (later Eagles) Lodge, built by IOOF Lodge No. 148, has been an integral part of community life in Carnation since its construction in 1895. The two-story building has a prominent gambrel roof which terminates at the second-story floor line, giving the structure a distinct barnlike appearance unusual for a social hall of this type and era. The lower roof pitches have diamond-cut patterned shingles, which were restored to the building in 1995 along with a ventilated cupola and flagpole which had been destroyed by lightning in 1914. The building is currently owned by the Snoqualmie Tribe, which maintains one of its principal village sites nearby.

### Hjertoos Farm
315 N.E. Fortieth Street, Carnation vicinity
*Hjertoos family, 1906*

With its prominent dairy barn and large late Victorian farmhouse, the Hjertoos Farm was developed by a Norwegian family who were part of a wave of settlers arriving in the lower Snoqualmie Valley in the 1880s. When the Hjertoos family purchased the farm in 1901 from the Shaw family, it included a two-story log house, a large house for boarders, and a substantial orchard. In 1905, the growing family built a two-story, wood frame farmhouse to replace the earlier structures. The elaborate two-story front porch, which had fallen into disrepair, was carefully reconstructed in 1988 based on historic documentation. The barn, built in 1910 for dairying, now supports a tree farm and farmer's market. The core of the historic farm property remains in the Hjertoos family.

### Quaale Log House
10101 W. Snoqualmie Valley Road N.E., Carnation
*Rasmus Quaale, 1903–5*

The first Euro-American settlers in the Snoqualmie Valley typically built log houses for temporary shelter until they could build more elaborate frame houses. The Quaale Log House, located on a high bench above the Snoqualmie River floodplain, is one of the few unaltered log buildings remaining in the valley today. Norwegian immigrant Rasmus Quaale constructed this two-story home between 1903 and 1905. Built from timbers logged on the property, the building is noteworthy for its hewn log construction with dovetail cornering. Rasmus and his wife, Segrid, lived in the log house until 1913, when they moved to a larger, wood frame house nearby.

**Vincent Schoolhouse**
8010 W. Snoqualmie Valley Road N.E., Carnation
*Designer unknown, 1905*

The small farming community of Vincent is located on the western side of the Snoqualmie Valley south of Carnation. In 1905 residents built a schoolhouse so their children could attend school close to their homes. The school housed all grade levels and included students from many pioneer families in the Snoqualmie Valley. About 20 students at a time attended the school. In the early years, teachers were typically hired for two- or three-month terms in the fall and spring—seasons when parents could release the children from their farming duties to attend school, and milder weather eased travel for the students from outlying farms. The school closed in 1942, but the Vincent Community Club still uses the building for social and community events.

**Fall City Hop Shed**
Fall City Riverfront Park, Fall City
*Designer unknown, 1880*

This hop shed in the Fall City area is the last remnant of what was the largest agricultural enterprise in King County during the 1880s: growing and exporting hops. Hops, an essential ingredient in brewing beer, became a major industry in valleys east and south of Seattle after hop aphids destroyed crops in traditional European hop growing centers. George Davis Rutherford built the rectangular building, measuring about 20 feet square, on a 1,500-acre hop farm near the Snoqualmie River. The building was used to dry hops before shipping, with the large vented cupola creating a draw for the heat generated by stoves. Falling prices, the high cost of supplies, and infestation by hop aphids brought an end to large-scale hop farming in the Snoqualmie Valley around the turn of the century. The building was moved to its present location in 1904 and converted for use as a storage shed. The Fall City Hop Shed Foundation has been instrumental in preservation of the shed and supervised its restoration in 1996.

**Fall City Masonic Hall**
33700 S.E. Forty-third Street, Fall City
*Designer unknown, 1895*

The Masonic Hall, which stands in the heart of Fall City, has been a focus of community life for over 100 years. The large, two-story wood-frame lodge rises above the peaks and gables of the surrounding homes. Its full-width front porch welcomes members and visitors. The Lodge provided a place to meet and socialize for members, who lived and worked in the Snoqualmie Valley's isolated farms or lumber camps. In its early years, the Lodge was known as a "Moon Lodge." Meetings were held close to the full moon so members who came from outside Fall City could travel to evening meetings by moonlight. The hall, still owned by the Masons, serves as a meeting place for community organizations and a center of community activity.

## August Lovegren House

8612 310th Avenue S.E., Preston
*August Lovegren, 1904*

See chapter 8.

## Neighbors-Bennett House

4317 337th Place S.E., Fall City
*Emerson Neighbors, 1904*

Built in 1904 by Fall City resident Emerson Neighbors, the house is the best local expression of Queen Anne vernacular architecture in the community. The home's most notable features are the high front gable created by a steeply pitched roof and the ornamented full width front porch. The upper half of the gable is clad with fish scale shingles, with a center diamond-shaped window. The low-pitched hip roof is supported by turned wooden posts. Band-sawn brackets on each post connect to a frieze of circular ornaments. The home's extensive flower and vegetable gardens, lovingly maintained by the present owner, recall the self-sufficiency of rural households in earlier times.

## Prescott-Harshman House

33429 Redmond–Fall City Road, Fall City
*Designer unknown, 1904*

The Prescott-Harshman house was built in 1904 on a prominent corner lot facing the main road through Fall City. Its elegant porch, tall narrow windows, and hipped roof reflect the influence of the Queen Anne style. Julia and Newton Harshman, who purchased the house in 1912 from the Prescotts, played an important role in expanding telephone service in the rural community. By 1905 residents in Fall City and

Tolt (now Carnation) banded together to connect telephone lines from their stores to the Northern Pacific Depot and establish a fledgling company. The Harshmans provided the first $300 in financial backing for the project and later moved the Fall City Switchboard to their newly purchased home in 1912. Julia operated the switchboard until her death. Her daughter then ran the board until 1951, when a dial system eliminated the need for a switchboard operation. The house, which had fallen into disrepair, was restored in the 1980s for use as office space.

*Railroad Avenue, Snoqualmie, 1897.*

## Snoqualmie Historic Commercial District

Railroad Avenue, Snoqualmie
*Designers unknown, 1889–1941*

Platted in 1889 in anticipation of the arrival of the Seattle, Lakeshore & Eastern Railroad in the upper Snoqualmie Valley, the town of Snoqualmie served as a commercial center for the northern portion of the upper Snoqualmie Valley. Major valley industries included the Snoqualmie Falls Electric Company power plant at Snoqualmie Falls and the mill operated by the Snoqualmie Lumber Company. Commercial development has historically centered along Railroad Avenue. Buildings standing in the district today trace the evolution of commercial building styles from wooden structures with boomtown facades to the stucco and brick cladding used in the 1920s. The 1890 Queen Anne style Railroad Depot, with a broad porch inset under the curve of its sweeping roof, has been individually designated as a Town of Snoqualmie Landmark, as has the two-story wooden 1902 I.O.O.F Hall which faces the depot.

## Northern Pacific Railway Steam Rotary Snowplow No. 10
Railroad Right-of-Way, Snoqualmie
*Designer unknown, 1907*

The heavy snowfalls in the Cascade range posed a challenge to providing year-round train service through the mountains. Rotary snowplows, invented in the late 19th century, provided rail crews with an effective tool for keeping lines open in winter. The Northern Pacific Railway Steam Rotary Snowplow No. 10 is a rare surviving example of a steam-driven rotary snowplow. Built in 1907 by the American Locomotive Company in Schenectady, New York, this plow cleared the snow on Stampede Pass between 1907 and 1964. The car's original wooden body was replaced with steel in the 1950s, but the cutting blades and rotating scoops that threw the snow clear of the tracks are original.

## Snoqualmie Odd Fellows Hall
38601 S.E. King Street, Snoqualmie
*Designer unknown, 1902*

The Snoqualmie Odd Fellows Hall was constructed in 1902 for IOOF Lodge No. 1196 in a commercial vernacular style. The rectangular two-story building is prominently sited next to the Snoqualmie Railroad Depot. The club organized local social activities and provided mutual aid to members. In addition to Odd Fellows gatherings, over the years the hall has been used for numerous community activities such as a benefit dances and card parties and has served as a polling place, unemployment office during the Great Depression, and a timber workers union hall.

## Snoqualmie Depot
38625 S.E. King Street, Snoqualmie
*Designer unknown, 1890*

The 1890 Snoqualmie Depot was constructed in the Queen Anne style from a design selected by the managers of the Seattle, Lake Shore & Eastern Railroad. Planned to join Seattle and eastern Washington via Snoqualmie Pass, the railroad never reached farther east than the North Bend area. Nonetheless, the railroad played an important role in the development of the Sammamish and Snoqualmie Valleys' agricultural and lumber industries. The depot is one of the most prominent structures in Snoqualmie's historic commercial core, and the oldest continuously oper-

ating train station in Washington State. The depot currently houses the Northwest Railway Museum, which maintains the region's largest collection of historic rolling stock and operates excursion trains between Snoqualmie and North Bend.

## Reinig Road Sycamore Corridor
Between 396th Drive S.E. and S.E. Seventy-ninth Street, Snoqualmie
*Designer unknown, 1929*

The sycamore trees growing on both sides of Reinig Road are among the last vestiges of the former company town of Snoqualmie Falls, located just east of the town of Snoqualmie on the Middle Fork of the Snoqualmie River. In 1916, the Snoqualmie Falls Lumber Company began developing housing and community facilities for the families of its growing workforce. Snoqualmie Falls had a community hall, barbershop, post office, hospital, and school. In 1929, the company planted a row of sycamore trees in front of the homes that flanked Reinig Road as part of a community beautification program. As business at the mill declined, the Weyerhaeuser Company decided to close the town. In 1958, 90 houses were moved from the town to new sites, and most of the other structures were demolished.

## Norman Bridge
Middle Fork Snoqualmie River
*King County Engineering Department, 1950*

The 295-foot-long Norman Bridge, spanning the Middle Fork of the Snoqualmie River near North Bend, is the only remaining example of a timber truss vehicular bridge in King County. The last of its type constructed by the King County Engineering Department, the 1950 bridge replicated the 1924 span that it replaced. By the time the Norman Bridge was built, concrete and steel trusses were commonly

used for bridge construction. However, the availability of relatively inexpensive large timbers in Washington kept timber bridges in use in the region.

### North Bend Masonic Hall
119 North Bend Way, North Bend
*Designer unknown, 1912*

The North Bend Masonic Hall is located in the heart of downtown North Bend. The two-story concrete building was designed with ground-floor commercial space and meeting space above. The Masons have hosted many community events at the hall over the years, including popular Saturday night dances. Like many other North Bend commercial buildings, the hall was given an Alpine look in the 1970s. In 1998, the Masons decided to remove the Alpine treatment and restore the building to its 1920s appearance.

### Camp North Bend
45509 S.E. 150th Street, North Bend
*Designer unknown, 1935*

Camp North Bend, located east of the town of North Bend at the base of Snoqualmie Pass, was constructed by and for the Civilian Conservation Corps (CCC) in 1935. Introduced by President Franklin D. Roosevelt in 1933, the CCC provided jobs for over 1.5 million unemployed men on conservation projects such as forestry stabilization, park improvements, and soil erosion control. Camp North Bend reflects the uniform design and building arrangement of CCC camp construction. Although over 4,000 CCC camps were built nationwide, Camp North Bend is one of the few of these "temporary" camps that remain intact. Remaining buildings at

the camp include a dining hall, barracks, office, Forest Service quarters, and an education building. Now known as Camp Waskowitz, the camp has housed the Highline School District's environmental education program since the 1950s.

## NORTHEASTERN KING COUNTY

### Skykomish Historic Commercial District
Railroad Avenue vicinity, Skykomish
*Designers unknown, 1893–1936*

The four-block-long Skykomish Historic Commercial District encompasses the heart of the historic railroading community of Skykomish. The 11 contributing buildings within the district document four periods of town history. Maloney's General Store (1893), the Great Northern Railroad Depot (1894), and Patrick McEvoy House (1897) come from the early days of the town, which was founded in 1893 with the railroad's arrival over Stevens Pass. The distinctive Skykomish Hotel (1904), Maloney's Warehouse (1906), and the Whistling Post Tavern (1905) were all built after a fire destroyed most of the commercial district in 1904. The Cascadia Hotel (1922), the Teacherage (c. 1914), Town Hall (1926), and the school's Manual Training building (1923) were built during a period when tunnel construction on the railroad spurred development. The landmark Skykomish School (1936), built by the Depression era federal Works Progress Administration, anchors the district's western end.

### Great Northern Depot
S.E. corner of Railroad Avenue and Fourth Street, Skykomish
*Designer unknown, c. 1890*

Constructed from standard Great Northern plans for rural train stations in the early 1890s, the Skykomish

Depot is one of only a handful of wood-frame Great Northern depots still standing in Washington State. When built, the rectangular one-story building with a gabled, wood shingle roof contained a passenger waiting room and office and likely a small freight room. The rail yard in Skykomish was expanded and improved in the early 1920s. At that time, the depot was moved across the yard and expanded by the addition of a large freight room. The depot is the only historic railroad building left in what was once a bustling rail yard at the western portal to the crossing of the Cascade Mountains. Passenger service ceased in the 1950s, and the depot is now used to support railroad maintenance work in the Skykomish area.

## Maloney's General Store
104 Railroad Avenue, Skykomish
*John Maloney, 1893*

John Maloney worked on the Great Northern Railroad's survey crew that established the initial route for the Stevens Pass rail line. Once the route was planned, Maloney purchased the land that would become the town of Skykomish. He built Maloney's General Store as a store and post office in 1893, the same year the rail line was completed. The boomtown facade of the store building faced the railroad tracks, which provided the only access to the town, and featured a high covered front porch and wooden sidewalk elevated above the mud of Railroad Avenue. John Maloney served as postmaster, mayor, and school board member, and had business interests in the Skykomish Lumber Company, Maloney Shingle Company, and Baring Granite Works. Over the years, the store building was expanded and remodeled but remained in use as a general store until the early 1990s. Between 1992 and 1996, the building

was carefully restored and the boomtown facade and front porch, which had been removed in the 1950s, were reconstructed based on historic photographs.

## Skykomish School and Teacherage
100 Railroad Avenue, Skykomish
*William Mallis, 1936; Designer unknown, 1914*

The Skykomish School is one of seven schools in Washington built under the auspices of the federal Works Progress Administration (WPA) during the Great Depression of the 1930s. As required by the WPA, the community provided building materials and the WPA provided funds to hire construction laborers. The school, designed by Seattle architect William Mallis and constructed by William Peterson, is a three-story flat-roof concrete structure with Streamlined Moderne detailing and Art Deco ornament. The original floor plan and many of the interior features, including woodwork and light fixtures, are intact. The Teacherage was built about 1914 to house the school's single female teachers. The rectangular building is of Craftsman design and detailing with a cross gable roof projecting on the east and west elevations. Both the school and the Teacherage (now the superintendent's residence) remain in use today.

## Skykomish Masonic Hall
108 Old Cascade Highway, Skykomish
*Designer unknown, 1924*

The Masonic Hall in Skykomish is a two and one-half story wood frame building, built facing the historic highway route through town. Construction of the Masonic Hall was a community effort. John Maloney Sr., the town founder and successful local businessman, donated the site. All funds for the project were raised among the local membership, and in a town of skilled craftsmen and laborers, all of the talent required to design, erect, and finish the two-story hall could be found close at hand. The Masons continue to meet in the building.

## SOUTHEASTERN KING COUNTY

### Elliott Farm
14207 Maple Valley Highway, Renton vicinity
*R. J. Elliott, 1909–11*

The prominent farmhouse and barns at the Elliott Farm, located in the Cedar River valley just east of Renton, reflect the development of small-scale dairy farming in the valley in the early 1900s. Homesteaders settled the Cedar River valley in the 1870s, cleared land for crops and pastures, and established small subsistence farms. As transportation and refrigeration technologies improved, dairy farming became the main agricultural activity in the area. The milk barn on the farm, built by R. J. Elliott between 1909 and 1910 along with four ancillary farm buildings, reflected Elliott's interest in the latest dairying practices. In 1911, he designed and built the 2.5-story, nine-room Craftsman style home on the farm. Today, neglect and encroaching urban development threaten the Elliott Farm.

### Lagesson Homestead
20201 S.E. 216th Street, Maple Valley
*Nils Peter Lagesson, 1890*

Nils Peter Lagesson, a Swedish immigrant, filed his homestead claim in Maple Valley in 1885 and five years later built a two-room, hewn log house and two barns on 29 acres of orchard, pasture, and cultivated land. He married Laura Nelson after a trip home to Sweden. In anticipation of Laura's parents moving to the farm, Lagesson built a second house in 1897. This house later became a bunkhouse for his sons.

The large barn features posts and beams hand-hewn by Lagesson. In addition to the houses and barn, the property includes a pumphouse, garage with gas pump, pig house, blacksmith shop, smokehouse, and wheathouse. These outbuildings illustrate the self-sufficient nature of this pioneer family.

### Lake Wilderness Lodge
22500 S.E. 248th Street, Maple Valley
*Young & Richardson, 1950*

Lake Wilderness Lodge, designed by the Seattle architectural firm Young & Richardson, opened in 1950. The building was developed by the Gaffney family, which had operated Gaffney's Lake Wilderness resort on the north end of Lake Wilderness in Maple Valley since the 1920s. The lodge provided overnight accommodations, a restaurant, and meeting spaces. The innovative design, which integrated the building into its sloping site while offering views of the lake and Mount Rainier beyond, received a prestigious American Institute of Architects National Honor Award in 1952. The resort became part of the King County Park system in 1964. Today the lodge is used as a recreation center.

### Maple Valley School
23015 S.E. 216th Way, Maple Valley
*Designer unknown, 1920*

In 1920, the Maple Valley School District opened its new brick two-story school, which was prominently located on a knoll above Maple Valley's commercial center. The school, with its fire-resistant brick construction, spacious classrooms, central heating, auditorium, and ample windows to bring in daylight, was a source of great community pride. As small rural districts consolidated into the Maple Valley School District, the school was built to accommodate students who had previously attended small community schools. Owned by the Tahoma School District, the school presently houses the Greater Maple Valley Historical Society.

### Olof and Mathilda Olson House and Barn
24206 S.E. 216th Street, Maple Valley
*Olof Olson, 1907; 1909*

The Olof and Mathilda Olson House sits on a plateau above the Cedar River about a mile east of Maple Val-

ley. The Olsons purchased their 80-acre parcel in 1898. Olof worked as a contractor for the Northern Pacific and Great Northern Railroads and specialized in tunnel construction. Mathilda managed operations of the family farm. Olson's work certainly influenced the couple's decision to build a poured-concrete house rather than a wood-frame house. The large two-story square house with a hip roof and broad eaves suggests the influence of the Prairie style. The barn, built in 1909, is noteworthy as one of the few historic barns in King County with barrel-vault construction. In the early 1990s, the pastures surrounding the house were developed as a links-style golf course, and the house was renovated for use as the course clubhouse and reception facility.

**Pacific Coast Coal Company Administration Building**
18825 S.E. Maple Valley Highway
*Designer unknown, 1927*

The Pacific Coast Coal Company administration building is the only intact structure associated with the once-active coal industry in the Cedar River valley between Renton and Maple Valley. In the early 1930s, the Pacific Coast Coal Company's New Black Diamond Mine was the top coal-producing facility in the state, employing nearly 300 people. The slope mine operation was located on the hillside behind the structure. The administration and shop building was constructed in 1927 as a combination office and machine shop for the coal mine. The long rectangular two-story post and beam industrial building features large windows to admit light into the workspaces, corrugated galvanized iron siding, and flat roof. The New Black Diamond Mine was the last large-scale slope mining facility built in King Coun-

ty. The mine's large washery, tramway, trestle, and railroad were dismantled when the mine closed in 1941.

**Miners' Cabin**
24311 Morgan Street, Black Diamond
*Designer unknown, 1910*

The mine workers in Black Diamond's coal mines lived, for the most part, in simple wood frame houses. Once prevalent, few of these houses remain today, and those that survive have been expanded or altered by changes to siding or other materials. While many mine families lived in houses on company-owned land, some miners constructed their own homes on private land near the company town. The small one-story wood-frame Miners' Cabin, located on land owned by Welsh miner Timothy Morgan, is said to have been built by two Italian miners. They lived in the house until the 1920s, when Morganville, a neighborhood just outside of the company owned town site, became the center of union activity during bitter labor disputes.

## SOUTHWESTERN KING COUNTY

**Carnegie Public Library**
306 Auburn Avenue N.E., Auburn
*David Myers, 1914*

The development of a public library in Auburn was part of a national movement spurred by the philanthropy of iron and steel magnate Andrew Carnegie. In 1911, the Auburn Library Board received $9,000 from the Carnegie Foundation to construct a building on property donated by the Ballard family. The Carnegie Public Library was designed by Seattle architect David Myers and built in 1914. The two-

story brick building reflects the restrained Neoclassical design and simple rectangular massing of Carnegie libraries built in the early 1900s throughout the country. The building currently houses a dance studio.

### Olson-Johnson Farm
28728 Green River Road S., Auburn
*Alfred Olson, c. 1874*

Located on a fertile shelf of land adjacent to the Green River known as Olson Canyon, the Olson-Johnson Farm was initially developed by Swedish immigrants Alfred and Mary Olson and later farmed by Mary's second husband, Eric Magnus Johnson. Because so many of the original structures remain in place, venturing into the canyon is like walking back in time. The farm ensemble includes a 1.5-story frame farmhouse built in 1902, a gable roof barn built in 1897, a weaving shed, workshop, smokehouse, and orchard. The city of Auburn acquired the 60-acre site in 1994 through funding from the King County Open Space Program.

### Neely Mansion
12303 S.E. Auburn–Black Diamond Road, Auburn
*Aaron and Sarah Neely, 1894*

Aaron and Sarah Neely built this large Classical Revival farmhouse on acreage that they cultivated in the Green River valley east of Auburn. The house, a prominent and impressive structure for a rural farming community, is one of the most ornate historic homes in unincorporated King County. Its simple and symmetrical form is embellished with decorative panels, sills, and scrollwork, as well as a frieze of garlands and ornate brackets below the eaves. A two-story portico, balconies, and an ornamented

pediment distinguish the structure. The home was an important social center in the valley, as the Neely's hosted gatherings for friends and neighbors with music and dancing. The nonprofit Neely Mansion Association has restored the house and operates it as a house museum.

### Hori Furo at the Neely Mansion
12303 S.E. Auburn–Black Diamond Road, Auburn
*Shigiechi Hori, 1930*

Built in 1930 by Shigiechi Hori, this building is an important reminder of daily life and traditional customs in this once predominantly Japanese agricultural community. The small single-story bathhouse was constructed adjacent to the Neely Mansion's rear porch. Shortly after 1900, the Neelys left their farmhouse and rented the property to a succession of tenants. For almost 65 years, Japanese and Filipino families managed the farm. Because laws prohibited Asians from owning property, Asians typically established long-term tenancy on farms. The Hori family leased the Neely property from 1930 to 1936.

### Reynolds Farm and Indian Agency
16816 S. 277th Street, Auburn
*Designer unknown, c. 1880*

The Reynolds Farm and Indian Agency is named for Charles A. Reynolds, who worked for the Office of Indian Affairs as the "farmer-in-charge" of the Muckleshoot Reservation from 1898 to 1928. As farmer-in-charge, Reynolds had administrative responsibility for activities such as court cases, road building, school attendance, and land allotments. The site contains an 1880s log house, likely built by an earlier resident of the property. The tall, narrow house, which features hewn logs and a shingle roof, is a rare example of the type of expedient construction favored by early Euro-American settlers. In 1914, Reynolds supervised the construction of the large farmhouse which still stands next to the log house.

**Erick Gustave Sanders Mansion**
5516 S. 277th Street, Auburn
*Erick Sanders, 1912*

Swedish immigrant Erick Sanders, a successful businessman and lumberman in Seattle and on Bainbridge Island, built this elaborate Craftsman house as a retirement home for himself and his wife, Sara. Sanders and several partners purchased 660 acres of farmland in the Green River valley west of Kent as an investment. On this land, they built the Standard Dairy, the Standard Mill, and Sanders's country home. Constructed with lumber from the mill, the house features stained glass salvaged from the Alaska-Yukon-Pacific Exposition and bricks left over from the construction of the West Valley Highway.

**Town of Selleck**
Kangley vicinity
*Pacific Lumber Company, 1908–39*

In 1908, the Pacific States Lumber Company built the town of Selleck around a new lumber mill located northeast of Black Diamond. The mill closed during the Great Depression and has since been torn down, but Selleck contains the largest concentration of original milltown structures in King County. The remaining buildings include half of the original single-story company houses, the more substantial Craftsman house of the mill superintendent, the community hall, and a two-story school. Among the

500 residents during the town's heyday in the 1920s were Japanese mill workers and their families who lived in an area called the Japanese Camp. While few historic structures remain in the Japanese Camp, a recent archaeological investigation has provided more information about this important part of the Selleck community.

## THEMATIC NOMINATIONS

### King County Bridges
Mount Si, Meadowbrook, Tolt, Stossel, Raging River, Fourteenth Avenue S.
*Various designers, 1904–51*

In 1997, following a study of all historic bridges owned by King County, the Landmarks and Heritage Commission selected six as significant representatives of the evolution of bridge engineering in King County for designation as King County Landmarks. Five bridges are in the Snoqualmie Valley: the Mount Si Bridge, spanning the Middle Fork of the Snoqualmie at the base of Mount Si (1904/1955); the Meadowbrook Bridge (1921) across the Snoqualmie in the community of Meadowbrook; the Tolt Bridge (1922), which spans the Snoqualmie at Tolt Hill Road south of Carnation; the Stossel Bridge (1951) over the Snoqualmie near Carnation Farms north of Carnation; and the Raging River Bridge (1915), which carried the Sunset Highway across the Raging River below Preston. The sixth bridge, the Fourteenth Avenue South Bridge (1931), spans the Duwamish River between the city of Tukwila and the South Park Community in unincorporated King County.

### Works Progress Administration Fieldhouses
Des Moines, Enumclaw, North Bend, Preston, White Center
*Designers unknown, 1938–40*

During the Great Depression, the federal Works Progress Administration made construction funds for public buildings available to local communities under an agreement where the communities would provide construction materials and the government would pay for the labor. These five landmark fieldhouses are among the buildings in King County created through this program. Designed in the Rustic style popularized by the National Park Service, the gabled buildings have half-log siding or full-log construction and wood shingle roofs. The building in Preston features a river rock exterior. Broad covered porches with oversized log support posts distinguish each building's facade, and a massive stone fireplace adorns each interior. All five of these structures remain in use as activity centers in county or city parks. (There are two others, now occupied by Ruth School in Burien and the Bellevue Highlands Senior Center.)

## REHABILITATION AND REUSE STORIES

Stretching from the tiny hamlet of Skykomish cradled in the Cascade Mountains to the shores of Vashon Island, and from the historic coal town of Black Diamond to the streetcar era suburbs of Shoreline, scores of important historic buildings are being brought back to new life. The wide variety of projects speaks to the commitment of the Metropolitan King County Council and the County Executive, the dedication of the Landmarks and Heritage Commission, and the enormous efforts of local municipalities, heritage organizations, and landmark property owners—all committed to preserving and enhancing the county's rich history. Nowhere is the vitality of this rehabilitation movement more striking than in the small cities, several of which are featured below.

### Skykomish

The town of Skykomish is tucked into a narrow valley along the picturesque Skykomish River in the foothills of the Cascade Mountains. Skykomish (meaning "inland people") takes its name from the Skykomish Tribe, who lived along the river from Monroe east to Index and beyond. Euro-American settlement did not occur in Skykomish until 1893, with the construction of the Great Northern Railroad across the Cascades.

The town was founded by John Maloney, a member of the survey team that was sent out to locate the best northern route across the Cascades. In 1890, knowing the route the train would follow, Maloney staked a claim on the South Fork of the Skykomish River. A siding was constructed and when the route was completed in 1893, he built a general store and post office. By the turn of the century, Skykomish was a thriving village with a population of 150. Mining and logging occurred in the surrounding forests, but the railroad was the lifeblood of the community.

It was during the 1920s that Skykomish peaked in population at about 1,000. The town boomed with construction workers, the local mill operated at peak capacity, the cross-state highway was completed, and numerous trains passed each day. Change quickened during and after World War II, as transportation technology grew increasingly sophisticated. Steam locomotives, displaced by diesel, disappeared in 1953. By the late 1950s, passenger service to Skykomish ended. In 1970 the Great Northern merged with the Chicago, Burlington & Quincy Railroad. By 1992, the substation and many other physical reminders of the railroad's presence in the community had been removed.

The timber industry declined over the years and eventually moved elsewhere, and over time mining also proved uneconomical. With these changes, the population of the town declined, stabilizing at about 200 in the 1960s–70s. However, increased use of Stevens Pass Ski Area, 15 miles to the east, more tourist attractions along State Route 2, and a growing number of people with mountain retreats have made Skykomish part of a larger recreational area for the ever-expanding and mobile population of Puget Sound. It was only a matter of time before property owners would engage the tools of historic preservation to enhance their community.

In 1993, the historic Skykomish School was in poor condition. Water damage from deteriorated windows was threatening the gymnasium floor and the entire building was in need of a paint job. Designed by architect William Mallis, and constructed in 1936 under the auspices of the Works Progress Administration, this handsome Art Deco–inspired building has been the heart of the community for many years. Still in use as a school and active community center in 1993, the strapped school district did not have the funds on hand to conduct the repair work.

Determined to find a way to repair and preserve the old school, Dr. Dennis McCrea, acting superintendent of the school district, sought out the assistance of the Landmarks and Heritage Program. Within a year after his initial phone call to the program, the town of Skykomish had entered into an interlocal agreement with King County for provision of historic preservation services, and one of the biggest recycling projects in the county was under way.

What started out as the restoration of a building turned into restoration of community spirit and

*The main street of early day Skykomish with the Skykomish Hotel at center.*

pride. Inspired by Dr. McCrea's enthusiasm, other property owners and residents began to stand up and take notice. Among them were Janet Garner and Rex Bakel, owners of Maloney's General Store, constructed in 1893 by the town's founder, John Maloney. Working hand in hand with Dr. McCrea, Garner and Bakel prepared landmark nominations for the school, Teacherage, and Maloney's store and all of the buildings were designated as Town of Skykomish Landmarks in 1994.

With support from King County's Suburban Heritage Special Grant Program and with hundreds of hours of volunteer labor, much of which was donated by students, the School District carefully restored and repaired deteriorated portions of the building. And with strong forward momentum, the district carried out restoration work on the adjacent Teacherage which, like the school, had suffered significant deterioration over the years.

But restoration of the school and Teacherage were just the beginning. Garner and Bakel had been painstakingly restoring Maloney's 1893 store for reuse as a combined residence and shop for their antique stove business since they purchased it in 1992. With support from a King County grant, the

*Maloney's General Store and Skykomish Hotel*

couple reconstructed the long-missing porch and false front of the store, returning it to its original prominence on the streetscape. The building is one of only a handful of early "boomtown" facade commercial buildings left in King County.

Upon enactment of the interlocal agreement for historic preservation services with King County, Garner was elected the first chairperson of the town's Design Review Committee, which adopted and implemented rules and procedures for reviewing changes to landmark properties. And with Bakel, a Town Council member, Garner was a catalyst for the establishment of a historic district overlay zone in the town's historic commercial core in 1997. The couple also worked closely with other community members to establish a local historical society which helped to complete the town's first comprehensive survey and inventory of historic resources, followed by design guidelines for alterations to buildings within the overlay zone, and completion of a walking-tour brochure.

The citizens of Skykomish continue to pump time and money into preservation of the past. In 1998, they worked with the county to designate Railroad Avenue as a Historic Commercial District, and at this writing plans are under way to nominate it for listing in the National Register of Historic Places. Restoration has been completed on the historic Masonic Hall, and the new owners of the Skykomish Hotel are just beginning renovation. The residents of Skykomish have brought new life and vitality to a community which was languishing on the sidelines.

## North Bend

South and west of Skykomish, the Snoqualmie River has carved out a broad, fertile valley in the shadow of the Cascade foothills. Home to the Snoqualmie people for thousands of years, the scenic valley's winding river, broad prairies, and wooded hillsides also attracted Euro-American settlers. The river was always the primary means of transportation, but in 1884 the arrival of the railroad initiated rapid change. Small settlements began to grow into a network of small towns that thrived on the burgeoning timber industry, followed by proliferation of hops farms and, later, dairy operations.

Today only a smattering of dairy farms are active in the valley, the lumber mills have moved on, and the hops farms have been gone for decades. Rapid change now characterizes the once small, bucolic agricultural communities of the area. The Snoqualmie Valley is fast becoming a bedroom community, acting as a net to catch the fallout from Seattle and east King County's explosive growth. As elected officials work to enact policies and programs to protect the environment, preserve the dwindling farmlands, reconstruct wildlife habitat, and maintain healthy amounts of open space, they are also working to preserve those elements of the historic environment that give these communities their special character: Snoqualmie's handsome train depot or Fall

City's venerable Masonic Hall or the historic commercial buildings in North Bend, presently disguised by applied Bavarian-inspired decoration.

Joan Simpson, mayor of North Bend, has been working with property owners and city and county officials on an ambitious campaign to restore North Bend's historic commercial area. The town's Alpine makeover dates back to the early 1970s when the construction of Interstate 90 diverted traffic more than a half-mile south of the existing downtown. In an attempt to attract travelers into the downtown, many merchants altered the facades of their buildings to reflect an Alpine aesthetic. Scroll-cut barge boards, balconies, gables, and other Swiss-style decorative elements were applied liberally over the old buildings' exteriors.

Despite these efforts to reinvigorate the old downtown, merchants continued to watch business decline. The Alpine facelift did not work, and by 1997 property owners and city officials were ready to try something new. That something was initiated in the form of an agreement with King County to provide historic preservation services to the city. The first step was completion of a comprehensive history of the downtown followed by documentation of all of the historic buildings. Historic photographs of the downtown, widely circulated during the study, served to stimulate interest in restoring the buildings to their original appearance. That, and the availability of financial incentives to property owners who landmark their buildings, led to the first pilot project in the downtown: renovation of the historic Masonic Hall.

The handsome, three-story, reinforced-concrete building was constructed in 1912 following a devastating fire which destroyed much of North Bend's downtown. And like many of the neighboring buildings, the Masonic Hall was subjected to the Alpine facelift of the 1970s, which covered all of its historic facade.

Encouraged by offers of support from the city and the county, Lodge members moved quickly to designate the building as a city of North Bend Landmark and to initiate restoration of the exterior. In addition to waiving permit fees, the city also hired restoration architect Les Tonkin to provide design and consultation to the Lodge members, and a $17,500 grant from King County supported much of the project. The faux facade was torn off and the elegant old building emerged again.

Just as its supporters hoped, the Masonic Hall

*North Bend, 1906*

project increased interest in the tools of historic preservation as a catalyst for downtown revitalization. At this writing, Art Skolnik, chairman of North Bend's Economic Development Commission, is advocating an even more active role by the city in supporting historic preservation. He would like to see a historic district designation for the downtown, and a formal facade improvement program through which the city could provide regular support to property owners—through economic incentives and relaxation of code requirements—to restore their buildings. The city has committed $20,000 to the 1999 downtown renovation effort and hopes to restore four more buildings during this year. Mayor Simpson is pleased. As a new millennium dawns, North Bend is poised to take its past into the present.

*Indian head corbel in Smith Tower lobby.*

*Chapter Seven*

# REHABILITATION
# AND REUSE

*To restore a building is not only to preserve it, to repair it, or to rebuild, but to bring it back to a state of completion such as may never have existed at any given moment.*

E. E. Viollet-le-Duc, Dictionnaire raisonné de l'architecture française du XIe au XVIe siècle, *1854–68*

Increasingly, landmarks that have been neglected or threatened with demolition have been recognized for their potential and adapted to new community uses. Most of these projects have required the cooperation of a variety of private and public organizations. All have involved creative risk-taking and vision. In Seattle, restoration and reuse projects during the early 1970s were fostered by Forward Thrust and federal Block Grant funding. Creative approaches to closed fire stations, bath houses, and houses of worship resulted in exceptionally well equipped dance and fine arts studios, theaters, and community centers.

In Seattle, a Downtown Land Use Plan approved in 1985 by the mayor and city council recognized the importance of the built environment through a number of policies that promoted preservation.

Specifically, the plan included a Transfer of Development Rights program that allows owners of designated landmarks in downtown Seattle to sell unused development rights from the site of the landmark to another site in the downtown, provided that the owner rehabilitates the landmark building. Owners of landmark buildings who demolished these resources were prohibited from receiving any of the many amenity bonuses available under the plan. Such actions would provide incentives to preserve and protect the landmark buildings in Seattle's Central Business District that, because of their comparatively small size and scale, did not provide a rate of return on investment commensurate with that of high-rise construction. The benefits of this program were not immediately seen because a downturn in the economy brought new development projects to a halt after the overbuilding of high-rises in the late 1980s.

Many preservation actions are eleventh-hour victories over the wrecking ball. Seattle has had its fair share of successes in this area, with the Pike Place Market topping the list. Uncertainty surrounding the fates of the Olympic Hotel and the 5th Avenue

Theatre, two of downtown's finest landmarks, generated sufficient outcry from individuals and civic groups to encourage serious evaluations of both structures for potential reuse and economic return. In the case of the Olympic, Urban Investment and Development Company and Four Seasons Hotels restored the public rooms and enlarged and redecorated guest rooms to re-create the grandeur of the original spaces. No fewer than 43 local businesses raised the money to meticulously restore the 1926 Chinese-inspired 5th Avenue Theatre for its new role as live performance space.

With Historic Seattle Preservation and Development Authority acting as catalyst to stimulate private-sector implementation, a number of important reuse projects turned fragile and underutilized properties into attractive, income-producing components of city neighborhoods. They were big projects and small, in the downtown and scattered throughout the city: the Mutual Life Building in Pioneer Square; Queen Anne High School and West Queen Anne Elementary School on Queen Anne Hill; the House of the Good Shepherd in Wallingford; an old fire station on Ballard's Market Street and another one on Capitol Hill's Harvard Avenue.

The timely purchase by Historic Seattle of the Stimson/Green mansion in 1975 saved it from an uncertain future. Carpenter Gothic residences on Twenty-third Avenue and Victorian houses on Fourteenth Avenue W. were brought back to life. Because of Historic Seattle's diligence, the city's first kindergarten, at Sixth Avenue S. and S. Main Street, was saved from demolition, and the Ward House, on Boren Avenue, was relocated to a safe site on E. Denny Way. The group even arranged to have a historic street clock repaired and installed in Pioneer Square to honor Earl Layman, the city's first Historic Preservation Officer, instrumental in administering the Pioneer Square Historic District and in establishing the city-wide preservation program.

While Seattle residents can pat themselves on the back for such successes, they should not ignore the many losses that have occurred. Significant monuments to Seattle's coming of age in the late 19th and early 20th century are gone: the Denny Hotel, the King County Courthouse, the Federal Building (U.S. Post Office), the Carnegie Library, Central School, the White-Henry-Stuart Building, the Metropolitan, Orpheum, Pantages and Music Hall theaters, the Burke Building, and hundreds of commercial buildings, churches, homes, and apart-

ment buildings representing nearly every popular style from the 1870s onward. For that reason, it is extremely important to preserve, protect, and maintain the best of what remains.

Chapter 4 discussed some of the rehabilitation in designated historic districts. This chapter and chapter 8 offer the reader a more detailed look at other outstanding and innovative rehabilitation and adaptive reuse projects that have kept Seattle's retail core intact and vital, encouraged in-town lifestyles, and maintained the architectural integrity and imagery of the city's varied neighborhoods. They range from early risk-taking ventures bringing people and business back into downtown to projects stimulated by the Tax Act legislation to recent efforts to provide affordable housing while saving historic structures.

In the Central Business District, in residential neighborhoods that surround the downtown, and in communities throughout King County, one can see the energy, commitment, and spirit of individual residents and users. They maintain, restore, and refurbish their early-20th-century homes, urge the Seattle School District to find new uses for closed neighborhood schools, and encourage new business into traditional local shopping areas in order to maintain the retail cores and strengthen neighborhood identity.

## The 1970s

### Fourteenth Avenue W. Residences
2000–2016 Fourteenth Avenue W.

This group of five residences was once part of a larger Finnish community extending several blocks along Smith Cove that, by 1915, served as the Slavic center of Seattle. Built between 1890 and 1910, these homes were usually oriented with their main living rooms facing west. Several had ample porches

*Few changes are noticeable to the exterior after the building's conversion to residential units.*

to take advantage of the breezes and views of the cove, which reached as far east as Fifteenth Avenue W. prior to the filling in of the tide flats for industry and commerce. These one- and two-story residences are simple late Victorian frame buildings with varied facades and ornamental treatments, including angled bays, a rectangular tower, porches with milled brackets and turned posts, and scallop shingles. In 1977–78, Historic Seattle Preservation and Development Authority purchased, refurbished, and sold these buildings with restrictive covenants, including facade easements that ensure respect for their characteristic vernacular style.

## Fire Station No. Twenty-five
1400 Harvard Avenue

The first of Seattle's brick firehouses, this Somervell & Coté–designed building of 1908–9 accommodated horse-drawn equipment until the last of these units was replaced in 1920 and it became the first firehouse in the city to be assigned motor apparatus. The sloping hill on which this firehouse was constructed necessitated the use of a terraced design for

*Motorized trucks outside the equipment bays of Fire Station No. Twenty -five,, c. 1920.*

the equipment bays. Dormitories and offices were located on the second floor of this L shaped station. The stepped bay arrangement turned out to be impractical and dangerous. Numerous accidents led to the installation of individual fire poles for each bay, and even to the placement of guardrails. The station's designation as a Seattle landmark and its listing on the National Register provided tax incentives for rehabilitation and renovation under the 1976 Tax

Reform Act. In 1977, Seattle transferred building ownership to Historic Seattle Preservation and Development Authority, who selected an owner/developer for the project. Two years later, it was sold with restrictive covenants to Commonwealth Pacific, which proposed a $1.6 million rental housing project.

In 1980, Stickney & Murphy were the firm responsible for renovation to create 16 units with lofts out of the interior. Units range in size from 738 to 1,237 square feet. Amenities includes one and one-half baths in each apartment, parquet floors, washer-dryer hookups, and elevator access, including a handicap accessible unit. Ground-floor units facing Harvard Avenue have private garden courts. Despite major interior changes, the cleaned brick exterior retains arched windows and doorways, and its tile roofed form bears the distinct characteristics of an early Seattle fire station.

## THE 1980s

### Four Seasons Olympic Hotel
411 University Street

Designed by the distinguished New York firm of George B. Post & Sons and opened in 1924, the Olympic Hotel was promptly acclaimed the grandest hotel west of Chicago. Its restrained Italian Renaissance facades, executed in light brick and terra-cotta, provided a dignified, sophisticated center for Seattle social life. Its exquisite interiors, rich with wood paneling, ornate plasterwork, and crystal and bronze chandeliers, set the stage for the city's premier events. Although the hotel has been continuously in use since its opening, it was unable to meet the needs of the convention trade which it accommodated as the flagship of the Westin Hotel chain from 1955 until 1979. That management demolished the landmark Metropolitan Theatre around which the hotel had been built in order to provide a large ballroom facility and driveway entrance to the hotel in 1962.

The property is owned by the University of Washington. In 1979, the university considered various alternatives for the site, including a demolition proposal. Outraged by the possibility of losing a building with both architectural and social significance, arts, preservation, and community groups pushed for the building's restoration and for its continued use as a hotel. In June 1979, the hotel was list-

*The Fourth Avenue and University Street facades of the Olympic Hotel rise over the concrete shell. The Metropolitan Theatre is far left.*

*An ornate spiral staircase rises shell-like from lower level shops and meeting rooms past the Spanish Ballroom foyer and to the mezzanine.*

*The arched windows and Italianate terra-cotta trim of the hotel inspired a new entrance to the Four Seasons Olympic Hotel facing University Street.*

ed in the National Register of Historic Places. The city was unable to protect it as a city of Seattle landmark because of its unique position as part of the university tract owned by the state of Washington. The university reviewed three restoration proposals by hotel chains and chose to lease the site to the Urban Investment and Development Company of Chicago and Four Seasons Hotels Limited, Toronto. Their plan was to rehabilitate the Olympic into a world-class luxury hotel.

Working with the NBBJ Group of Seattle, interior designer Frank Nicholson of Concord, Massachusetts, and residential designer John North, the partnership invested $55 million to restore the hotel's grand public spaces and integrate new construction

in a sympathetic manner. Upper floors of the hotel were rebuilt to create larger guest rooms and suites; 756 rooms were reduced to 451 more-spacious rooms. The ballroom addition was demolished and a new Garden Court Lounge was constructed with five two-story Palladian windows similar to windows of the public rooms elsewhere in the hotel. A new glass-walled spa complex was added on a second-floor terrace facing south, its form influenced by 19th- and early-20th-century conservatories. Additional meeting rooms were designed to complement the elegantly restored Spanish Ballroom and its adjacent foyer. Other public spaces, including the lobby and the Georgian dining room, were reconfigured to suit the more intimate character of a smaller hotel and updated with the finest materials available, including imported oak paneling, 11 kinds of marble, hand-woven carpets, antiques, and richly textured fabrics. Restoration included the original silverware, including coffeepots, chafing dishes, and candelabra.

The exterior required tuck-pointing and cleaning brick and replacing missing cast iron trim and marquee fascia with a glass reinforced polyester resin to simulate cast iron. Glass reinforced concrete replicated damaged terra-cotta and was used for all new construction. The care taken to re-create the ambiance of Seattle's premier gathering place while providing handsome and comfortable facilities to meet the needs of today's traveler earned this project nationwide recognition and respect.

## 5th Avenue Theatre
1308 Fifth Avenue

The 5th Avenue Theatre and the Italianate Skinner Building which surrounds it were designed by respected local architect R. C. Reamer. His early work included Old Faithful Inn and other lodges and shelters at Yellowstone Park. In Seattle, his firm was responsible for a number of prestigious buildings, such as the 1411 Fourth Avenue and Great Northern Buildings, the Seattle Times headquarters, and the Meany Hotel.

The magnificent interiors of the 5th Avenue Theatre, opened in 1926, were modeled after the Summer Palace, the Temple of Heavenly Peace, and the Throne Room of the Imperial Palace in Peking's Forbidden City. Its ornate walls and domed ceiling, with its guardian dragon centerpiece, duplicate in plaster the traditional Chinese heavy timber

*Restored auditorium of the 5th Avenue Theatre is dominated by the golden dragon and pearl of perfection chandelier.*

columns, beams, and coffering for which Imperial China was known. Interior design was largely the work of Gustav Liljestrom, trained in China and chief designer for the Gump Company in San Francisco. As with many such theaters from coast to coast, the 2,400-seat house became uneconomical as a motion picture house and closed its doors in 1978. As was the case with the Olympic Hotel, the city was unable to protect it as a designated landmark because of its unique position as a part of the university tract owned by the State of Washington. Nevertheless, the threat of its destruction to make way for a shopping mall or office space brought 43 of the area's leading businesses together in a rare showing of support. The

5th Avenue Theatre Association, a nonprofit organization, was founded for the express purpose of providing Seattle with a much needed performing arts facility. The association comprised 43 local leading businesses, individuals, and organizations that underwrote the loans necessary to renovate the theater and guaranteed losses during the first few years of its operation.

Theater architect Richard McCann, who had worked for and then taken over the firm of B. Marcus Priteca, was in charge of the renovation. The number of seats was reduced to just over 2,100, the slope of the main floor was adjusted for better sight lines, new ventilation, air-conditioning, stage light-

*Opening night crowds fill Fifth Avenue in September 1926.*

ing, and sound systems were installed, and the interior walls and ceilings were meticulously cleaned and, where necessary, repainted in colors matching the originals as closely as possible. New carpeting, reupholstering of original furnishings, and restoring lighting fixtures re-created the exotic ambiance of the theater as it must have been on opening night in 1926.

The $2.6 million renovation was unique in American theater history because the 5th Avenue was the first theater of that scale to be developed without any public funding. The association was established with the long-range goal of having net revenues from the theater fund other cultural activities in the state of Washington. At this writing, the theater has established a $1 million endowment through the Seattle Foundation to support internships in local theater. Its Musical Theatre Association has a base of nearly 33,000 subscribers, making it a remarkably successful regional cultural resource.

## Waterfront Place
Western and First Avenues
Madison Street to Seneca Street

With the discovery of gold in the Klondike and the influx of newcomers to Seattle, new transient lodg-

*Restored buildings along First Avenue were joined by a new building (Watermark Tower) housing retail, offices, and condominiums.*

ing, restaurants, and commercial buildings were built along upper First Avenue, close to the railroad depot and steamship terminals. Compared to the simple red-brick buildings of 1890, these turn-of-the-century buildings were more refined, sophisticated examples of Beaux Arts classicism. The Cornerstone Development Company restored the facades of a number of these buildings along the west side of First Avenue between Madison and Spring Streets. The interiors were adapted to new hotel, office, and residential purposes as part of a much larger project incorporating old and new construction in what had been a six-block area of deteriorating and abandoned buildings. The project, called Waterfront Place, includes the Globe Building (1001–11 First Avenue), Beebe Building (1013 First Avenue), Hotel Cecil (1019–23 First Avenue), Grand Pacific (1115–17 First Avenue), Colonial Building (1119–23 First Avenue), Coleman Building (94–96 Spring Street), and National Building (1001–24 Western Avenue).

*Globe Building, corner of First Avenue and Madison Street, now the Alexis Hotel.*

*Workmen complete facade restoration of the Globe Building.*

## Alexis Hotel
1007 First Avenue

The Alexis, a 54-room European style luxury hotel, emerged from the gutted interior of a 1901 hotel building that had been converted to a parking garage in the 1940s. In a 1982, $5.2 million renovation by the Bumgardner Partnership, the original brick and terra-cotta facade was cleaned and repointed, new marquees were designed for the entries, and balconies were reinstalled. An original arch and light

court on the south side of the building were reopened, allowing the evolution of the guest room floors into two wings. Fifteen plan configurations, nine different color schemes, and a variety of amenities, including fireplaces, built-in bars, custom furniture and antiques, reinforce the individuality of each room or suite of rooms. The public spaces evoke the grace of early day hotels without literal interpretation of any former period or style. The lobby, dining room, and bar rely upon coffered ceilings and skylights to provide a warm and inviting environment.

## Arlington and Grand Pacific Buildings
First Avenue between Madison and Spring Streets

Originally turn-of-the-century hotels, these four buildings have heavy timber frames and exterior brick bearing walls with extensive Beaux Arts styled terra-cotta ornament. In a $8.9 million project supervised by the Bumgardner Partnership, the facades were completely restored and interiors joined in pairs with new common circulation for residential, parking, retail, and office uses. The buildings now house 80 apartments and condominiums, ranging from studios to two-bedroom and two-story units, with a variety of plan arrangements that acknowledge the generous windows, high ceilings, ornament, and embellished facades of each structure. In the Arlington, 7 of 43 units have roof terraces. In the Grand Pacific,16 units surround a two-story interior atrium, while many of the 37 units have exterior terraces or original wrought iron balconies. New storefronts of carefully detailed wood and glass are designed to blend with the c. 1900 facades.

**Arctic Club Building**
700 Third Avenue

The Arctic Club was a social club composed of the region's prominent citizens and was headquartered in the Morrison Hotel at Third Avenue and Jefferson Street. As the club grew, a building on the corner of Third and Cherry was commissioned. Designed by A. Warren Gould in 1913 and completed in 1917, the cream-color terra-cotta-faced building provided flexible office space and beautifully detailed club interiors. The decorative theme included distinctive polychrome terra-cotta walrus heads adorning the third-floor exterior and a life-size polar bear replica placed over the Third Avenue club entrance. Multicolored matte-glaze terra-cotta in submarine blue and peach adorn the elaborate top story, main cornice, and spandrel sections. Alaska marble was used in the main corridors leading to office spaces, and the club lobby was finished in imitation Caen stone. The club had wood paneled meeting rooms on the second floor and a main lounge dominated by a fireplace with a mantel of glazed tile depicting Mount Rainier and Lake Washington. The most significant feature of the club remains the 60-foot-square dining room, surmounted by a stained-glass dome and its walls and ceiling ornamented with fruit and vegetable friezes. In 1971, when the Arctic Club merged with the College Club, the furnishings were auctioned, and in 1973 the space was taken over by city of Seattle offices.

The building was refurbished in 1984 as quality office space and the Dome Room restored. Renovation by Stickney & Murphy for Carma Development and Foster Marshall included the installation of new entrance doors, a marquee and retail store fronts, cleaning and repair of terra-cotta, installation of air-conditioning, ventilation, and plumbing systems, rehabilitation of elevators, and restoration of the Dome Room. Unfortunately, the mahogany wood-

*Arctic Club Building.*

*The ornate vegetable frieze in the Dome Room is treated with gilt.*

work throughout the second floor was painted at that time. The walruses adorning the facade also received fiberglass replica tusks to replace the terra-cotta originals that had been removed years ago as a precaution against earthquake damage. By the mid-1990s, the walruses had begun to crack. It became apparent that the grout used to attach these tusks had absorbed water, expanded, and damaged the terra-cotta heads. In 1997, a cast was made from one of the original walrus heads, and new terra-cotta heads were created to replace the most severely damaged ones.

*Franklin High School as it was built.*

## University Methodist Episcopal Church/ Brooklyn Square
4142 Brooklyn Avenue N.E.

The University Methodist Episcopal Church was one of a number of early-20th-century Protestant houses of worship that cast aside the Catholic symbolism of nave and cruciform and emphasized an auditorium arrangement. The building's nearly square two-story central sanctuary is clad in narrow shiplap siding and covered with a pitched roof with smaller side gables. An octagonal tower originally supported a belfry and spire reaching 125 feet in height. The church features a large number of floral-patterned colored-glass windows and some Palladian styled windows. The Methodist congregation originated in 1891 in Seattle, meeting in the Latona Schoolhouse. The Brooklyn Avenue church was designed by Tacoma architect G. W. Bullard and built in 1906–7 to serve as a religious focal point for visitors to the Alaska-Yukon-Pacific Exposition in 1909. Following the fair, the church served the community as the "university chapel." When a larger church was built nearby in 1926, the old church served other religious and secular groups.

The words "Save Me" were painted in red on the front door of the abandoned and decaying building in 1977. Beneath, in black, someone had scrawled "Why?" No one chose to respond positively to the question until 1984, when the Forty-second and Brooklyn Associates and the architectural firm of Anderson, Koch & Duarte began restoration and remodeling plans for restaurants and retail. The lofty ceilings, stained-glass windows, and woodwork of the main sanctuary were preserved while new ground-level storefronts and a small inside shopping mall were provided.

## Franklin High School
3013 S. Mount Baker Boulevard

With its dominant red-tile roof and distinguished Renaissance facade of buff brick and terra-cotta, Franklin High School was once considered "the most beautiful school west of the Mississippi." It was and continues to be a significant visual and cultural landmark in the Rainier Valley. The original design by School Architect Edgar Blair in 1911, occupied in 1912, was expanded in 1925. In 1958, a gymnasium and other additions destroyed or blocked views of the principal facade.

Neighborhood support in the form of a "Save Franklin" campaign countered a Seattle School District decision to demolish the building based on inaccurate early estimates of the costs for seismic and systems repair and the difficulty of adapting it to meet state educational specifications for flexible classroom space. The school was designated a landmark in 1986, encouraging the school district to rethink its position. According to Elizabeth Wales, a school board member at the time, "By designating Franklin as a landmark site, it gave us time to go back and find a solution. It made us look and look again."

The three-year fight to save the school involved public hearings, petition drives, and feasibility studies that reflected grassroots participation at its best. Instead of demolishing the distinctive building, the school board in 1987 accepted a compromise plan that retained the north, west, and south facades, as well as the roof and cupola, while building essentially a new facility inside and in additional space. The offending newer gym and additions were razed, the original building was renovated, and new and respectful additions were developed by Bassetti Norton Metler Rekevics Architects in 1989–90 at a cost of $19.3 million.

Franklin High School is a model of successful collaboration among owner, community, and design

*The new commons space.*

team. The architects worked with school officials, neighbors, students, alumni, and preservationists to develop a plan which would allow for the restoration of the school. The refurbishment and additions to the landmark required a design approach that was sensitive to site, context, program requirements, and community involvement. The unreinforced masonry building presented a complex seismic problem to the design team. The solution preserved the masonry facade by structurally tying the existing building to a new addition. Rather than trying to copy or compete with the grandeur of the original Neoclassical structure, the design for the new addition's east facade complements the existing design while taking advantage of modern construction methods and materials. The primary exterior wall elements consist of a concrete base, brick veneer, and a concrete cornice. Terra-cotta removed from the original east facade was reused or replicated for use in the string

course of the new addition. Inside, the former auditorium, with its elegant coffered ceiling and tall arched windows, was converted into "the commons."

The scope of work included a new auditorium and stage, media center, art classrooms, and science and vocational technology labs. Site design was also an important consideration, providing pedestrian pathways and numerous gathering and socializing spaces, as well as a multipiece steel sculpture entitled The Keys of Learning integrated with site walls accented with colorful tiles that provide seating areas. The northwest entry portal was reinforced as the main point of access to the building, providing a clear link with Mount Baker Boulevard. The project received awards from the National Trust, Seattle Chapter AIA, and the Association of King County Historical Organizations.

*Architect Val Thomas added French doors and patios on both east and west sides of the former auditorium to bring light into a spacious multilevel residence.*

*West Queen Anne Elementary School before additions were made.*

## West Queen Anne Elementary School
515 W. Galer Street

Visually a landmark atop Queen Anne Hill, the building is one of the earliest brick schools extant. To replace a clapboard "shack school" that had been built on the hastily cleared site in 1890, the Seattle School District approved a brick building designed by the firm of Skillings & Corner. It was erected in 1895–6 and subsequently added to in 1900 and 1902 to provide a nearly symmetric plan. Its dignified Romanesque styled facade featured semiround and segmental arched window openings, a shake

roof, and dormers. In 1916, School Architect Edgar Blair designed a compatible 10-room south wing and auditorium.

Closed since 1981, its continued presence in the neighborhood was ensured by a privately financed redevelopment of the building into condominium and rental units (which later converted to condominiums) with underground parking, private gardens, and landscaped grounds. The project, encouraged by the efforts of Historic Seattle Preservation and Development Authority and the Seattle School District Properties Management section, was designed by Cardwell/Thomas and implemented by West Queen Anne Associates, a limited partnership.

The $3.8 million complex respects the formality of form and plan of the Romanesque structure. The playground has been transformed into a landscaped garden sited over a new 55-space parking garage. A paved circular court, centered between the wings of the 1896–1902 section of the building, is flanked by formal lawns and a central fountain. From the court, a staircase rises to the new front entrance to the building. Forty-nine units, both one and two story, range from 600 to 1,400 square feet on the four levels of the renovated building. Units on the ground floor have private gardens. The two principal classroom floors, with high ceilings, vertical fir wainscoting, and multipaned and arched windows, provide a variety of studio/one-bedroom and two-bedroom units. The former attic has been converted into 12 two-story units with cathedral ceilings and decks. Because of its hilltop setting, many units in the building have superb views. The resulting units are warm, inviting spaces that reflect today's lifestyles while incorporating the craftsmanship and materials of an earlier time. This project received a 1985 National Trust Honor Award.

## Interlake Public School/Wallingford Center
4416 Wallingford Avenue N.

In 1902, architect James Stephen won a competition for the design of a model school that would meet Seattle School District needs during a period of unprecedented growth. Stephen's design called for a three-story eight-room rectangular frame building that could be easily enlarged by the addition of wings at either end. The floor plans for all schools would be almost identical, but facade treatment, fenestration, and trim could be varied for each building to provide a unique identity. All the buildings would have excel-

lent natural lighting conditions and efficient, functional plans. Stephen was then hired by the District as the School Architect and oversaw construction of over 20 grammar schools of this type. Interlake Public School (1904) is essentially a replication of the initial model plan school, Green Lake Elementary (demolished). It has an I-shaped plan generated by its central section (1904) and two identical north and south pavilions (1908). It features a pedimented main entrance pavilion with an Ionic columned portico and an entablature bearing the name of the school.

When Interlake Public School was closed in 1981, the Seattle School District Property Management staff sought proposals to utilize the building to serve the community. A 99-year lease was arranged with Lorig Associates, a local developer who adapted the building to market rate rental apartments and two floors of retail space in 1982–83. The architectural firm of Tonkin/Greissinger designed 24 studio/one-bedroom apartments on the third floor with 26,000 square feet of retail on the lower two floors. Maple floors, fluted wood columns, and corridor archways have been preserved on the main floor, and Alaskan marble salvaged from the rest-

*The columned entrance portico of Interlake School was restored and repainted.*

*Corridor archways and columns were retained and floors were enlivened with painted geometric designs.*

rooms was reused to form a new entrance stairway. In its new role, the school continues to serve as a community landmark for the Wallingford neighborhood.

# THE 1990S

## Victorian Row Apartments
1234–38 S. King Street

Seattle's only surviving 19th century frame row apartment building reopened its doors as 14 low-income apartments after seven months of refurbishing and reconstruction in 1993. Built in 1891 to meet the needs of a growing housing market, this handsome Victorian building was moved to its present location earlier in this century after the city widened and regraded Jackson Street and the adjoining streets of the present International District. It represents a type of dwelling that was an early prototype for multiple-family units. With its two-story rectangular bays, scalloped skirting, and gabled entrance porches with spindle work, turned posts, and paneled doors, it resembles the attached Victorian row houses that were commonplace in 19th-century American cities, including Seattle. Inside, millwork with intricately profiled window and door surrounds, decorative corner blocks, wainscoting in the entries and kitchens, and brass hardware date from its construction.

Although the building was a designated Seattle historic landmark as early as 1977 and was listed in the National Register of Historic Places, its condition had deteriorated because the longtime property owner, Stacia Champie, was unable to afford repairs. Faced with condemnation of the rear porches by the Seattle Fire Department in 1990, and unable to

*The restored and colorful facade is a rhythmic repetition of square bays and porches.*

secure financing to augment assistance from the rental rehabilitation programs of the Department of Community Development, Champie approached Historic Seattle to undertake this project as a general partner.

Historic Seattle combined resources from the city of Seattle, the National Equity Fund, and Pacific First Bank in order to generate nearly $1.5 million in construction and permanent financing costs to complete the project. The firm of Stickney & Murphy, architects for the Bel-Boy project and with an outstanding record in restoration and adaptive reuse, was chosen to carry out the program. Sven Larsen was the project architect. Briere Skoegard Company was the general contractor, with Mike Cochrane as site superintendent. The property is managed by the Seattle Housing Resources Group.

The flats have been reconfigured from the original 12 into 14 units with a combined 11,400 square feet of space. When built, there were 4 three-bedroom units on either end of the building, and 8 two-bedroom units. Now there is more variety, with 2 studio, 2 one-bedroom, 6 two-bedroom, and 4 three-bedroom units. The apartments range from 360 to 860 square feet. The foundation has been stabilized, mechanical and plumbing systems upgrad-

*Victorian Row had been minimally maintained for many years.*

ed, a fire sprinkler system installed, and rear porches rebuilt. The exterior features and interiors remain essentially unaltered, although the bathrooms and kitchens have been enlarged and modernized.

Color chips were analyzed to determine the original colors. The intricate brass hardware was stripped of its paint and restored. Trim moldings, wainscoting, pocket doors, and other original features were cleaned and reused. Even the glazed windows were refurbished and reinstalled. For Ron Murphy, "It's exciting to work on a building that has been continuously occupied for 100 years and is still virtually intact. This humble, overlooked building will now attract people's attention for the way it contributes to its neighborhood."

Similar rehabilitation programs completed by Historic Seattle are the Bel-Boy project and the William B. Phillips residence. The former project involved six turn-of-the-century residences and boardinghouses that were converted into low- and moderate-income housing south of E. Pike Street in 1988. The Neoclassical Phillips residence, an unusual double house on E. Union Street that was vacant for a decade and the subject of demolition rumors, by 1994 was providing multifamily housing behind its elegant facade.

### St. James Cathedral
Ninth Avenue and Marion Street

Seattle's Roman Catholic cathedral was designed by the nationally prominent partnership of Heins & La Farge, best known for their early design work for St. John the Divine in New York, the largest cathedral in the world. W. Marbury Somervell was the local supervising architect, assisted by Joseph S. Coté, his future partner. Planned as early as 1903 and completed in 1907, this Beaux Arts interpretation of the monumental works of the Italian Renaissance commands a prominent site on First Hill above the Central Business District. Originally designed in a cruciform plan with a central altar, the buff-colored brick-clad building has rich terra-cotta ornamentation. The building relies heavily on structural concrete and steel for internal supports. Two identical square-based towers with octagonal belfries and cupolas rise 165 feet on either side of the west facade. The formal entrance between the towers has the aspect of a triumphal arch, nearly 60 feet high and encompassing three portals. An ambitious central dome rising 120 feet above an exceptionally wide crossing collapsed under the weight of a heavy snowfall in 1916. Subsequent reconstruction efforts by

*The central plan intended in the original design of St. James has been restored.*

*The towers of St. James Cathedral dominate First Hill.*

architect John Graham Sr. in 1916–17 left St. James without a dome and with an altered interior plan, including additional columns and piers to support a future dome at the crossing of the nave and the transepts. Despite the intent of the original designers to have a central altar, the cathedral opted for an altar at the far east end of the sanctuary.

The original interiors were quite plain because of the shortage of funds. The 1917 refurbishment by John Graham Company included, in addition to the structural bracing, an Italian Renaissance style frieze and cornice work. In 1950, another refurbishment was undertaken, during which, among other changes, acoustical tiles were attached to the ceiling to deaden the sound, and the walls and ceilings were painted and decorated.

In 1994, the Bumgardner Architects completed a major renovation of the building and its interiors that incorporated liturgical changes with a new seating plan, central altar, and oculus; baptismal font; devotional shrines; acoustical and lighting improvements; pipe organ restoration; new bells; artwork and furnishings; seismic strengthening; ventilation, electrical, fire safety, and barrier-free access improvements; and roofing restoration and replacement.

Driving forces in the renovation were to change the focus of liturgical action to the midst of the assembly for full participation by all, to create an excellent place for musical performance, and to provide flexibility for liturgical and civic uses while respecting the classical architecture and historic features. By introducing a central oculus that echoes the original dome in its location and focusing purpose and by removing the columns and partitions added in 1917, the architects have returned the building closer to its original design. They also uncovered and restored terrazzo flooring that had been hidden by carpeting since the 1950 renovation, removed the acoustical ceiling and developed a new molded plaster coffered ceiling that aids the building's natural acoustics and incorporates lighting. The marbleized columns are now set off with "Dutch metal" gilded capitals, and the wall and ceiling features are painted with compatible colors.

The $4.3 million renovation of the cathedral marks a positive and productive cooperative effort between St. James Parish, the Roman Catholic Archdiocese, the architects, and the Seattle Landmarks Preservation Board, which reviewed and commented upon changes to exterior and interior.

## Paramount Theatre
901 Pine Street

Constructed during 1927–28 and opened as the Seattle Theatre, the 3,000-seat Paramount was billed as the "largest and most beautiful theatre west of Chicago." Its architects, Rapp & Rapp, were responsible for the New York Paramount and many other motion picture palaces throughout the nation. In Seattle, they affiliated with B. Marcus Priteca, renowned for his beautifully designed and acoustically superb theaters for Alexander Pantages and the Warner Brothers and Orpheum chains. It is believed that in this case, he was largely responsible for the studio apartments rather than the theater itself. While the building was externally quite restrained, the designers spared no expense to provide the public with a lavish interior, modeled predominantly after French Renaissance palaces. A progression of spaces leads from box office to colonnaded foyer and into a grand hall with two magnificent bronze and crystal chandeliers high overhead and three tiers of lobbies. A white and gold player grand piano was located in an upper-floor lobby, called the salon de musique, to entertain during intermissions. The

*The Paramount Theatre (originally the Seattle Theatre) and Studio Building during its opening, 1928.*

*The grand staircase with Czechoslovakian cut glass chandelier.*

boldly ornamented auditorium utilized inverted domes with hidden lights, draperies, and textured walls and ceilings with many carved ornamental surfaces to create distortion free sound. The Paramount Wurlitzer orchestra pipe organ was the largest in the world when it was installed. The Great Depression closed the theater temporarily. When it reopened, it was strictly a movie house. During years of changing ownership and management, nearly all of the original sculpture, ornate furniture, and paintings disappeared from the theater. Fortunately, its mighty Wurlitzer was left intact.

In 1981, under the ownership of the Volotin Investment Company, refurbishment of the theater proceeded with the supervision of Ray Shepardson, whose credits included renovation of Playhouse Square in Cleveland. The renovation, largely cosmetic, included cleaning all walls and ceilings; disassembling, cleaning, polishing, and restringing the crystal chandeliers; installing new carpeting, upholstery, and curtain; and upgrading the sound system. The theater was reopened in October 1981 as a live concert hall. Changing management was unable to make the hall a financial and cultural success.

A second, more comprehensive refurbishment was undertaken by the Seattle Landmark Association under new owner Ida Cole and architects from NBBJ, with John Savo as project manager. Work began in 1994 and culminated in the March 1995 grand reopening. By filling in the wedge of ground where Pike Street meets the freeway with a 47-foot addition to the building, the Paramount gained a proper loading lock, a deeper stage, and new dressing rooms. Inside, decorative ceilings and walls were cleaned, patched, and refinished where needed to closely approximate original finishes, glazing, and gilding; carpet and seat fabrics were replaced with fabrics that complement the brown and gold tones of the decorative walls; lighting fixtures were repaired and cleaned; and adequate rest rooms were installed to accommodate the large number of users during intermissions. Structural, seismic, heating, air-conditioning, lighting, and sound upgrades were accomplished. A hydraulic floor that makes it possible to turn raked seating to flat floor "festival" seating and ballroom space in less than an hour was planned but not installed until several years later. To the public the most visible sign of the theater's rejuvenation was the cleaning of exterior brick and cast stone that removed years of soil and carbon deposits, and the restoration of the marquee and vertical neon sign. The project cost $37 million, and the theater's transformation is evidence of private vision inspiring private and public cooperation.

## Coliseum Theatre/Banana Republic
1506 Fifth Avenue

Conceived in 1914 by C. D. Stimson and J. Gottstein and opened in 1916, the Coliseum was advertised as the first major theater in the world designed exclusively for the showing of motion pictures. While far from the truth, the exaggeration cer-

*Coliseum Theatre opening night, 1916.*

*Even in its decline, the Coliseum sported the most flamboyant classical terra-cotta facade in the Northwest.*

tainly didn't hurt local ticket sales. The Coliseum Theatre's innovative design and acoustics did influence theaters nationwide and were prototypes for the American motion picture palace. Its exuberant facade is an adaptation of Italian Renaissance styling in white glazed terra-cotta. The richly ornamented building is composed of a series of arched panels and niches embellished with scrolled brackets; festoons of fruit, flowers, and leaves; urns and garlands. Origi-

*The facade was restored and reconstructed with a new corner entrance and a reversible retail interior.*

nally, the cornice and the Roman styled incised letters of the name "Colisevm" were illuminated by lights placed in the recesses. A marquee along the length of the ground floor culminated at the corner ticket booth, a vestibule under a great coffered half-dome crowned by a glowing cupola of art glass.

The theater designer, B. Marcus Priteca, began his practice in Seattle in 1909 and, in 1911, became the sole architect for Alexander Pantages, a local theater entrepreneur who created an entertainment empire in the United States and Canada. During his lifetime, Priteca designed 60 major theaters and over 160 minor theaters for Pantages, Warner, and other clients. In 1950, he supervised a modernization of the interior that obliterated the proscenium and many of its significant lobby features. At that time, a new marquee was constructed with a revolving neon cylinder. It was to have been topped by a gold Oscar statue, which never materialized. When the theater finally closed its doors, concerns were voiced about the viability of the building on its valuable corner location in the middle of the commercial district.

A solution came in the guise of a major clothing retailer, Banana Republic, which was looking for a prestigious location for a flagship store downtown. The theater's cavernous interior offered the owners an opportunity to install a flexible arrangement of retail space with few structural barriers. NBBJ restored the exterior, where most of the damage to the terra-cotta skin had been at the retail level in an assortment of storefront changes over time. Terra-cotta was either recast or replaced with concrete in the same color and finish made by Architectural Reproductions of Portland, Oregon. The 1950 era marquee was removed and replaced by an illuminated steel and glass "window" that fits into the curving wall which was once the backdrop for the glass dome. Minute details were important, down to the lost horns on terra-cotta steer heads, which were rebuilt out of Bondo, a common auto-body filler.

The interiors were designed by internationally recognized architect Robert M. Stern, whose Postmodern approach included archways and ornamental bas-reliefs that echo the theater's design and classical period style. The store is actually a self contained "building within a building." In the event that someone should at some point in the future wish to reconvert the building into a theater, the improvements can be removed. While it was necessary to remove the mezzanine, the ramps, and the lobby of the old theater, the balcony, the ceiling, and the proscenium of the theater are largely intact survivors above the roof of the store.

## Log House Museum Building
3003 Sixty-first Avenue S.W.

One of most telling stories of grassroots preservation is that of the Southwest Seattle Historical Society and their four-year drive to turn an unused log home in the historic Alki Beach neighborhood into "The Birthplace of Seattle" museum. While never officially documented, this small log dwelling is believed to

*The Log House Museum as completed.*

*Damaged logs were removed and new logs were carved and hoisted into place.*

have been designed and built during 1903–4 as part of a group of buildings on the Bernard family estate designed by Fred L. Fehren. The log construction, porch, windows, and interior ceiling treatment of this house relate closely to the main house, Fir Lodge (now the Alki Homestead Restaurant).

The Southwest Seattle Historical Society, founded in 1984, began the process in earnest during planning meetings in 1993 that stimulated a campaign to "Save the Log House." Thousands of Alki residents cast ballots in favor of the museum project in March 1994. The group assumed title and raised over a half million dollars to begin renovation and conversion. This included $170,000 in Metro mitigation funds and contributions that flowed in from individuals, corporations, foundations, and local businesses. David Leavengood, a specialist in museums and in log structures, was hired for the design work, which included repairs to the foundation, roof, and walls, replacement of a large number of rotted logs, rebuilding of the porch, installation of accessibility ramps, and refurbishment of altered and unaltered interior spaces to provide exhibition space.

Initial construction began in December 1996. The society requested funds and received $189,000 from the Capital Projects for Washington Heritage Fund to complete the annex and interior/exterior restoration. It enabled the museum to open, on schedule, on November 13, 1997—the 146th anniversary of the Denny Party Landing at Alki. The museum's mission is to be "a place to celebrate the unique history of the Duwamish Peninsula and the Birthplace of Seattle." As an educational and interpretive center, it provides a base for preserving and

*Frederick and Nelson Department Store, c. 1940.*

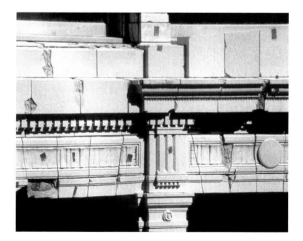

*Damaged terra-cotta awaits restoration.*

sharing community history, presenting exhibitions and hosting special heritage events. The museum has received awards from the Washington Museum Association and the Washington Trust for Historic Preservation.

### Frederick and Nelson Department Store/ Nordstrom

500–524 Pine Street

This department store was the cornerstone of the newly forming retail district when it opened its doors. D. E. Frederick's radical step, labeled "Frederick's Folly" by fellow retailers, businessmen, and financiers at the time, proved itself a sound financial move. It signaled the eventual move of major retail, including the Bon Marché, from Second Avenue eastward along Pine Street. John Graham Company designed the original five-story terra-cotta-clad structure in a "Neorenaissance" style. Conceived in 1916, the building was completed and open by 1919. It was expanded by five additional floors in 1952. These, along with its two basement levels, provided 700,000 square feet. The addition had a simplified terra-cotta skin, and the upgrading included filling in of the end window bays, modernization of the ground floor, and elimination of the elaborate cornice that terminated the shorter building. The closure of the store in 1992 left a void in the city's retail center and concern about its future health. Financial support by the city of an adjoining parking garage that is now part of Pacific Place made the rehabilitation of the building possible.

In its new role as the flagship store and offices for Nordstrom, the building exterior has been refurbished. Its structure has been seismically upgraded, its systems have been completely replaced, and an entirely new interior has been developed by Callison Architecture that includes 380,000 square feet of retail and corporate offices on levels 6 through 10.

The 14-month makeover of the exterior began with in-depth investigation of the terra-cotta and windows. According to Mark Morden, AIA, a terra-cotta consultant with Wiss, Janney, Elstner Associates, Inc., "most of the damage to the terra-cotta was concentrated on the original lower five floors caused by the added weight of the 1952 upper levels, which overstressed the older, lower-level terra-cotta." To correct this condition, the reconstructed facade includes new expansion joints. According to project architect Nate Thomas, "damaged tiles were repaired or replaced, corroded support steel was replaced with stainless steel, and mortar joints were tuck-pointed."

The wood frames of all 1,746 windows were restored; new sashes were fabricated to match the original design and installed with energy-efficient glass. Through careful planning of the store layout, fewer windows are blocked off than before, and offices, stockrooms, and an alterations shop are located on the perimeter to take advantage of natural light.

### Ford Assembly Plant/Craftsman Press/Shurgard
1155 Valley Street

This five-story concrete- and masonry-clad industrial building on south Lake Union was the first Seattle

*Ford Assembly Plant during its second use as a factory for Fuller Paints, c. 1920, prior to becoming Craftsman Press.*

assembly plant for Ford Motor Company, opened in 1913. It represents the emergence of more efficient assembly methods, from "static," in which the automobile was assembled in one place with parts and workers moving around it, to "assembly line," in which chain-driven assembly lines were hung from the ceilings or off the floors. Gravity slides and the elevator were used to move assembled components from the top floor downward until the completed vehicles rolled off the final ramp to be tested and moved into the showroom level, where they were sold. The success of this building gave John Graham Sr. the opportunity to design Ford assembly facilities in seven other cities. The building operated as Craftsman Press prior to its purchase and rehabilitation for headquarters and storage facility by Shurgard Storage Center, Inc., with design work by Fuller Sears.

The $4.1 million renovation of the 177,000-square-foot building was carried out with the goal of restoring the building's original openness by removing most of the filled-in window openings from the Craftsman Press era. The poor condition of the existing industrial sash forced replacement, but the company spent $500,000 to replicate their configuration and profiles. They preserved the terra-cotta surrounds that once framed the ground floor display windows for the automobile showroom and matched original brick in locations that needed replacement. Another original feature of the building, the monogram "F" on the showroom capitals,

*The refurbished building closely resembles its early look because new windows replicate the industrial sash. Signage has been placed where it was historically.*

has also been preserved. The lower floors are reserved for public storage. The company offices are housed in the top two floors of the building, to take advantage of expansive views shared by the entire staff. The focal point is an interior stairway between the two floors that rises around a mock lighthouse—the symbol of the company—to a clerestory that pops through the roof and brings light into the stairwell.

*Entrance porch, Stimson residence on First Hill, 1901.*

1207

# Chapter Eight

# At Home:
# The Personal Side
# of Preservation

The previous chapters have highlighted the great rewards that come from official landmarks programs, the incentives to owners and developers of historic properties, and the initiative of those who take risks to save, restore, and reuse significant reminders of the region's built heritage. However, they also make clear that city and county government, nonprofit organizations, and a small group of well-meaning historic preservation professionals, architects, and planners cannot hope to be watchdogs for a metropolitan area of 1.6 million people in King County.

Fortunately, for every designated landmark property that is protected by the city or the county, many more buildings are protected simply because their owners love and respect them. This is particularly true of residences, where people share their lives with family, celebrate special occasions, and do most of their growing up. The personal attachments people form with their homes make for some of the most memorable examples of preservation, conservation, and good stewardship.

Simple clapboard houses of locally cut and sawn wood, manors of brick, stone, and terra-cotta inspired by centuries-old European traditions, and wood and glass modernist boxes—all represent aspects of the residential heritage of Puget Sound. Many Seattle neighborhoods are filled with buildings copied from pattern books and periodicals that spread design ideas across the country. In the same way, bungalows and Craftsman homes offered inexpensive and well-appointed housing for working-class families during the first quarter of the century. Revival styled residences in the Georgian, Dutch Colonial, English Tudor, and Italianate styles are comparable to those in older communities on the East Coast and Midwest because Seattle builders followed national trends and popular theories about domestic life, social interaction, and manners. On occasion, the reverse has been true; local architects have forged new ground that has focused nationwide attention on the Pacific Northwest. In particular, designers have responded sensitively to the region's topography, climate, and light qualities to develop domestic architecture that uses local building materials and fits well with its natural surroundings.

The following personal stories reveal the importance people place upon their homes and the efforts they make to respect and maintain community landmarks for future generations. They also reveal that buildings do not have to be museums, and that by understanding the design intents, materials, and stylistic vocabulary of these buildings, it is possible to adapt, expand, and modernize without defacing and destructively altering them.

The homes are described chronologically, from perhaps the earliest extant house in King County to a late example of master architect Frank Lloyd Wright's work for a Normandy Park couple who still take pleasure in their hand-built home. These stories give meaning to the phrase *grassroots preservation*.

## THE PIONEER PERIOD

### First Growth

From their kitchen window, Paul and Judy Thomas have a view of one of several huge cedar stumps that dot their three-acre property and are constant reminders of the provenance of their timber home. Judy says, "We've been told it is the oldest inhabited log structure in King County."

Theirs is a handmade house built by a Swedish immigrant over a century ago on a quarter section tract of densely wooded land. The couple can only guess the year—about 1875—from dated newspapers stuffed in the cracks between the timbers to keep out drafts. The homesteader used skilled woodworking techniques brought from the Old World.

According to restoration architect Peter Steinbrueck, the house is neither a log house nor a timber frame but is timber stave construction using interlocking squared timbers aligned vertically. All lumber used in the original construction was either hand-sawn or, more likely, split from the huge cedar trees felled just yards from the house. Each piece has chamfered edges, and they come together with dowels and ties at the bottom. The house was laid out symmetrically with six nearly equal rooms on the 30 x 40 foot first floor and a large open space beneath the roof for additional living quarters as need arose. Story has it that the homesteader left his wife and family for Alaska without finishing the second floor.

Paul and Judy lived in the house for twenty years without making substantial changes, except to make a usable upstairs bathroom and put in a basement where there had only been a crawl space. But by the time they were finished raising two children, they were ready to make some long awaited improvements, including an expanded covered porch and outdoor deck, a larger kitchen and dining room, a new bathroom, and a stone fireplace.

*In extending the kitchen, architect Peter Steinbrueck reused wood salvaged from two inside walls. A new covered porch with a single unifying shed roof extends the length of the house.*

They initially contacted Peter Steinbrueck because of the reputation his father, the late Victor Steinbrueck, had in the preservation community. Growing up in that arena had a strong impact upon Peter's value system. Much of his residential work ties old and new together as seamlessly as possible by respecting traditional materials, structure, and methods. Judy Thomas feels he has accomplished that with their house: "He wasn't trying to impose new things on it; he was trying to work with its components."

Their goal was to preserve the house and restore its original design integrity. The exterior, which had been exposed to over a century of harsh weathering and had never been painted or stained, needed extensive repair and restoration. Many of the old double-hung wood windows were badly deteriorated, joints leaked, and some wall timbers were deeply rot damaged.

With the expertise of Ernst & Donovan Ltd., the general contractors, all repairs and structural alterations were carried out using exactly the same methods, materials, and joinery techniques employed in the original construction. Timbers that could be

*The house is built of split cedar held together with pegs at top and bottom and with dowels that run through the notched bottoms of the timbers.*

saved were reused, and new timbers were fashioned on-site to match the old. That did not make for a fast-track project. Steinbrueck says, "Since much of the original construction joinery was concealed, duplicating it was a learning process, as parts of the house were disassembled and their details were revealed." Okem—a by-product of the linen-making process combined with creosote—fills the cracks that were once filled with newspapers and old blue jeans. Headers were placed above new single-paned windows to prevent future water damage.

The kitchen addition was the major challenge for the architect. "The original house was symmetrical, and the wood was aged over a century. To make the addition appear seamless, timbers from two interior walls were used to piece together the additional exterior facades, and a new covered porch with a single unifying shed roof extends the length of the house. We strictly duplicated joinery techniques. The interlocking timbers that made up the walls had to be carefully disassembled and reassembled in the same

order." The effort has preserved the house and retained its integrity.

For the Thomases, the house continues to reveal its history as former residents return to visit. Seventy-five year-old Eleanor Parker remembered planting the holly tree out front when her family lived here in the first decades of the century. Her family rented it to Japanese truck gardeners in the 1930s. One of their children came back and recalled her dad taking the wagon to the Pike Place Market daily. She asked Paul and Judy if they had ever found her dolly in the wall (her sister had hid it). Since the Thomases have found newspapers and blue jeans, they wouldn't be a bit surprised if, someday, the doll surfaces too.

## Unpretentious but Proud Victorian

There were once hundreds of Italianate Victorian houses in early Seattle neighborhoods. They were not grand mansions but simple, sturdy homes for laborers in the mills and at the wharves. Frequently

The 1890 Fremont Victorian is painted three shades of "drab" (a respectable name for a color in the late 19th century).

The parlor is a studied approach to the Victorian period, with 1870 era reproduction wallpaper, Axminster carpet, and a coal burning stove.

they were the first homes for immigrants to Seattle from northern Europe. Most of these homes were demolished or "remuddled" to serve new generations who saw no intrinsic value in "restoring" them. It was difficult to see the value in obsolete kitchens and bathrooms, drafty high-ceilinged rooms, inadequate heating systems, and almost nonexistent closet space. "Modernizing" was the way to go.

Greg Ahmann finds value and beauty in pioneer Seattle buildings. His purchase in 1984 of a Fremont mill worker's home has led to a career change. A former deputy prosecuting attorney in Everett, Greg shifted his focus to restoring and refurbishing historic buildings. He learned his skills from family members, books, and building suppliers and contractors. Mostly, he learned as he worked on several rundown properties in Seattle's Central Area that he has bought, restored, and resold.

He found his diamond in the rough in the shadow of the Aurora Bridge: a two-story, bay-windowed building with a bit of scrollwork and fish scale shingles. Greg says, "The people who owned this house before me liked it in spite of how old it was and not because of how old it was." He paid $70,000 for the 1,500-square-foot house and, with the exception of $2,400 paid to a contractor for some demolition and

framing, has done everything himself to restore and renovate it.

Swedish immigrant Victor Nelson was 27 years old when he moved to the new house with his 25-year-old wife in 1890. He drove a delivery wagon for a steam laundry on Lake Union. Two Norwegian women lived in the house in the second decade of the century and rented out the upstairs. Subsequent owners applied various enclosures, walls, and window replacements in an effort to bend the house to their needs.

The house represents nine years of ongoing refurbishing. Greg first tackled the dining room and adjacent study (originally a bedroom). Because these rooms were virtually intact, they simply required paint, wallpapers, returning picture moldings to the walls, installing new baseboards, and repairing inoperable windows. Where the original hardware no longer existed, he salvaged appropriate period pieces.

In contrast to the dining room, the kitchen required a major overhaul. Greg hired a contractor to do demolition and framing, but did all the finish work himself. He approached the rest of the house with the same eye to detail and pocket for bargains. For example, period balusters from a salvage shop returned the modernized stairway to its 19th-century appearance at one-third the cost of specially milled duplicates of the originals. The front parlor became his "museum room," showcasing an antique coal burning stove with English Victorian reproduction tile, 1870 era reproduction wallpaper, and Axminster wall-to-wall carpet.

Upstairs, he encountered difficulties covering the old walls, which are not lathe and plaster. "The builders put 1 x 12 shiplap over 2 x 4 studs on the inside. They layered burlap over that. In some cases, I've found three layers of wallpaper. Drywall had been applied on top of that by later homeowners, and more layers of wallpaper. Then they painted it." That may explain why, when Greg bought the house, there was no molding except in the upstairs hall, where the original wall reveals shiplap seams.

The last bit of work included repainting the exterior three shades of "drab," with brilliant amber accents. In Victorian times, "drab" was a respectable name for a color. Greg points out it was not until recently that it has become a pejorative adjective. Drab is similar to taupe or tan.

Throughout the restoration process, Greg went the extra mile. When he needed to replace fish scale shingles at the very top of the house, he actually made them by hand. He uses hand tools instead of modern equipment and admits that he is slow, "But when it's done, I always like the way it looks."

**Preserved in Preston**

Jack and Virginia O'Malley own a picturesque old house with a pond in Preston, a historic mill town east of Issaquah. But it isn't just any old house. It came with impressive credentials. Built in 1904 by August Lovegren, a Swedish immigrant and owner of the Preston Mill, it was the most palatial house in town. Its site on the hill overlooked the shingle mill, the town that developed around the mill, and the Raging River beyond.

Responding to the demand for cedar shingles after the 1889 Seattle fire, Lovegren and five other immigrants located a large stand of cedar southeast of Seattle and, in 1892, purchased acreage and built a shingle mill. With the advantages of the railroad and natural resources from the river and the forested slopes of the Cascade foothills, the lumber concern prospered, bringing many workers to Preston—the majority of them Swedish immigrants.

By 1904, Lovegren had designed and built a home in the popular Colonial Revival style with a number of dormers and window bays. Its most dis-

*The southwest corner of the house is filled with Lovegren family members and friends at a Christmas 1904 gathering.*

tinctive feature was a wraparound verandah of handsome turned balusters and posts at both the first and second floors. The grounds included a fountain fronting the house and lawn, a carriage house, and a greenhouse heated by steam piped up from the sawmill.

By the time the O'Malleys saw the property, the outbuildings no longer existed, and a fire had destroyed the verandah and the topmost dormer. Previous owners had substituted two smaller south and west entry porches, recycling the original columns as supports, but had never replaced the missing dormer. Despite these changes, what swayed the O'Malleys was the remarkable state of benign neglect that had preserved most of the interiors. The two oak and tile fireplaces, original brass lighting fixtures and hardware, intricate spindle work trim, and all the fir and maple woodwork and picture molding were intact.

What they didn't necessarily anticipate when they moved in during November 1994 was all the expensive behind-the-scenes work that needed to be accomplished prior to tackling the cosmetic upgrading of the house. Years of deferred maintenance, negligent repairs, and resident termites, carpenter ants, and worms had caused leakage, dry rot to most of the exterior window walls, and settling. However, in less than two years, most of the problems were solved.

Two layers of asphalt roofing and shake were removed and the roof was rebuilt and sheathed in new shakes. A number of rotted outside walls were replaced; a new dormer was constructed; a home office was carved out of raw attic space; the structural system was reinforced; a new electrical system was

*The most visible part of restoration work has been rebuilding the wraparound verandah and the attic dormer. Balusters will come later.*

*Despite years of neglect, the delicate sawn spindle work screens that embellish the stairwell are still intact.*

installed; and a new kitchen and bath were completed. With the reconstruction of the wraparound porch and installation of a window bay that had been removed years earlier, the house finally took on the gracious appeal it had when it was new. As a King County landmark, the owners have benefited from grants-in-aid for some of their restoration work.

To guide their restoration, the O'Malleys were fortunate enough to have historic photographs sent to them by a relative of August Lovegren. These left no doubt about the look of the attic dormer, the original porches, and the missing window bay, and also showed the landscaping and the fountain areas.

Family connections have also provided a bit more knowledge about how the rooms were used. A back bedroom on the first floor had apparently been a school room and study room. With nine surviving children, it might simply have been the location for tutoring the Lovegrens. But it could possibly have been opened to children of other families as well until a schoolhouse was built in town. Original wallpapers in the sewing room behind the stairs illustrate nursery rhymes. Apparently the Lovegren children would read these nursery rhymes to their mother, an accomplished seamstress, while she was sewing.

With much of the hidden but necessary work completed, Virginia now looks to the next stage—interior plaster, wallpapers, and floors. The couple also wants to restore the pond and the old plantings. According to Jack: "Our intention for buying this was as a hobby. It fell into place, even though it wasn't exactly the right time, with me almost ready to retire. At times we looked at ourselves and thought, 'What in the heck did we ever do this for?' But for the most part, we're really tickled we have it, and we're pinching ourselves because it's real." Pride comes from knowing that they are caretakers to history, owning a home that was a pioneer's.

**Central Area Restoration**

The experience of Ray and Zita Hachiya gives people hope. They transformed a house that looked like it should be condemned into comfortable living space, and did it on a limited budget. The house on which they worked their miracles is a two-story frame dwelling in Seattle's Central Area. The neighborhood has some of the city's earliest extant housing, although much of what survives shows the marks of years of neglect, quick-fix remodeling, and vandalism.

Their house was the first building to rise on the newly platted Walla Walla Addition to the city in 1890—not surprising given that the original owner, J. F. Brewer, was the attorney for the landowner who platted the addition. Early records show that sawmill and bank owner Henry Yesler financed the house. John and Adora Brewer lived there for 10 years. The next owners, the Gleasons, built a smaller house behind it for their daughter when she married. According to the rumor mill, when she divorced, her

*In 1985, this boarded up derelict had become a source for salvage and firewood seekers.*

*With new windows, doors, repaired siding, and a multicolored paint job, the 1890 house is as good as new.*

ex-husband moved across the alley and became a bootlegger.

Long-term ownership—and maintenance— went downhill from then on. Tax records from the 1930s show that the house was sold ten times in a 12-year period. When Zita Hachiya saw it in May 1985, the kindest words one could say was that it was structurally sound but lacked "street appeal." A recent owner had begun to restore it, going so far as putting in a new concrete foundation and bringing wiring and plumbing up to the house. For Zita, the tiny 3" x 5" foreclosure sign was serendipity. In their search for a Victorian, she and Ray had been considering a nearby house. Zita was encouraged to look at this house as well, but initially refused. "I had driven by several years before when someone was restoring it and I coveted it so, I said I would never go past that house again."

The foreclosure sign drove her to action immediately. She went to the bank and, informed that the first person with cash could have the house, she signed papers, went home to tell her husband, and they bought it the next day for $37,000. She spent

time at the King County archives to locate tax records and late 1930s photos—not just for this house but for every house on the block so she could envision the entire neighborhood context. She found out that theirs was the only house with 11-foot ceilings downstairs and that rooms in their house were larger than in others nearby. While its finishes were more middle class than top end, she says, "Ours was fairly commanding at that time."

With a $70,000 restoration loan in hand, the couple spent the next year making the house livable. They put up Sheetrock—most of the lathe and plaster walls were gone or damaged. All the original glass was gone; some of the windows had been decorated with colored square borders. They found colored glass shards in the flower bed below them. They installed new clear-paned windows but had a stained-glass window designed for the prominent dining room bay and above the entrance door. The small main-floor bathroom may have been carved out of the pantry when indoor plumbing was brought into the house early in the century. For convenience and the luxury of a large bathtub, they

*Silk curtains frame the bowed window of the front parlor. Aesthetic period late-19th-century papers with cherry blossoms were inspired by Japanese design.*

decided to turn a fourth bedroom upstairs into a large bathroom.

The fir floors were unsalvageable and, for expediency and cost savings, were patched and carpeted. However, the couple stripped and replaced woodwork that had been painted, punctured with lock hardware, and exposed to the weather. They replaced exterior wood siding that had been stolen for firewood. "One day we came here and there was a child taking one of the porch pillars down the street." Not everything was missing. Although the Eastlake style sun ray millwork at the peak of the gable was gone, fish scale shingles were still there. Front porch and stair hall balusters were missing, but the upstairs porch was intact, as was the paneling of the rounded north bay.

With the essential work complete, in 1991 Zita started on a path that has turned the house into a showroom for historic wallpapers reproduced by Bradbury & Bradbury, a company based in Benicia, California. Each room has its own period style, from the Aesthetic period parlor to the Neoclassical

entrance hallway to the Anglo-Japanese den, the William Morris period dining room, and the deer and rabbit decorated master bedroom. Rooms have as many as 10 different patterns of hand-silk-screened papers in wall and ceiling treatments.

Zita had been collecting antiques for a long time, but it took finding this house to really figure out her period: high and late Victorian. Nevertheless, the house is filled with objects that span the late 19th and early 20th centuries. "It's not reasonable to think that someone moved in one day and bought everything brand new. They brought things from other houses and may have lived here for decades, acquiring pieces over time."

### The Lofts: Pioneer Square Adaptation

The Lofts was designed by the architectural firm of Josenhans & Allan and built in 1904 by the Trustee Company. In its lifetime, it has housed various businesses, including a paper company, wholesale pharmaceuticals, and office furniture. In its 1995–97 renovation and upgrade by Triple T Group and ARC Architects for Charlwood Pacific Properties Ltd., the removal of gray paint revealed the original beauty of its fir plank flooring, supporting masonry, and old-growth fir ceiling beams and floor joists. Each of the floors is divided into two front units with approximately 1,900 square feet of space and two rear units with approximately 1,300 square feet. Satterberg Desonier Domo Interior Design worked with the architects' layouts and chose lighting, paint colors, and finish materials.

One couple, Bob and Nancy Woodford, bought

*One of the original brick archways leads from the entrance foyer into the kitchen. The advantage of the top-floor units is the skylights that bring light into the deep interiors.*

*From Third Avenue S., the brick facade of the Lofts looks nearly as it did in 1904. Chicago style pivoting windows are still in place, although they now hold thermopane glass.*

## CITY AND COUNTY COME OF AGE

### A Capital House for Capitol Hill

The family names associated with palatial residences on Seattle's Millionaire's Row recall the days when lumber, banking, shipbuilding, and retail were rapidly turning the city into an up-to-date metropolis. Stretching along Fourteenth Avenue E. leading into Volunteer Park from E. Aloha to E. Prospect Streets were the homes of Nathan Eckstein, a vice president of Schwabacher Brothers Hardware; Thomas Russell, the owner of Tenino Stone Quarries; Cyrus Clapp of a major investment company; David Skinner, the founder of the Port Blakely Mill Company and Skinner & Eddy Shipyard; W. A. Stuart, founder of Pacific Coast Condensed Milk Company (later to become Carnation); and C. H. Cobb, lumber company owner. Topping the list was James Moore, the developer of much of this area of Capitol Hill.

While their homes were distinctive, none probably got into the press in as infamous a way as did the $100,000 home of George H. Parker, completed in 1909 by architect Frederick Sexton. At more than 7,500 square feet, it was one of the most impressive Colonial Revival houses in the city. But the money that built the house had come from a stock embezzlement scheme, which landed George H. Parker in prison.

Parker's death in 1926 was just the beginning of another colorful chapter in the history of the house. In 1929, his widow sold it to Eugen Fersen, a Russian baron and the only acknowledged illegitimate son of Czar Nicholas II. He brought a large amount of furniture from his Paris apartment, where he had the good fortune to be staying at the time of the Russian Revolution. The 1,000-room family castle in St. Petersburg had been confiscated by the Bolsheviks, and this Capitol Hill house became its substitute, bedecked with red and purple satin festoons—the colors of the Russian royal family. In the 1940s, Fersen founded a religious organization called The Lightbearers, and the house became its headquarters for the next 40 years.

David and Ruth Walsh McIntyre were housahunting in 1987, and they remember well their first view of the draped and darkened interior, with its equally dark, heavily carved furnishings. The elderly followers of Fersen, who had died in 1956, continued the religious rites; they wore black robes, carried

and combined two rear top-floor units to provide 2,650 square feet of space to make their dream of living in downtown Seattle a reality. As a warehouse, the building had a handsome supporting masonry wall down its center punctuated with arches. These were filled in to make solid walls between units. But in the Woodfords' double unit, arches serve as connectors to the entrance foyer/living area, the kitchen/dining area, and the master bedroom.

The shaft that housed a water-powered hydraulic elevator is now a conversation piece. It was actually used during reconstruction, before the elevator cab was dismantled. Plans had called for enclosing the shaft, but the Woodfords said, "no," and its pulley wheels, suspended from the top of the shaft, have become a defining feature between the dining room and master bedroom.

Their cost for the two units was just under $500,000. But, as Nancy is quick to point out, "If we had found a high-rise with this square footage and a view, it would have cost a million." And the advantage of this small building is that they have few neighbors and less building traffic. "What I think is so exciting is that we are in a huge city, but because of the neighborhood feeling of Pioneer Square, if you want to get involved in the community, you can."

*The Colonial Revival house has two-story-high Corinthian columns and pilasters. Originally, the facade was covered with wood shingles instead of stucco. It is missing balustrades on second- and third-floor porches.*

*A Rookwood della robbia fruit frieze frames the fireplace in the oak-paneled dining room. The Arts and Crafts era chandelier is by Tiffany Company.*

candles, worshipped the morning light, and kept the windows permanently blacked out. Signs of the zodiac were painted in the basement billiard room. A Rasputin-like portrait of the late baron, with dark sunken eyes and prominent cheekbones, was a constant reminder of their founder.

Fortunately for the McIntyres, the house had been maintained in a state of benign neglect—what the new owners refer to kindly as "a patina of grime." They saw past that to appreciate rooms which combine the formality of Classical Revival style and beautifully finished hardwoods with the informality and rustic qualities of the American Arts and Crafts period.

The drawing room and the library are dressed in mahogany. In the drawing room, Moravian tile designed by Henry Chapman Mercer brings the Arts and Crafts period to the formal Classical Revival mantel. In the bookcase-lined library with its Romanesque hearth, Rookwood scenic tiles of shoreline, trees, and distant mountains are catalogue items that recall Lake Washington Boulevard. Also original to the room are lighting fixtures with scenic painted shades.

In the oak-paneled dining room, the ceiling is painted with oak leaves, palms, and roses. The fireplace surround is composed of Rookwood glazed tile in a fruit pattern. An Art Nouveau Arts and Crafts period bronze chandelier hangs above the dining room table and chairs—the original Parker pieces, which passed to the baron and then came to the new owners. By the time the McIntyres moved in, the tapestries on the upper walls had deteriorated and needed to be removed.

In the entry hall, a mirrored glass ceiling was an early-day change made by Parker. He had gone on an

ocean voyage and, on seeing the captain's dining room, decided that he wanted this mirror treatment. Two granddaughters remembered the house when they were little girls and heard stories passed down. There was a furor over that change, but Parker had stood his ground. Fortunately, his pleasure in the stained-glass window in the stair landing did not waiver, and it still exists. Parker's granddaughters recall that grandfather insisted on the Tiffany Company doing that and the lighting fixtures.

The baron covered up the magnificent hand-painted and -stenciled pendant designs by gluing red velvet onto the walls of the entrance hall, now the focus of restoration efforts. When the tattered fabric was removed from the stair hall walls, damage occurred to the stenciled patterns beneath. Artist Debbie Huls re-created them to match the intact ones surrounding the entrance door. She brought the pattern into the main-floor powder room as well. Huls also applied her talents in the oak-paneled breakfast room, which had been a damp space with peeling canvas wall coverings.

While restoration is the intent in the principal rooms, the McIntyres have had to completely reconstruct the kitchen based upon clues in the butler's pantry, where the cabinetry and flooring were intact. David made molds of original hardware in order to duplicate this for the new cabinets. The couple had most of the stained fir molding reconstructed too, so it is difficult to determined where the old ends and the new begins. The complex pattern of gold, pink, black, and celadon green hexagons that composed the original floor was also reproduced.

The McIntyres have just scratched the surface of repairs and restoration. But as they move from room to room and recount the "before" and "after" stories, it's clear that the pleasure has been in the learning process, and in seeing the results as, under their watchful custodianship, the rooms come out of the dark ages of the baron into the polish and shine that greeted the Parkers in 1909.

## Authentic Arts and Crafts

Seattle's older homes are usually remodeled and renovated. Rarely do owners take the time or devote academic scholarship to faithfully restore, replicate, and reconstruct, using authentic reproduction pieces when the right hardware, molding, or doorknob is not available. Cost and time have a lot to do with such decisions, but the curiosity to delve into the history of the house, its style, and the period in which it was built is also involved. For Olivia Dresher, restoration and reconstruction seemed the only way to go.

When she acquired her 1918 Wallingford Craftsman house in 1992 for $168,000, the two-bedroom, one-bath house had been the testing ground for the previous owner/architect's "when I get to it" school of refurbishing. The exterior and nearly every room were "in process"—taken apart but never completed. Olivia recalls: "It was a complete disaster. Wires were hanging everywhere, ceilings were falling down, woodwork was painted over. We truly rescued a dead house."

The upside of its condition, and the principal reason Olivia had bought the house in the first place. were that, after looking at nearly 100 houses, "This was the only one that hadn't been remuddled totally." At least most of the woodwork and a good number of the windows were intact. And there were no cottage cheese ceilings. Still, Olivia says, "It took vision to see what this house would become." She, her design partner, Victor Munoz, and interior designer Laurie Taylor of Ivy Hill Interiors made the transformation happen over the next two years, ably assisted by Chambers Building Contractors.

Olivia had been interested in English and American Arts and Crafts for some time prior to purchasing the house. But it was the house project that focused her interest. "All of us who have been working on this house have a love and appreciation for Craftsman homes and Craftsman style, and once we had the opportunity to work on a house, we really started doing research. In the process I must have discovered 100 different resources. I read everything, called people, walked around neighborhoods, and studied Craftsman houses. My collection of books kept growing. Laurie discovered American Bungalow magazine."

In the restoration, they decided to use authentic period pieces wherever possible, and they involved many craftspeople and artists who specialize in Arts and Crafts period building parts, hardware, furniture, textiles, wall and floor coverings, and accessories. When they couldn't find what they wanted locally, they tracked down the best sources nationally.

On the main floor, the living room, dining room, kitchen, and stair received attention first. The stairs needed additional support posts to hold them up, and a design in a Stickley bungalow book did the trick. Improper south-facing windows were replaced with double-pane windows that closely matched the originals in the living room, with new brass hardware to match. Oak floors were refinished, the mottled buff bricks of the fireplace were cleaned, and cracked floor tiles were replaced. William Morris pattern reproduction rugs now carpet the living room, music room, and stairs. Heavy draperies, or "portieres," were made to separate the dining and living rooms from the kitchen.

The dining room was the least altered room in the house, although its fir box beams had been painted, along with the built-in buffet. The furniture had long ago lost drawers and beveled-glass doors. By researching similar built-ins of the period, they reconstructed the hutch, its dividers, doors, and cab-

*Simplicity of design and honesty of materials characteristic of the Arts and Crafts period are reflected in the living room.*

*William Morris wallpapers, refinished beams and sideboard, and an embroidered portiere make the dining room one of the purest Arts and Crafts spaces in this house. French doors open to a new office.*

inet faces. They bought reproduction hinges for the hutch and for the period kitchen. The refinished wood beams and moldings were paired with Compton wallpapers by William Morris to make this one of the most authentic-looking Arts and Crafts period rooms.

For Olivia, it was important that nothing in the house be modern. "All the latches and the switch plates are old-fashioned. I don't have anything modern in the kitchen, no garbage disposal or dishwasher. I have a 1923 stove." She had the five panel doors that were part of the original house replicated. Paneled and painted kitchen cabinets have new nickel pulls. Even the refrigerator/freezer has old-fashioned panels and cane to match the cabinets. In expanding the house, Olivia had the beams and wood trim of the dining room replicated for her office, opted for turn-of-the-century fixtures in the powder room, and chose to construct an old-fashioned back porch instead of the more typical wood deck.

Upstairs, the master bedroom is now Olivia's library and music teaching room. When she purchased the house, wood windows and trim moldings in this room had been painted white, and there were no fixtures. The only untouched feature was the window seat under the ribbon of east-facing windows. A sloping corner of the room underneath the roof now shelters a storage closet for Olivia's musical instruments. New divided light windows on the south wall reproduce the appearance of the original windows. The room features some wonderful Arts and Crafts period touches, including a Mackintosh rose frieze

and matching curtains and stenciled and embroidered pillows.

Olivia recalls the nearly two years of weekly meetings to talk about fabrics, wall and floor coverings, and paint colors, and the expensive decisions made along the way: over $300,000 for basic construction and reconstruction and an additional $12,000 for interior design work, exclusive of designer fees. "It was extravagant and exciting and evolved in unexpected directions. Every single nook and cranny has been given total attention. Nothing has been slapped together. Every little detail has been totally researched and given care, down to the bumper stops and the latches. It's just the way I wanted it."

### Beaux Arts Village

In 1908, fifty acres of forest on the east shore of Lake Washington was purchased by a local group calling themselves the Beaux Arts Society. Cofounders Frank Calvert and Alfred Renfro planned a community of artists, architects, and craftspeople where they could "live together, work together, and play together." Their interest in the popular American Arts and Crafts movement and obvious efforts to emulate Elbert Hubbard's famed Roycroft community near Buffalo, New York, would result in Craftsman styled homes on half-acre lots in the verdant woodland setting. Over one thousand feet of waterfront was retained for a community park and boat moorage.

At the center of the project, 10 acres was set aside for Atelier Square, which was to eventually include workshops for the Beaux Arts Academy in an Arts and Crafts building, a clubhouse, tennis court, and cricket and sketching ground "for healthful recreation by members of the Beaux Arts Society." The clubhouse was to be completely outfitted with furniture, fixtures, tapestries, and accessories made in the Arts and Crafts workshop. This part of the plan was never accomplished.

The emblem of the Beaux Arts Society was the Beaux Arts cottage, an Arts and Crafts bungalow partly constructed of logs. According to the founders, "It is a refinement of the pioneer cabin of the West, and emblematic of the 'home.'" Calvert and Renfro were the first to build their rustic woodland chalets, and other members followed suit.

One of these early homes, a two and one-half story log and cedar building, also has the distinction of some notoriety. In 1915, it was rented to a yoga cult, and alleged nudist practices and illicit behaviors

*This Beaux Arts Village log and cedar home was inspired by the American Arts and Crafts movement.*

made Seattle headlines for many weeks. This 3,000-square-foot home was bought by Marnie Ross and her husband in 1989. They engaged local architect Robert Hoshide to direct the extensive renovation work. Some very basic things had to be done. The "monstrous octopus in the basement" had to be replaced with a fuel-efficient gas furnace. Flexible duct pipe was woven into whatever wall spaces were available. That sometimes meant building up the floors of closets or placing closets back to back with duct spaces between them. The log construction made insulation very difficult. They needed to allow for air circulation, especially under the roof, to prevent rot.

Traces of a 1940 era remodel had to be undone. While the exterior log and cedar and most of the windows were intact, the window frames had been painted an inappropriate turquoise. Inside, the beautiful river rock chimney of the fireplace had been hidden by a painted plywood wall of shelves and china cabinets when the open porch at the back of the house was converted into a dining room. The original dining room had been used as a bedroom/study by former owners, who installed French doors to separate it from the living room. The lower part of the stairway had been enclosed. And

*The lower stairway banisters and log risers were newly made to match the remaining originals.*

*The granite and river stone hearth, with its segmental arch and log mantel, is the focus of the living room, giving it the ambiance of a hunting lodge.*

lowered ceilings hid the roof timbers and board and batten.

According to Marnie, determining what had to be done was largely trial and error. "The contractor made holes in various places and we peered inside. It was a crowbar experience. What started to be a budget of $50,000 rapidly turned into a budget of $150,000. We wound up removing added ceilings to expose the wood beams in the bedrooms upstairs. We brought in new logs and a timber post to replace the wall between the kitchen and dining room. New hand-cut banisters were made to match the upper banisters and split-log steps."

The family was lucky to find a talented finish carpenter who designed and crafted the stairway. They hired a log finder to search out logs of specific diameters. The stone hearth was beautiful, but poor maintenance had resulted in two chimney fires. The chimney box had to be rebuilt. The wood floors needed some patching and refinishing. Because several walls were removed, they needed to add new flooring and cover up the location of old heat registers. The balcony overlooking the family room (the enclosed back porch) also needed attention.

Since the house had no fixtures, they chose new Arts and Crafts reproduction sconces and ceiling fixtures. They augmented this period lighting with track lighting in the living room that illuminates the granite and river stone hearth. As with all the other new systems, wiring was difficult to do, since there were no spaces between the floors for laying new electrical wires.

After six months in full-blown construction and an equal amount of time in only slightly less chaotic conditions, the house was done. But even as order was restored, the couple began planning a major family room addition, which Robert Hoshide of Hoshide Williams designed and which earned the grand prize in the National Trust Great American Homes Awards program in 1995.

## Bungalow Meets Prairie

Mount Baker Park was the first city neighborhood to be integrated into the Olmsted Brothers' comprehensive plan for parks and boulevards. That accounts for the pleasant way in which streets follow hillside contours and afford wonderful views of Lake Washington and the Cascade Mountains.

In 1907, the Hunter Tract Improvement Company sought to create an exclusive upper-income residential district adjacent to the park. They did this through deed restrictions that limited the number of houses on a lot, the minimum cost for these houses, a requirement that every house have a basement, and insisting there be "no outhouses or stables, and no animals, except domestic pets."

*The Ellsworth Storey house was first published in* Bungalow Magazine *in March 1916.*

BUNGALOW MAGAZINE

25 CENTS

MARCH 1916

SUPPLEMENT BUNGALOW WITH COMPLETE WORKING DRAWINGS, SPECIFICATIONS AND BILL OF MATERIAL

The firm's efforts paid off. The area has an outstanding mix of architect-designed residences and builder homes and bungalows. One of the latter was designed by one of the city's best-loved architects, Ellsworth Storey (1879–1960).

The home of Jerry and Vreni Watt, built in 1916 and the featured building in Jud Yoho's *Bungalow Magazine* of March 1916, shows the influence upon Storey of the Arts and Crafts movement and of the Prairie style architecture of Frank Lloyd Wright in Storey's native Chicago. The Watts' home is a three-bedroom, 1,700-square-foot, stucco California bungalow with references to the Prairie style in the wide projecting eaves, the bold square columns that support the pergola, and the bands of windows, which, all told, number 37, and make the house into one great sunroom.

As a featured home in the *Bungalow Magazine,* this bungalow had been photographed inside and out, every board and nail used in the construction of the house was documented, and full working drawings and details were provided so that "any capable builder should experience no difficulty in duplicating this bungalow." This article provided the Watts with invaluable documentation when they took on the task of undoing the damage of previous owners' upgrades to kitchen and bathroom.

Outside, brick window boxes had been removed. A green fiberglass canopy was supported by two 4 x 4 posts, the original large-scaled columns having long ago disappeared. The new owners have rebuilt the entrance columns and trellis, opting for slightly smaller columns and a wet weather glass canopy. They took to heart the *Bungalow Magazine* criticism of this part of the original design, "the supporting pil-

*The house today looks very much as it did originally, although the trellised canopy has been rebuilt, and the pylons are slightly smaller in scale.*

lars look far too massive for the light weight which they are expected to support."

Inside, the brick-trimmed fireplace had been painted over. French doors to the dining room had been removed. None of the lighting fixtures remained, nor did any of the wood paneling in the dining room. At some point the upper half of the wall between the kitchen and dining room had been removed for a bar and pass-through, and the kitchen had received a 1960 era makeover. The bathroom had also been redone, and green vinyl covered the walls.

In reconstructing the kitchen, the Watts rebuilt the breakfast nook, and their architect, Joseph Greif, designed cabinetry that looks as though it had always been there. But instead of the simple glass—pane cabinets shown in the *Bungalow Magazine* article, these cabinets incorporate the distinctive diagonal and triangular details that were Storey's trademark.

## THE DAWN OF THE MODERN ERA

### Housing between the Wars

The push and pull of "progress" in America is told in its residential communities developed between the world wars. Architects were exposed to the exciting theoretical ideas of European designers—Walter Gropius, Ludwig Mies van der Rohe, Robert Mallet-Stevens, and Le Corbusier—who promoted austere cubist houses with flat roofs, white stucco walls, minimal ornament, and large expanses of glass. Le Corbusier's famed demonstration residence, described as a "machine for living," evoked awe and controversy at the Paris Exposition of Decorative and Industrial Arts in 1925.

American architects may have been excited by these design breakthroughs, but rarely did they have the opportunity to explore the possibilities on their own turf. Their ideas would invariably be tempered by a client who had grown up in a Tudor Revival, Colonial, or Georgian house and sought a similar residence to prove that he or she had "made it." Seattle, after all, was not freewheeling Los Angeles, which had a less rigid, more open attitude toward newness. Beginning with Frank Lloyd Wright's concrete block houses in the late 1920s, Richard Neutra, Rudolph Shindler, and later Charles Eames made modernism a visible reality in the Hollywood hills.

But in most of America, homemakers were reading Elsie de Wolfe's *The House in Good Taste,* which encouraged comfortable traditional interiors. At the same time, the popular magazines *House Beautiful* and *House and Garden* were mouthpieces and sales tools for historically inspired residential design. Seattle simply followed the traditional attitudes shaping residential neighborhoods throughout America. Between the wars, it was a fertile ground for romantic brick and half-timbered English and French cottages and country homes and Spanish colonial

*Thiry's design predates the "split level" houses that would become the American suburban home dream after World War II. From the entry, stairs lead up to the main floor and down to the family room.*

mini-mansions. But not all architects chose to follow the expected norm.

One Seattle architect who was excited about the new architecture and made efforts to make it his own was Paul Thiry. Thiry is respected for his valuable contributions as supervising architect of the Century 21 exposition grounds (now Seattle Center) and for the designs of the Coliseum on the site, the Museum of History and Industry in Montlake, and many churches, including St. Demetrios Greek Orthodox Church. His talents in the broader field of urban design led to master plans for Western Washington University in Bellingham and for Pennsylvania Avenue in Washington, D.C.

In the mid-1930s, however, just beginning his own practice, he built houses for himself and other clients in traditional neighborhoods like Capitol Hill, Leschi, Denny Blaine, and Madison Park. He and contractor Edwin C. Edwards developed some double lots on the hillside above Lake Washington Boulevard near Denny Blaine. Several were historic revival styled homes that "fit right in." But Thiry's home and the home he designed for Edwards were in the "modern" style and drew mixed reviews from many passersby. Even as late as 1979, former owner

*A curved surface makes the original fireplace wall a sculptural feature. To the right, the glass block that once was part of an outside wall now faces into the sunroom.*

*The white modernist box with corner windows was a radical departure from typical Seattle homes.*

Eve Alvord recalls a friend's terse comments, "Oh, that house—maybe graphics will help."

Current owners, artist Norman Lundin and his wife, Dr. Shirley Johnson, are enjoying the fruits of the labors of Chap and Eve Alvord III, who lived there over a decade and directed two periods of expansion and refurbishing. Before beginning their project, they contacted Thiry, then in his eighties and still managing an architectural office. Eve recalls telling him, "We want the addition to stay with your vision." Thiry made some preliminary sketches but it fell to architect Rob Widmeyer to realize the vision in 1981 and 1987.

Widmeyer appreciated the historic importance of this house. It represented "an architectural experiment, with its open plan, simple expression of structure, and industrial sash. It expressed confidence in the new modernism. It was also a house that was easy to alter and make additions to." In 1981, a master bedroom, breakfast nook, and sunroom were added to the rear of the house. In 1987, the master bedroom was extended further, above a new main floor library and a basement guest room.

Widmeyer used Thiry's vocabulary of simple boxes, punctuated with corner industrial sash windows, varied ceiling heights and raised areas, curved walls, metal railings, and occasional glass block to make his addition read like the original while allowing it to grow to approximately 3,800 square feet. New aluminum thermopane windows were installed with the same proportions as the original metal sash, and the mullions were painted black on the outside to read as closely as possible to the originals. The original glass block in the living room was matched for the adjoining sun room and a curving glass block wall defines a breakfast nook that replaces an exteri-

or brick patio. By using glass French doors to separate the living and dining rooms from the sunroom and library, the architect has succeeded in retaining the open feeling of the original house. The exterior facade, painted taupe instead of the cool white of the original, is less strident in its assertion of "modern." But the house remains a remarkably crisp, clean, and fresh piece of architecture, as up-to-date today as it was ahead of its time in 1936 Seattle. It is a credit to Thiry's vision.

## The Wright Place

In 1956, on less than an acre in Normandy Park covered in blackberry vine, salal, and seedlings, arose a remarkably sophisticated residence that is both prominent architectural statement and respectful of its wooded bluff. The owners, Bill and Elizabeth Tracy, knew they could count on their architect—Frank Lloyd Wright—to do that.

The Tracys had seen and admired many of Wright's buildings, especially his "textile" block houses, such as the Aline Barnsdall residence (1917–21) and Charles Ennis residence (1924–26) in Los Angeles. Textured concrete block provided Wright with a versatile medium for a rich tapestry of ornamental forms. By the time the Tracys were ready to build their own home, Wright had gained national attention for his Usonian homes. Begun in the late 1930s and continuing through the 1950s, his solution to affordable housing consisted of a standard plan based on a modular system. It usually consisted of a living/dining room designed around a central hearth, a utilitarian kitchen, and three bedrooms squeezed into 1,200 square feet and incorporating built-in furniture and storage.

But Wright hadn't been their first choice. They

*Construction proceeds with the raising of the exterior walls.*

*Concrete blocks form windows, walls, and the roof of the Tracy residence. Ceiling heights vary from 6 1/2 to 11 1/2 feet.*

had brought Seattle architect Milton Stricker out to the site, thinking he might do the house. When he saw the wooded view lot, Stricker, a Wright apprentice at the Taliesin Fellowship, thought it was so dramatic that he suggested Wright design it. Stricker wrote on their behalf, describing them and the site. It helped their case when the Tracys told Wright that Ray Brandes had agreed to build the house for them. Brandes had already completed a house to Wright's design in Issaquah in 1951.

While Wright never came out to see the lot, with good aerial photographs, topographic maps that revealed the elevations and views, and a list of facts the clients drew up ("He wanted a complete description of our lifestyle and us"), Wright went to work on a 1,200 square foot, three-bedroom house on one level. Bill remembers, "When the preliminaries came in we were overjoyed. . . . One of the remarkable things about this design was what that genius was able to make out of such a small lot." Construction came to $25,000—not including the countless hours it took the couple to manufacture the blocks.

The house got off to a slow start. They had approached Wright in 1954, but they needed another year to gather enough money for the project. Ray Brandes cleared the lot in April 1955. Into construc-

tion in the late summer, there was a steel strike, and they couldn't get rebar for the concrete. That caused a delay of several weeks. But once they got started, it went rapidly, taking a little more than four months to build. The couple moved in the day after Thanksgiving, 1956.

Bill, whose background was in architecture and civil engineering, naturally took special interest in the condition of the concrete used in the blocks. "I had test cylinders poured about every month." He added more rebar than was called for in the codes, and made the ceiling blocks an inch thicker than had been stipulated in Wright's drawings.

The couple built all the blocks themselves (1,700 all told, in 11 different forms) on acreage that adjoined their rented duplex. They took the block drawings to a metal fabricator, Century Metalworks, where they made shop drawings for steel forms. Milton Stricker made some of the plywood forms. Elizabeth Tracy remembers the time-consuming task because each block had to be exact and the forms had to be perfect. "I made blocks in the morning. Bill come home from work and after dinner he would pull what I had made and he'd make some. We did that every day for five days out of the week. You had to keep the forms in process all the time. The wood-

*The west-facing side of the house is defined by a series of French doors divided by textile block piers, with an operable corner door. The dining room table and chairs were constructed from Wright's design drawings.*

en forms tended to take up moisture, would get swelled and rough. Then you couldn't pull them for danger of breaking the block. I would spend the afternoons refinishing them, sanding them down, varnishing them. He [Bill] finally got the idea of covering them with sheet aluminum."

Ray Brandes rented a truck with a hydraulic tailgate to move the blocks to the site, where they were unloaded on high ground. A handcart and gangplanks were used to move the blocks from there to the construction site. With roof blocks weighing 160 pounds and parapet blocks (the blocks joining the roof and walls) weighing 180 pounds, they were very difficult to hoist. They worked on steel scaffolding with six by six timbers on top. The building varies in height from 6'6" in bedrooms, 8'6" in living and dining areas, and 11'6" in kitchen and bathroom (blocks are 1 foot high and base block is 6 inches). Brandes constructed the low roof first and moved up to the higher roofs from that. Elizabeth watched the building process and recalls, "when it came to lining ceiling blocks, they worked days getting those exact."

In theory, Wright's blocks were intended to be a modular system that could be efficiently constructed to provide an inexpensive housing solution. The Tracys' construction experience negated that. "It's a good way to build a work of art, but it's not practical. . . . The blocks have to be handmade. Finding a contractor able to put them together is unrealistic. Only about 23 of these textile block buildings were completed; they are too difficult to put up. They are so heavy, and there are no mortar joints between the blocks, so they had to be precisely located. That posed quite a problem, getting a 180 pound object accurately located. The completed roof weighs in at 37 tons. When he [Ray] finished this building, he said he'd never build another one and he justified himself by saying 'I'd much rather pick up a two by four than a concrete block.'"

Brandes and his crew did all the construction and the interior woodwork of solid redwood and redwood plywood. Wright sent design plans for furniture, as well. While Tracy had little experience in woodworking, he built living room seating and dining room chairs, and Elizabeth finished them. Wright's drawings also called for indirect lighting, using light boxes hidden within bookshelves and piers. Bill Tracy recalls, "When I looked at the electrical drawings and saw no ceiling lights, I really wondered if they hadn't made a mistake. Then I realized that Wright was well known for his lighting and resolved to go ahead and build it as he wanted. It's been very satisfactory."

The house is compact but comfortable, unlike some of Wright's work, where very narrow hallways and low ceilings can spark claustrophobia. The concrete block and redwood wall system also does not accommodate art well. Bill Tracy puts it, "The structure is so decorative, that when you try to add anything more it's really difficult." Of course this had been Wright's intent. He had once insisted, "Furniture, pictures, and bric-a-brac are unnecessary because the walls can be made to include them or be them."

The decorative quality of the materials—the contrasting dark wood and light concrete, the vertical and horizontal planes and angles formed by the textile block—has made it a pleasure for forty years according to Elizabeth. "We have new experiences almost every day in this house because of the shadows and the picturesque patterns that are formed. We never tire of it." Bill agrees, "Wright told some client, 'You'll see something different in your house every day,' and I know what he means. It's very true."

*The Burke Building demolition, 1971.*

# APPENDICES

## APPENDIX A

### OBITUARIES

It would take many pages to list significant local buildings that have been lost in the past 150 years as natural disasters (fire and earthquake) and man-made change (regrading, highways, commercial and residential construction) have reshaped the topography, replaced older buildings, and filled open space. This section simply acknowledges some losses over the past few decades that, because they are recent, may jog the memories of local residents.

### *Demolished Designated Landmarks*

#### Green Lake Public School
2400 N. Sixty-fifth Street
*James Stephen, 1901–2; 1907*

In an effort to accommodate the growth of Seattle's school-age population, the Seattle School Board in 1901 adapted a model school plan by architect James Stephen that would allow its frame grammar school buildings to expand as enrollments grew. The plan was first implemented with the erection of Green Lake Public School, completed in 1902. Green Lake was built in two phases, starting with a central two-story frame portion and a north wing and ending with a complementary eight-room south wing in 1907 that generated an I-shape. Green Lake was enriched with an Ionic portico leading to a round arched portal, a pediment with elliptical window, and refined lintels, cornice moldings, and a continuous entablature and cornice with dentil molding. It was demolished by the Seattle School District for open space.

#### Jolly Roger Roadhouse
8721 Lake City Way N.E.
*Designer unknown, 1929*

This was the last extant and intact roadhouse in the greater Seattle area. Built in 1929 on what was the Bothell Highway, the roadhouse was a response to the advent of the automobile and the Prohibition era. Roadhouses sprang up along highways outside city limits to illegally dispense liquor, as well as pro-

vide a place for dining, dancing, and other "wicked" entertainments. The Jolly Roger, with its white maple dance floor, bar, and secret rooms for gambling and prostitution, was a fortified enclosure; its architecture included a setback octagonal lookout tower that allowed the management to observe the highway and warn the guests of a police raid. The Jolly Roger was a reminder of the Roaring Twenties lifestyle, Prohibition, and the advent of businesses catering to the automobile trade, which has so dramatically changed the landscape of America. It was destroyed in an arson fire.

### Martha Washington School
6612 Fifty-seventh Avenue S.
*Floyd Naramore, 1920–21; 1928*

Martha Washington School consisted of three Georgian brick buildings that originally housed the administration office, classrooms, dormitory, and gymnasium of a school operated by the Seattle School District for delinquent and troubled girls. The prototype for this school had been developed at the turn of the century by Major and Mrs. Cicero Newell to aid neglected, indigent, and unfortunate children. In 1919, the school district purchased nine acres of land south of Bailey Peninsula (now Seward Park) and developed the grounds for a Girls Parental School. Apart from the buildings, the grounds included a rare grove of Oregon white oak, which, though represented west of the Cascades from the Columbia River north through Puget Sound, are not present in Seattle to any extent. The site also included one of the largest madrona trees in the city and perhaps in the county as well. The buildings were razed by the Parks Department for open space, despite the preparation of an alternative building use feasibility study by Historic Seattle.

### Music Hall Theatre
702 Olive Way
*Sherwood Ford, 1927–28*

Despite its youth and size, Seattle has a remarkably vivid and broad-ranging reputation as the home and training ground for theater entrepreneurs and designers who ultimately established enormous national and international empires: John Cort, Alexander Pantages, Sullivan and Considine, B. Marcus Priteca, and E. W. Houghton. Only a few of Seattle's many legitimate stage houses, vaudeville and motion picture palaces, and downtown and neighborhood motion picture theaters are still intact. The Music Hall was one of the casualties. Designed with a flamboyant Spanish Baroque exterior, with fluted columns and rich decorative bas-reliefs surrounding its colored-glass windows, this showplace hosted Fanny Brice, George Jessel, Martha Graham, Yehudi Menuhin, Katherine Hepburn, and many other stars of the world of music and drama under various changing ownerships. Interior features included a mock timber ceiling in the lobby, ornate chandeliers, and scrollwork surrounding the proscenium. The theme of Spanish exploration was exploited in the maritime images of ships' wheels and prows that embellished the organ grilles. A lovely mezzanine lounge extended along the Olive Street side of the building, lit by the filtered light of tall colored glass windows. The Clise family, owners of the property, took action to eliminate controls over the landmark structure so it could be replaced by a hotel. Lengthy Landmarks Preservation Board meetings and hearings before the city hearings examiner finally resulted in a ruling for the owners. The building was demolished, the hotel plans disintegrated, and the site served as an interim parking lot. A commercial and residential project is now being constructed.

### Temple de Hirsch Sinai
Fifteenth Avenue E. and E. Union Street
*J. F. Everett, 1907–8*

Temple de Hirsch Sinai congregation is the oldest (1897) and the largest Jewish congregation in the Puget Sound region. Its members include outstanding civic leaders and businessmen who have contributed greatly to the growth of the community and to the Northwest. Named for Baron de Hirsch, a benefactor who assisted Eastern European Jews in their efforts to reach America and start new lives, the

*Temple de Hirsch Sinai sanctuary, 1908.*

temple was completed in 1908 in the Neoclassical style. Clad in buff-colored brick with terra-cotta trim, its west front consisted of a Doric columned entrance portico flanked by two substantial bell towers. Both towers originally terminated in rich Baroque belfries and cupolas, later removed. The main sanctuary was neo-Palladian in form and detailing. Oriented east-west, it terminated at the east end in the rostrum and bema, surmounted by the ark and Torah, above which was a stained-glass window of Moses. There was a shallow barrel-vaulted cross-ribbed ceiling with four equal cross-vaulted bays supported by Tuscan columns. Balconies were placed at the sides and rear of the sanctuary, glass lunettes were located at the ends of the cross vaults, and extremely high arched windows appeared on both the north and south walls. The temple, long vacant and decaying, was demolished in 1992, and only a few remnants of the dignified facade stand watch over the site today.

### Landmarks No Longer Listed or Controlled by the City of Seattle

### First United Methodist Church
811 Fifth Avenue
*James Schack & Daniel Huntington, 1907–10*

The Seattle First United Methodist Congregation, founded in 1853, outgrew its frame church of 1855

and a more commodious, Gothic styled 1889 building at Third Avenue and Marion Street. As commerce pressed into this area of town, the church purchased a site on Fifth Avenue and Marion Street for a major building that could accommodate over 2,000 worshippers. The church broke away from tradition in a number of ways. Its Beaux Arts styling and its central plan relied upon Roman and Renaissance building forms. First Methodist was progressive in housing under one roof the functions of a major community center for its members as well as the more traditional religious functions. James Schack and Daniel Huntington designed a light-colored brick and terra-cotta facade with a distinctive orange-tile-covered central dome. The 66-foot-high sanctuary is surrounded by opalescent arched windows and ringed by seating galleries and an organ loft. At each of the four corners of the church are vestibules containing staircases leading to balconies and community rooms. The church's tile roof and dome and the undulating brick facade add color and form to the dense, high-rise character of this section of downtown.

### Swedish Tabernacle/First Covenant Church
1500 Bellevue Avenue
*John A. Creutzer, 1906*

A Swedish Mission Church was organized by Swedish immigrants in 1889. The present building, the congregation's third, is a relatively unaltered example of Renaissance-inspired eclecticism. The two and one half story rectangular base, faced in ashlar blocks of smooth-faced sandstone, is organized into bays, the central ones recessed behind engaged Tuscan columns or pilasters. A Doric entablature and a broad pediment unify the central bay. The church's most readily identifiable feature is an elliptical dome surmounted by a classical styled cupola consisting of a columned drum and a round dome. The ribbed dome is supported by a ring of marbleized columns in the large centric auditorium. A series of circular windows punctuate the lower portion of the dome between the ribs, providing natural light to the interior. A large chandelier hangs from the center of the dome. Because of its prominent location along the bend of Pike Street as it rises toward Capitol Hill, the domed church terminates an important visual corridor and strongly contributes to the distinctive identity of its surrounding neighborhood.

## W. T. *Preston* Snag Boat

Anacortes, Washington
*U.S. Army Corps of Engineers, 1915; 1940 (relocated)*

The W. T. *Preston* was built in 1915 at shipyards on Bainbridge Island and named the *Swinomish*. It is the last of a line of snag boats originating in 1880 and designed for operation in shallow water for channel clearing and dredging. It is a steam-powered stern propelled craft that has been rebuilt several times (the present hull dates from 1940), but its steam engines are original, and the ship's red, white, and black hull, tall smokestacks, and stern paddle wheels are distinctive, having the character of a Mississippi riverboat. As the *Swinomish*, this boat participated in the dredging of the government ship canal and, along with Admiral Perry's flagship, sailed through the Ballard locks and the canal on opening day in July 1917. Until its purchase by the Anacortes Museum and its relocation there, the W. T. *Preston* was a familiar site on Seattle waterways.

## S.S. *San Mateo*

Fraser River, British Columbia
*Southern Pacific; Golden Gate Ferries, 1922 (relocated and decaying)*

The *San Mateo* is a 55-car and passenger ferry with the distinction of being the last remaining steam-powered auto ferry left in the United States. Built in San Francisco in 1922 and operated there until 1940, the boat was purchased by the Puget Sound Navigation Company and transferred to the Washington State Ferry System in 1951 to operate in Washington waters. The ferry has a double-ended steel hull, wooden superstructure, and single stack located amidships and is propelled by two steam triple expansion engines. Historic Seattle Preservation and Development Authority acquired the vessel in 1976 to oversee renovation and reuse. Ownership was transferred to a private nonprofit organization, Northwest Seaport, which encouraged local interest in a maritime museum of which the *San Mateo* would be a part. Sadly, the boat was forced to move from its Lake Union moorage. It was sold to Canadian interests who have been unable to pursue restoration. It is presently decaying on the banks of the Fraser River in British Columbia.

## Designated Landmarks That Have Been Significantly Altered

### Austin A. Bell Building
2326 First Avenue
*Elmer Fisher, 1889–90 (only two exterior walls remain)*

### Brooklyn Building
1222 Second Avenue
*Designer unknown, 1890 (only two exterior walls remain)*

### Coliseum Theater
Fifth Avenue and Pike Street
*B. Marcus Priteca, 1916 (significant interior changes)*

### Italianate Victorian Pair
208–210 Thirteenth Avenue S.
Now at 1414 S. Washington Street
*Designer unknown, 1901 (one burned; the other moved)*

## Demolished Nondesignated Landmarks

In addition, a number of fine buildings that were not designated landmarks were demolished for new construction (some of which never occurred). Below is a small sampling.

### American Savings Bank/Empire Building
Second Avenue (imploded)
*A. Warren Gould, 1904-6 (demolished for First Interstate Bank)*

### Ballard High School
Fifteenth Avenue N.W. and N.W. Sixty-fifth Street
*Edgar Blair, 1912 (demolished for a new school)*

### Burke Building
Second Avenue and Marion Street
*Elmer Fisher, 1889-91 (demolished for new Federal Building)*

### Estabrook Building
Second Avenue at Union
*E. W. Houghton, 1901–2 (demolished for office block)*

### Fraser Paterson Department Store/J. C. Penney
Second Avenue at Pike Street
*John Graham Company, 1930 (demolished for Newmark Tower)*

**Hambach Country Estate**
International Blvd. north of S. 196th, city of SeaTac
*Lawton & Moldenhour, 1917–30 (demolished by city of SeaTac, no plans for site)*

**Hanson Baking Company complex**
Lower Queen Anne, included church and factory
*Various designers, dates (demolished for shopping center)*

**Hubbel Building**
704 Union Street
*Henry Bittman, 1922 (demolished for 2 Union Square)*

**Majestic/Palace Hippodrome**
Second Avenue and Spring Street
*E. W. Houghton, 1908-9 (demolished for Seattle Trust Building, now Key Bank)*

**McDougal Building (Bon Marché)/J. C. Penney**
Second Avenue at Union Street
*John Graham Company, 1912 (demolished for Newmark Tower)*

**McKay Apartment Hotel**
711 Pike Street
*John Graham Sr., 1914 (demolished for Washington State Convention and Trade Center)*

**Music Box Theatre**
Fifth Avenue between Pike and Union Streets
*Henry Bittman, 1928 (demolished for City Centre Building)*

**Perry Hotel/Cabrini Hospital**
Madison Street and Boren Avenue
*Somervell & Coté, 1906-7 (demolished for proposed senior housing, not built)*

**Savoy Hotel**
Second Avenue near University Street
*James Schack, Olof Hansen, 1905–6 (demolished for Washington Mutual Tower)*

**Waldorf Towers Hotel/Apartments**
706 Pike Street
*Henderson Ryan, 1906–7 (demolished for expansion of the Washington State Convention and Trade Center)*

# Appendix B

## The Landmark Designation Process in Seattle

In order to be designated, the object, building, or site must be at least 25 years old; must have "significant character, interest, or value as part of the development, heritage, or cultural characteristics of the city, state, or nation," and must be the location of or associated in a significant way with an important historical event or figure or with a significant aspect of the cultural, political, or economic heritage of the community, city, state, or nation; or must embody distinctive visible characteristics of an architectural style or be the outstanding work of a designer or builder; or must be an easily identifiable visual feature of the city because of its prominence of spatial location or contrasts of siting, age, or scale. Consequently, the built resource may qualify for landmark status on any number of social, cultural, architectural, or urban design related levels.

Nominations for landmark status may be requested by any person or group. Nominations are considered at Board meetings held every two weeks. Should a property be nominated, another public meeting is scheduled within 30–60 days at which time public testimony is heard. If the Board designates a property, controls and incentives for the landmark are negotiated by the Board staff with the owner. Controls define those features of the landmark to be preserved and the process of obtaining a Certificate of Approval for changes to these features. Incentives may include zoning variances or energy, fire, and building code exemptions, as well as financial incentives.

When agreements have been reached with the owner, a designating ordinance is requested from the City Council. A Hearing Examiner may modify the Board's recommendations should a property owner object to landmark status or disagree on controls and incentives.

### Design Review Guidelines

Protection of individual landmarks and properties located within landmark districts is provided by design review of modifications to the exteriors (and, in some cases, interiors) of buildings. For example, in the landmark districts of Columbia City and Harvard/Belmont, application review committees, composed in part by people who live or own businesses in these areas, review applications for alterations to protected buildings and landscape elements. They make recommendations to the Landmarks Preservation Board. Similarly, when the Department of Construction and Land Use (DCLU) reviews plans involving historic properties, these plans are circulated to the relevant committees for approval prior to the issuance of permits for construction projects. The DCLU is notified of Board actions so that plan examiners and building inspectors can refer to these decisions in approving or denying permits and in ongoing construction inspections.

The advocacy role of design review committees, the Seattle Landmarks Board and District Boards in protecting properties not directly under their jurisdiction should be noted. These groups often comment on Environmental Impact Statements when proposed developments threaten the stability and physical well-being of historic properties. Through comment, the various Boards and review committees can have significant input in protecting historic properties that may not be directly controlled by them, thus nurturing a preservation ethic among development interests.

Design review guidelines vary from district to district, depending upon the special characteristics of each area. In some cases, the Department of Interior's Standards for Rehabilitation and Guidelines for Rehabilitating Historic Buildings have been adopted, reconciling local review guidelines with state and federal design review standards.

For further information, contact the Urban Conservation Division, Department of Neighborhoods, City of Seattle, 700 Third Avenue, Seattle, WA 98104-1848. Telephone (206) 684-0228.

# Appendix C

## The Landmark Designation Process in King County

Anyone may nominate a building, site, object, structure, or district for consideration as a King County Landmark. A standard nomination form (available upon request from the King County Landmarks and Heritage Program, Office of Cultural Resources) must be completed and filed with the Historic Preservation Officer. Submitted forms are reviewed by the Historic Preservation Officer for completeness prior to being forwarded to the Landmarks and Heritage Commission for consideration. The following steps are followed to complete the nomination process:

1. Applicant files the nomination form with the Historic Preservation Officer, who reviews the form for completeness and requests additional information as needed.

2. The Historic Preservation Officer schedules a public hearing for the Landmarks and Heritage Commission to consider the nomination. The applicant, the owner, and any parties of interest are notified in writing of the meeting date at least 30 days and not more than 45 days before the meeting.

At the public hearing, the Landmarks and Heritage Commission receives evidence and hears arguments as to whether or not the nominated property meets the criteria for designation. In order to be designated, a nominated building, site, structure, object, or district must be more than 40 years old; possess integrity of location, design, setting, materials, workmanship, feeling, and association; and, meet at least one of the following criteria:

1. Be associated with events that have made a significant contribution to the broad patterns of national, state, or local history; or

2. Be associated with the life of a person or persons significant in national, state, or local history; or

3. Embody the distinctive characteristics of a type, period, style, or method of design or construction, or represent a significant and distinguishable entity whose components may lack individual distinction; or

4. Yield or be likely to yield information important in prehistory or history; or

5. Be an outstanding work of a designer or builder who has made a substantial contribution to the art.

If the Landmarks and Heritage Commission determines that the property meets the designation criteria, it identifies what elements of the property will be subject to design review. These elements, called "features of significance," typically include the exterior of the property if it is a building and the parcel on which it is sited. If significant historic interior features are present, interior space may also be included in the designation.

If a property is designated, the design controls go into effect immediately, and the property owner becomes eligible to apply for incentive programs. If the determination is negative, the proceedings terminate. A designation report is issued approving or rejecting the nomination within 14 calendar days of the public meeting at which the decision is made. The designation report is filed with the County Recorder, owner, Building and Land Division Manager, applicant, and other parties of record.

Once a property has been designated as a King County Landmark, it is subject to design review procedures any time the owner wishes to make significant changes to the designated features of significance or wishes to move or demolish the building. The process is as follows:

1. An application for a Certificate of Appropriateness is filed with the Historic Preservation Officer.

2. A consultation meeting is held between the applicant, the Historic Preservation Officer and members of the Design Review Committee of the Landmarks and Heritage Commission.

3. If all parties agree, a recommendation for approval is brought before the Landmarks and Heritage Commission at its next regularly scheduled meeting.

4. If all parties do not agree, a public hearing is scheduled by the Landmarks and Heritage Commission within 30 days of receipt of the application.

5. Notice of the public hearing is mailed at least 10 days prior to the date of the hearing.

6. The public hearing is held. If the Commission declines to issue a Certificate of Appropriateness, a written report is forwarded to the King County

Council within 90 days of the application date. Copies are sent to all parties of record and the Clerk of the Council.

The nomination, designation, Certificate of Appropriateness process, and appeal procedures are described in detail in King County Code 20.62.

All Landmarks and Heritage Commission decisions may be appealed to the King County Council within 30 days of notice of the decision.

For further information, contact the King County Landmarks and Heritage Program, King County Office of Cultural Resources, 506 Second Avenue, Suite 200, Seattle, WA 98104-2307. Telephone (206) 296-7580, 1-800-325-6165.

# APPENDIX D

## STATE AND NATIONAL REGISTER PROPERTIES IN KING COUNTY

This listing, current as of January 1999, is provided by the agency below. There may be discrepancies between the property names and locations listed here and those used in the previous chapters. For further information, contact:

Washington State Department of Community, Trade, and Economic Development
Office of Archaeology and Historic Preservation
420 Golf Club Road S.E., Suite 201
Post Office Box 48343
Olympia, WA  98504-8343
Telephone  (360) 407-0752
Fax (360) 407-6217

** indicates properties listed as National Historic Landmarks.
* indicates properties listed in the Washington Heritage Register only. All others are listed in the National Register of Historic Places and the Washington Heritage Register.

Auburn, AUBURN PUBLIC LIBRARY, 306 Auburn Avenue  (NR 8/3/82)

Auburn, OSCAR BLOMEEN HOUSE, 324 B Street Northeast  (NR 6/21/91)

Auburn, PATTON BRIDGE, State Route 18 and Green Valley Road  (NR 2/8/95)

Auburn vicinity, AARON NEELY SR. MANSION, East of Auburn off WA 18  (NR 10/15/74)

*Bellevue, WILBERTON TRESTLE, Spans Mercer Slough  (3/13/81)

Bellevue, FREDERICK WINTERS HOUSE, 2102 Bellevue Way Southeast  (NR 4/21/92)

Berne vicinity, STEVENS PASS HISTORIC DISTRICT, West of Berne, on U.S. 2 (NR 10/22/76)

*Black Diamond, BLACK DIAMOND DEPOT, 32627 Railroad and Baker Streets (2/25/83)

*Black Diamond vicinity, GREEN RIVER GORGE HISTORIC DISTRICT, Green River Gorge, south of Black Diamond  (12/9/70)

*Black Diamond vicinity, UNION STUMP, Off Robert Drive at Morgan Road  (12/9/70)

*Bothell, ANDREW AND AUGUSTA BECK-STROM LOG CABIN, Park at Bothell Landing, 9919 Northeast 180th  (12/9/70)

Bothell, BOTHELL CEMETERY, 108th Avenue Northeast and Northeast 180th Street  (NR 2/16/96)

*Bothell, BOTHELL'S FIRST SCHOOL-HOUSE, Park  (12/9/70)

*Bothell, BOTHELL-LAKE FOREST PARK BRICK HIGHWAY, Jaunita Drive and WA 522  (12/9/70)

*Bothell, S. J. BOWER HOUSE, 17611 Eason Avenue  (2/23/90)

Bothell, DR. REUBEN CHASE HOUSE, 17819 113th Avenue Northeast  (NR 8/27/90)

Bothell, FAUST-RYAN HOUSE, 18604 104th Avenue  (NR 5/19/94)

Bothell, LILLY KIRK HOUSE, 19619 100th Avenue Northeast  (NR 3/9/95)

*Bothell, W. A. HANNAN RESIDENCE, 10222 Main Street  (12/9/70)

Bothell, HARPER THORNTON HOUSE, 17424 95th Avenue NE  (NR 9/17/97)

*Bothell, JAMES SKIRVING HOUSE, 10425 East Riverside Drive  (8/21/92)

Bothell, SORENSON HOUSE, 10011 West Riverside Drive  (NR 3/9/95)

Bothell, ST. EDWARDS STATE PARK, 14445 Juanita Drive NE

*Clyde Hill, THE MOORINGS, 1401 92nd Avenue Northeast  (8/26/77)

*Des Moines, COVENANT BEACH CHURCH CAMP (DES MOINES BEACH PARK), Cliff Avenue and 220th Street  (11/18/88)

Enumclaw, LOUIS AND ELLEN OLSON HOUSE, 1513 Griffin Avenue  (NR 8/30/84)

*Fall City vicinity, FALL CITY CEMETERY, WA 522, one mile south of Fall City  (12/9/70)

*Fall City vicinity, HOP CURING SHED, Fall City Community Park  (12/9/70)

Issaquah, BRANDES HOUSE, 2202 212th Avenue Southeast  (NR 12/14/94)

Issaquah, ISSAQUAH (SEATTLE, LAKE SHORE, AND EASTERN) DEPOT, Rainier Avenue North  (NR 9/13/90)

*Issaquah, ISSAQUAH SPORTSMEN'S CLUB, 23600 SE Evans Street  (9/25/98)

Issaquah, PICKERING FARM, 21809 Southeast 56th Avenue  (NR 7/7/83)

*Kent, CARNATION MILK FACTORY, 203 Meeker Street  (12/9/70)

*Kent, DAVID F. NEELY HOUSE, 23691 Russell Road  (5/20/77)

Kent, ERICK GUSTAVE SANDERS MAN-SION, 5516 South 277th Street  (NR 11/6/86)

*Kent vicinity, ALVORD'S LANDING, Southwest of Kent on River Road  (12/9/70)

*Kent vicinity, LANGSTON'S LANDING, West and Willis Streets  (12/9/70)

*Kent vicinity, MADDOCKSVILLE LANDING, One mile northwest of Kent on Russell Road  (12/9/70)

*Kent vicinity, WHITE RIVER MASSACRE SITE, Between Kent and Auburn  (8/31/73)

Kirkland, PETER KIRK BUILDING, 620 Market Street (NR 8/14/73)

Kirkland, KIRKLAND WOMAN'S CLUB, 407 First Street (NR 1/26/90)

Kirkland, LOOMIS HOUSE, 304 Eighth Avenue West (NR 8/3/82)

Kirkland, LOUIS S. MARSH HOUSE, 6604 Lake Washington Boulevard (NR 6/30/89)

Kirkland, MASONIC LODGE BUILDING, 700 Market Street (NR 8/3/82)

Kirkland, JOSHUA SEARS BUILDING, 701 Market Street (NR 8/3/82)

*Kirkland, TOURIST II , 25 Lake Shore Plaza, Marina Park (NR 4/15/97)

Kirkland, DR. TRUEBLOOD HOUSE, 127 Seventh Avenue (NR 8/3/82)

Lake Forest Park, HARRY WURDEMANN HOUSE, 17602 Bothell Way Northeast (NR 12/27/90)

*Lester vicinity, STAMPEDE PASS TUNNEL, Through summit of Cascade Range at Stampede Pass (3/13/81)

Medina, JAMES G. EDDY HOUSE AND GROUNDS, 1005 Evergreen Point Road (NR 2/19/82)

*Medina, MEDINA CITY HALL, 501 Evergreen Point Road (12/9/70)

Mercer Island, LAKEVIEW SCHOOL (SUNNY-BEAM SCHOOL), Island Crest Way and Southeast 68th Street (NR 6/16/88)

*Newcastle, NEWCASTLE CEMETERY, Southwest of 69th Way and 129th intersection (10/10/80)

Newcastle, PACIFIC COAST COMPANY HOUSE NO. 75, North of Renton at 7210 138th Street Southeast (NR 12/21/79)

North Bend, CAMP NORTH BEND, 45509 Southeast 150th Street (NR 4/29/93)

North Bend, CEDAR FALLS HISTORIC DISTRICT, 20030 Cedar Falls Road SE (NR 7/9/97)

North Bend, NORTH BEND RANGER STATION, 42404 Southeast North Bend Way (NR 3/6/91)

North Bend vicinity, NORMAN BRIDGE, Old 428th Avenue Southeast, across the North Fork, Snoqualmie River (NR 7/19/94)

*North Bend vicinity, SNOQUALMIE PASS WAGON ROAD, At Denny Creek (12/9/70)

*Redmond, MARYMOOR FARM DUTCH WINDMILL, 6046 Lake Sammamish Parkway Northeast (4/20/73)

Redmond, THE YELLOWSTONE ROAD, 196th Street between Fall City Highway and 80th Northeast (NR 12/2/74)

Redmond vicinity, JAMES W. CLISE HOUSE, 6046 West Lake Sammamish Parkway Northeast (NR 6/19/73)

Redmond vicinity, MARYMOOR PREHISTORIC INDIAN SITE, 6046 West Lake Sammamish Parkway Northeast (NR 11/20/70)

*Renton, RENTON COAL MINE HOIST FOUNDATION, South of Benson Road and Grady Way intersection (12/5/75)

*Renton, RENTON FIRE STATION, Houser Way and Mill Avenue (11/17/78)

*Renton, RENTON SUBSTATION, SNOQUALMIE FALLS POWER COMPANY, 1017 South Third Street (11/19/82)

Seattle, 12TH AVENUE SOUTH BRIDGE, Dearborn Street (NR 7/16/82)

Seattle, 14TH AVENUE SOUTH BRIDGE, Spans Duwamish River (NR 7/16/82)

**Seattle, *ADVENTURESS* [SCHOONER], Lake Union Drydock (NHL 4/11/89)

Seattle, ALASKA TRADE BUILDING (UNION RECORD BUILDING), 1915-1919 First Avenue (NR 5/6/71)

*Seattle, ALEXANDER HALL, SEATTLE PACIFIC COLLEGE, Seattle Pacific College campus (SR 12/9/70)

*Seattle, ALKI BEACH PARK, 65th Southwest to 58th Southwest (12/9/70)

Seattle, ALKI POINT LIGHT STATION, Tip of Alki Point off Alki Beach Avenue Southwest (NR 1977)

Seattle, ARBORETUM SEWER TRESTLE, 26th Avenue East at Washington Park (NR 7/16/82)

*Seattle, ARCHITECTURE HALL (BAGLEY HALL), UNIVERSITY OF WASHINGTON, University of Washington campus (12/9/70)

Seattle, ARCTIC BUILDING, 306 Cherry Street (NR 11/28/78)

Seattle, ASSAY OFFICE (GERMAN CLUB), 613 Ninth Avenue (NR 3/16/72)

Seattle, AURORA AVENUE (GEORGE WAHINGTON MEMORIAL) BRIDGE, WA Aurora Avenue (NR 7/16/82)

*Seattle, BAKER STREET HOUSE, 2002 Northwest 60th Street (2/18/98)

Seattle, BALLARD AVENUE HISTORIC DISTRICT, Ballard Avenue from Northwest Market to Northwest Dock Street (NR 7/1/76)

Seattle, BALLARD BRIDGE, Spans Lake Washington Ship Canal (NR 7/16/82)

Seattle, BALLARD CARNEGIE LIBRARY, 2026 Northwest Market Street (NR 6/15/79)

Seattle, BALLARD-HOWE HOUSE, 22 West Highland Drive (NR 6/15/79)

Seattle, RICHARD A. BALLINGER HOUSE, 1733 39th Avenue (NR 5/28/76)

Seattle, BARNES BUILDING, 2320–2322 First Avenue (NR 2/24/75)

*Seattle, BATTLE OF SEATTLE SITE, Third and Jefferson (12/9/70)

Seattle, BELL APARTMENTS, 2326 First Avenue (NR 7/12/74)

Seattle, JESSE C. BOWLESS HOUSE, 2540 Shoreland Drive South (NR 11/6/86)

Seattle, BUILDING NO. 105, BOEING AIRPLANE COMPANY (E. W. HEATH SHIPYARD), 200 Southwest Michigan Street (NR 8/26/71)

Seattle, BUTTERWORTH BUILDING, 1921 First Avenue (NR 5/14/71)

Seattle, CAMLIN HOTEL, 1619 Ninth Avenue (NR 3/25/99)

*Seattle, CARSON BOREN HOME SITE, Second and Cherry Streets (12/9/70)

Seattle, CHELSEA FAMILY HOTEL, 620 West Olympic Place (NR 12/14/78)

Seattle, CHINATOWN HISTORIC DISTRICT, Roughly bounded by Main, Jackson, I-5, Weller, and Fifth (NR 11/6/86)

Seattle, CHINESE BAPTIST CHURCH, 925 South King Street (NR 7/31/86)

Seattle, CHITTENDEN LOCKS AND LAKE WASHINGTON SHIP CANAL HISTORIC DISTRICT, Salmon Bay (NR 12/14/78)

Seattle, CHURCH OF THE BLESSED SACRAMENT, PRIORY, AND SCHOOL, 5040-5041 Ninth Avenue Northeast (NR 1/12/84)

*Seattle, CLARK HALL, UNIVERSITY OF WASHINGTON, University of Washington campus (12/9/70)

Seattle, COBB BUILDING, 1301–1309 Fourth Avenue (NR 8/3/84)

Seattle, COLISEUM THEATER, Fifth Avenue and Pike Street (NR 7/7/75)

Seattle, COLMAN BUILDING, 811 First Avenue (NR 3/16/72)

*Seattle, COLMAN DOCK SITE, Pier 52 (9/6/74)

Seattle, COLONIAL HOTEL, 1119–1123 First Avenue (NR 4/29/82)

Seattle, COLUMBIA CITY HISTORIC DISTRICT, Roughly bounded by South Hudson and South Alaska Streets, 35th and Rainier Avenues (NR 9/8/80)

Seattle, CORNISH SCHOOL, 710 East Roy Street (NR 8/29/77)

Seattle, COWEN PARK BRIDGE, 15th Avenue Northeast (NR 7/16/82)

Seattle, DE LA MAR APARTMENTS, 115 West Olympic Place (NR 8/18/80)

*Seattle, DENNY HALL, UNIVERSITY OF WASHINGTON, University of Washington campus (12/9/70)

*Seattle, ARTHUR DENNY HOME SITE, Second Avenue and Union Street (5/31/74)

*Seattle, DENNY PARK, Denny Way and Dexter Avenue North (12/9/70)

Seattle, DUNN GARDENS, 13533 Northshire Road Northwest (NR 12/15/94)

**Seattle, DUWAMISH [FIREBOAT], Lake Washington Ship Canal, Chittenden Locks (NHL 6/29/89)

Seattle, DUWAMISH NO. 1 ARCHAEOLOGICAL SITE, South of Elliott Bay (NR 10/18/77)

Seattle, EAGLES AUDITORIUM BUILDING, 1416 Seventh Avenue (NR 7/14/83)

Seattle, EMMANUEL LUTHERAN CHURCH, 1215 Thomas Street (NR 2/25/82)

Seattle, FEDERAL OFFICE BUILDING, 909 First Avenue (NR 4/30/79)

Seattle, PIERRE P. FERRY HOUSE, 1531 Tenth Avenue East (NR 4/18/79)

*Seattle, FERRY SERVICE TO WEST SEATTLE, Foot of Madison Street (9/6/74)

**Seattle, FIR [VESSEL], Lake Union (NHL 4/11/89)

*Seattle, FIRE STATION NO. 7, 402 15th Avenue East (7/28/72)

Seattle, FIRE STATION NO. 18 (BALLARD FIRE STATION), 5427 Russell Avenue Northwest (NR 6/19/73)

Seattle, FIRE STATION NO. 23, 18th Avenue and Columbia Street (NR 9/10/71)

Seattle, FIRE STATION NO. 25, 1400 Harvard Avenue (NR 4/14/72)

*Seattle, FIRST CATHOLIC HOSPITAL SITE, Fifth Avenue (3/8/74)

Seattle, FIRST METHODIST PROTESTANT CHURCH OF SEATTLE, 128 Sixteenth Avenue East (NR 5/14/93)

*Seattle, FIRST POST OFFICE SITE, First Avenue (12/9/70)

*Seattle, FIRST PUBLIC SCHOOL SITE, Third Avenue (12/9/70)

*Seattle, FIRST SERVICE STATION SITE, Holgate Street and Alaskan Way (12/9/70)

Seattle, FORT LAWTON, Discovery Park (NR 8/15/78)

**Seattle, *ARTHUR FOSS* [TUGBOAT], Central Waterfront at Moss Bay (NHL 4/11/89)

Seattle, FOURTH AVENUE BUILDING, 1411 Fourth Avenue (NR 5/28/91)

Seattle, FREMONT BRIDGE, Spans Lake Washington Ship Canal (NR 7/16/82)

Seattle, FREMONT BUILDING, 3419 Fremont Avenue North (NR 11/12/92)

Seattle, CAROLINE KLINE GALLAND HOUSE, 1605 17th Avenue (NR 2/8/80)

Seattle, GLOBE BUILDING, BEEBE BUILDING, AND HOTEL CECIL, 1001–1023 First Avenue (NR 4/29/82)

*Seattle, GORST FIELD, 5400 West Marginal Way Southwest (12/9/70)

Seattle, J. S. GRAHAM STORE, 119 Pine Street (NR 12/7/89)

*Seattle, GRAND CENTRAL HOTEL BUILDING, 214 First Avenue South (within Pioneer Square-Skid Road Historic District) (10/1/71)

Seattle, GRAND PACIFIC HOTEL, 1115-1117 First Avenue (NR 5/13/82)

*Seattle, GREAT WHITE FLEET DISEMBARKATION SITE, Pier 64 (12/9/70)

Seattle, GUIRY AND SCHOLLESTAD BUILDINGS, 2101–2111 First Avenue (NR 8/29/85)

Seattle, HARVARD/BELMONT HISTORIC DISTRICT, Roughly bounded by Bellevue Place, Broadway, Boylston, and Harvard Avenues (NR 5/13/82)

Seattle, SAMUEL HILL HOUSE, 814 East Highland Drive (NR 5/3/76)

*Seattle, HILLCREST APARTMENTS, 1616 East Howell Street (11/21/80)

Seattle, HOGE BUILDING, 705 Second Avenue (NR 4/14/83)

Seattle, HOLYOKE BUILDING, 1018–1022 First Avenue (NR 6/3/76)

Seattle, HOME OF THE GOOD SHEPHERD, Sunnyside North and 50th Street (NR 5/23/78)

*Seattle, HOSPITAL SHIP *IDAHO,* Foot of South Washington Street (SR 12/9/70)

Seattle, HULL BUILDING (A-1 LAUNDRY BUILDING), 2401-5 First Avenue (NR 1/27/83)

Seattle, SAMUEL HYDE HOUSE, 3726 East Madison Street (NR 4/12/82)

Seattle, IMMIGRANT STATION AND ASSAY OFFICE, 815 Airport Way South (NR 1/25/79)

Seattle, INTERLAKE PUBLIC SCHOOL, 4416 Wallingford Avenue North (NR 7/14/83)

Seattle, IRON PERGOLA, First Avenue and Yesler Way (NR 8/26/71)

Seattle, KING STREET STATION, Third Street South and South King Street (NR 4/13/73)

Seattle, JOSEPH KRAUS HOUSE, 2812 Mount St. Helens Place (NR 2/25/82)

Seattle, LEAMINGTON HOTEL AND APARTMENTS, 317 Marion Street (NR 5/13/94)

Seattle, ELIZA FERRY LEARY HOUSE, 1551 Tenth Avenue East (NR 4/14/72)

*Seattle, LEWIS HALL, UNIVERSITY OF WASHINGTON, University of Washington campus (12/9/70)

*Seattle, LIST-BUSSELL HOUSE, 1630 36th Avenue (2/28/86)

Seattle, LYON BUILDING, 607 Third Avenue (NR 6/30/95)

*Seattle, MAPLE DONATION CLAIM (BOEING FIELD), Airport Way (12/9/70)

Seattle, R. D. MERRILL HOUSE, 919 Harvard Avenue East  (NR 8/22/77)

*Seattle, MIIKE MARU ARRIVAL SITE, Alaskan Way  (12/9/70)

Seattle, MONTLAKE BRIDGE, Spans Lake Union Ship Canal  (NR 7/16/82)

Seattle, MOORE THEATRE AND HOTEL, 1932 Second Avenue  (NR 8/30/74)

Seattle, MOUNT BAKER RIDGE TUNNEL, East of WA 90  (NR 7/16/82)

Seattle, LACEY V. MURROW BRIDGE, Lake Washington  (NR 4/29/87)

Seattle, NATIONAL BUILDING, 1006-1024 Western Avenue  (NR 04/29/82)

Seattle, NAVAL MILITARY HANGAR-UNIVERSITY SHELL HOUSE, University of Washington campus  (NR 7/1/75)

Seattle, NEW WASHINGTON HOTEL (JOSEPHINIUM), 1902 Second Avenue  (NR 9/28/89)

Seattle, NIHON GO GAKKO (JAPANESE LAN-GUAGE SCHOOL), 1414 South Weller Street  (NR 6/23/82)

Seattle, NIPPON KAN, 622 South Washington Street  (NR 5/22/78)

*Seattle, NORTH QUEEN ANNE DRIVE BRIDGE, Spans ravine of Second Avenue North  (3/13/81)

Seattle, NORTHERN LIFE TOWER (SEATTLE TOWER), 1212 Third Avenue  (NR 5/30/75)

*Seattle, OBSERVATORY, UNIVERSITY OF WASHINGTON, University of Washington campus  (12/9/70)

Seattle, OLD GEORGETOWN CITY HALL, 6202 13th Avenue South  (NR 4/14/83)

Seattle, OLD PUBLIC SAFETY BUILDING, Fourth Avenue and Terrace Street; Fifth Avenue and Yesler Way  (NR 6/19/73)

Seattle, OLYMPIC COLD STORAGE, 1201 Western Avenue  (NR 11/14/97)

Seattle, OLYMPIC HOTEL, 1200–1220 Fourth Avenue  (NR 6/15/79)

Seattle, PARAMOUNT THEATRE, 901 Pine Street  (NR 10/9/74)

Seattle, PARK DEPARTMENT, DIVISION OF PLAYGROUNDS, 301 Terry Avenue  (NR 3/16/72)

*Seattle, PARRINGTON HALL, UNIVERSITY OF WASHINGTON, University of Washington campus  (12/9/70)

Seattle, WILLIAM PARSON'S HOUSE, 2706 Harvard Avenue East  (NR 6/21/91)

Seattle, WILLIAM PHILLIPS HOUSE (PHILLIPS-HEG HOUSE), 711–713 East Union Street  (NR 4/29/93)

Seattle, PIKE PLACE PUBLIC MARKET HIS-TORIC DISTRICT, Roughly bounded by First and Western Avenues, Virginia and Pike Streets  (NR 3/13/70)

**Seattle, PIONEER BUILDING, PERGOLA AND TOTEM POLE, First Avenue, Yesler Way and Cherry Street  (NHL 5/5/77)

Seattle, PIONEER HALL, 1642 43rd Avenue East  (NR 6/5/70)

Seattle, PIONEER SQUARE-SKID ROAD HIS-TORIC DISTRICT (and expansion), Roughly bounded by Second Avenue, South King Street, Western Avenue, and Columbia Street  (NR 6/22/70)

Seattle, QUEEN ANNE CLUB, 1530 Queen Anne Avenue North  (NR 1/27/83)

Seattle, QUEEN ANNE HIGH SCHOOL, 215 Galer Street  (NR 11/21/85)

Seattle, QUEEN ANNE PUBLIC SCHOOL, 515 West Galer Street (NR 7/30/75)

Seattle, RAINIER CLUB, 810 Fourth Avenue (NR 4/22/76)

Seattle, RAVENNA PARK BRIDGE, 20th Avenue, spans Ravenna Park Ravine (NR 7/16/82)

Seattle, RAYMOND-OGDEN MANSION, 702 35th Avenue (NR 6/15/79)

Seattle, REDELSHEIMER-OSTRANDER HOUSE, 200 40th Avenue East (NR 1/12/90)

**Seattle, *RELIEF* [LIGHTSHIP], Ballard (NHL 4/11/89)

Seattle, JUDGE JAMES T. RONALD HOUSE, 421 30th Street (NR 2/20/75)

*Seattle, ROUND THE WORLD FLIGHT SITE (SAND POINT NAVAL AIR STATION), WA 513 (12/9/70)

*Seattle, ROW HOUSES ON 23RD AVENUE, 806–828 23rd Avenue (12/9/70)

*Seattle, SALMON BAY GREAT NORTHERN RAILROAD BRIDGE, Spans Salmon Bay (3/13/81)

Seattle, S.S. *SAN MATEO* [ VESSEL], South end of Lake Union (NR 4/7/71)

Seattle, SCHMITZ PARK BRIDGE, Spans Schmitz Park Ravine (NR 7/16/82)

Seattle, SCHOONER *ZODIAC* (SCHOONER *CALIFORNIA*), Lake Union Dry Dock (NR 4/29/82)

Seattle, SEATTLE, CHIEF OF THE SUQUAMISH STATUE, Fifth Avenue, Denny Way, and Cedar Street (NR 4/19/84)

**Seattle, SEATTLE ELECTRIC COMPANY, GEORGETOWN STEAM PLANT, King County Airport (NHL 7/27/84)

Seattle, SEATTLE PUBLIC LIBRARY-FRE-MONT BRANCH, 731 North 35th Street (NR 8/3/82)

Seattle, SEATTLE PUBLIC LIBRARY-GREEN LAKE BRANCH, 7364 East Green Lake Drive North (NR 8/3/82)

Seattle, SEATTLE PUBLIC LIBRARY-QUEEN ANNE BRANCH, 400 West Garfield Street (NR 8/3/82)

Seattle, SEATTLE PUBLIC LIBRARY-UNIVERSITY BRANCH, 5009 Roosevelt Way Northeast (NR 8/3/82)

Seattle, SEATTLE PUBLIC LIBRARY-WEST SEATTLE BRANCH, 2306 42nd Avenue Southwest (NR 8/3/82)

*Seattle, SEWARD SCHOOL LUNCHROOM AND GYMNASIUM, East Louisa between East Franklin and East Boylston (11/30/73)

Seattle, SKINNER BUILDING (5TH AVENUE THEATRE), 1300–1334 Fifth Avenue (NR 11/28/78)

*Seattle, START OF 1889 SEATTLE FIRE SITE, First Avenue (5/31/74)

Seattle, STIMSON-GREEN HOUSE, 1204 Minor Avenue (NR 5/4/76)

*Seattle, STIMSON-GRIFFITHS HOUSE, 405 West Highland Drive (5/20/77)

Seattle, ELLSWORTH STOREY COTTAGES HISTORIC DISTRICT, 1706–1816 South Lake Washington Boulevard and 1725–1729 South 36th Avenue (NR 7/6/76)

Seattle, ELLSWORTH STOREY RESIDENCES, 260 and 270 East Dorffel Drive (NR 4/14/72)

Seattle, STUART RESIDENCE AND GAR-DENS, 619 West Comstock (NR 4/14/83)

Seattle, SUMMIT SCHOOL, East Union Street and Summit Avenue (NR 10/4/79)

Seattle, WILL H. THOMPSON HOUSE, 3119 South Day Street (NR 11/29/79)
Seattle, TIMES BUILDING, 414 Olive Way (NR 1/27/83)

*Seattle, TON OF GOLD AND SAILING OF WILLAPA SITE, Foot of Pike Street (12/9/70)
Seattle, TRACY HOUSE, 18971 Edgecliff Drive Southwest (NR 6/1/95)

Seattle, TRIANGLE HOTEL AND BAR, 551 First Avenue South (NR 5/03/76)

Seattle, TRINITY CHURCH, 609 Eighth Avenue (NR 9/26/91)

Seattle, TURNER-KOEPF HOUSE (JEFFERSON PARK LADIES IMPROVEMENT CLUB), 2336 15th Avenue South (NR 4/22/76)

Seattle, UNION STATION, Fourth Avenue South and South Jackson Streets (NR 8/30/74)

Seattle, UNITED SHOPPING TOWER (NORTHWESTERN MUTUAL INSURANCE BUILDING), 217 Pine Street (NR 8/18/80)

Seattle, U.S. COURTHOUSE, 1010 Fifth Avenue (NR 1/8/80)

Seattle, U.S. IMMIGRATION BUILDING, 84 Union Street (NR 0/14/87)

Seattle, U.S. MARINE HOSPITAL, 1131 14th Avenue South (NR 12/21/79)

*Seattle, U.S.S. *NEBRASKA* LAUNCHING (SKINNER AND EDDY SHIPYARD), Pier 42 (3/8/74)

Seattle, UNIVERSITY BRIDGE, Spans Lake Washington Ship Canal (NR 7/16/82)

*Seattle, UNIVERSITY METHODIST EPISCOPAL CHURCH, 4142 Brooklyn Avenue (3/24/78)

*Seattle, UNIVERSITY OF WASHINGTON COLUMNS, University of Washington campus (12/9/70)

Seattle, VICTORIAN APARTMENTS, 1234–1238 South King Street (NR 12/18/90)
**Seattle, *VIRGINIA V* [PASSENGER FERRY], Lake Washington Ship Canal (NHL 4/24/73)

Seattle, WILLIAM VOLKER BUILDING, 1000 Lenora Street (NR 10/13/83)

Seattle, VOLUNTEER PARK, Bounded by East Prospect and East Galer Streets, Federal and East 15th Avenues (NR 5/3/76)

Seattle, WAGNER HOUSEBOAT (THE OLD BOATHOUSE), 2770 Westlake Avenue North (NR 2/19/82)

Seattle, WALLINGFORD FIRE AND POLICE STATION, 1629 North 45th Street (NR 1/27/83)

Seattle, WARD HOUSE, 520 East Denny Way (NR 3/16/72)

Seattle, WASHINGTON STREET PUBLIC BOAT LANDING FACILITY, South Washington Street west of Alaskan Way (NR 6/10/74)

*Seattle, WASHINGTON TERRITORIAL UNIVERSITY SITE, Seneca Street (12/9/70)

Seattle, WAWONA [SCHOONER], South end of Lake Union (NR 7/1/70)

Seattle, WEST POINT LIGHT STATION, West of Fort Lawton (NR 8/16/77)

Seattle, WILKE FARMHOUSE, 1920 Second Street North (NR 11/1/74)

Seattle, YE COLLEGE INN, 4000 University Way Northeast (NR 2/25/82)

*Seattle, YESLER HOUSES, 103, 107, and 109 23rd Avenue (12/2/96)

*Seattle, YESLER TERRACE LOW INCOME HOUSING PROJECT, 903 Yesler Way (5/29/81)

*Seattle, YESLER WHARF AND DECATUR ANCHORAGE SITE, Foot of Yesler Way (11/14/69)

Selleck, SELLECK HISTORIC DISTRICT, Southeast 252nd  (NR 3/16/89)

Shoreline, WILLIAM E. BOEING HOUSE, Huckleberry Lane, The Highlands  (NR 12/16/88)
Skykomish, MALONEY'S GENERAL STORE, 104 Railroad Avenue West  (NR 7/9/97)

Skykomish, SKYKOMISH/GREAT NORTH-ERN DEPOT, Southeast corner of Railroad Avenue and 4th Street (NR 4/14/97)

Snoqualmie, SNOQUALMIE DEPOT, 109 King Street  (NR 07/24/74)

Snoqualmie, SNOQUALMIE FALLS HISTORIC DISTRICT, Snoqualmie Falls  (NR 10/24/92)

Snoqualmie, SNOQUALMIE FALLS CAVITY GENERATING STATION, North of Snoqualmie River  (NR 4/23/76)

Snoqualmie, SNOQUALMIE SCHOOL CAM-PUS, Silva and King Streets  (NR 3/16/89)

*Snoqualmie Falls, SNOQUALMIE PASS WAGON ROAD, At Denny Creek (12/9/70)

Tukwila, JAMES NELSEN HOUSE, 15643 West Valley Road  (5/25/90)

Tukwila, TUKWILA SCHOOL, 14475 59th Avenue South  (NR 11/29/79)

Vashon, MUKAI COLD PROCESS FRUIT BARRELLING PLANT, 18005-18017 107th Avenue Southwest  (NR 9/26/94)

Vashon-Maury Island, DOCKTON HOTEL, Southwest 260th Street and 99th Avenue South-west  (NR 7/28/83)

*Vashon vicinity, LEWIS CASS BEALL HOUSE, 91st Avenue Southwest  (8/23/91)

Woodinville vicinity, HOLLYWOOD FARM, Southeast of Woodinville at 14111 Northeast 145th Street  (NR 12/15/78)

# Suggested Reading

The following are some selected books for learning about Seattle and King County architecture, history, culture, and preservation. Some of these are currently out of print but can be found in libraries and at local historical societies. The King County Landmarks and Heritage Program in the King County Office of Cultural Resources has compiled a number of excellent bibliographies that range from general history to specific geographic areas, neighborhoods, and themes. They are listed below by title, and are continually being updated. For copies, contact that office at 506 Second Avenue, Suite 200, Seattle, WA 98104-2307, (206) 296-7580. The Seattle Public Library has compiled bibliographies and referral guides to assist people in researching their homes and in finding appropriate architecture and design books. Contact the Fine and Performing Arts Department, Seattle Public Library, 4th Floor, 1000 Fourth Avenue, Seattle, WA 98101, (206) 386-4613. Relevant architectural drawings, photographs, ephemera, and archival materials can also be found at Special Collections, Manuscripts, and University Archives, Allen Library, Box 352900, University of Washington, Seattle, WA 98195-2900, (206) 543-1929 or at the library of the Museum of History and Industry, 2700 24th Avenue East, Seattle WA 98112, (206) 324-1125, in addition to the Washington State Historical Society in Tacoma and many smaller historical societies and museums throughout King County.

Avner, Jane A., and Meta Buttnick. *Historic Jewish Seattle: A Tour Guide.* Seattle: Washington State Jewish Historical Society, 1995.

Bagley, Clarence B. *History of Seattle from the Earliest Settlement to the Present Time.* 3 vols. Seattle: S. J. Clarke Publishing Co., 1916.

————. *History of King County.* 4 vols. Chicago: S. J. Clarke Co., 1929. Reprint, Auburn: White River Valley Historical Society, 1979.

Berner, Richard C. *Seattle, 1900–1920: From Boomtown, Urban Turbulence, to Restoration.* Seattle: Charles Press, 1991.

————. *Seattle, 1921-1940: From Boom to Bust.* Seattle: Charles Press, 1992.

Booth, T. William, and William H. Wilson. *Carl F. Gould: A Life in Architecture and the Arts.* Seattle: University of Washington Press, 1995.

Buerge, David. *Seattle in the 1880s.* Seattle: Historical Society of Seattle and King County, 1986.

Calvert, Frank, ed. *Homes and Gardens of the Pacific Coast:.* Vol. 1. Seattle: Beaux Arts Society Publishers, 1913.

*Central District Historical and Cultural Resources.* Seattle: Historic Seattle Preservation and Development Authority, 1995.

Chew, Ron, ed. *Reflections of Seattle's Chinese Americans: The First Hundred Years.* Seattle: University of Washington Press/Wing Luke Museum, 1994.

Crowley, Walt. *National Trust Guide: Seattle. America's Guide for Architecture and History Travelers.* New York: Preservation Press, John Wiley & Sons, 1998.

Dorpat, Paul. *Seattle Now and Then.* 3 vols. Seattle: Tartu Publications, 1984–89.

Eals, Clay, ed. *West Side Story.* Seattle: West Seattle Herald/White Center News, 1987.

Hanford, Cornelius H. *Seattle and Environs, 1852–1924.* 3 vols. Seattle: Seattle Pioneer Publishing Co., 1924.

Hines, Neal O. *Denny's Knoll: A History of the Metropolitan Tract in Seattle.* Seattle: University of Washington Press, 1980.

*Historic Preservation in Seattle: A Guide to Incentives and Procedures.* Seattle: Department of Community Development, City of Seattle, July 1991.

Hutchinson, Charles J. *History and Progress of King County, Washington.* Seattle: H. C. Piggott Printing Concern, 1916.

*Impressions of Imagination: Terra-Cotta Seattle.* Seattle: Allied Arts of Seattle, 1986.

Jones, Nard. *Seattle.* Garden City, N.Y.: Doubleday & Co., 1972.

Kreisman, Lawrence. *Apartments by Anhalt.* Seattle: Office of Urban Conservation, 1978. Reprint, Seattle: Kreisman Exhibit Design, 1982.

————. *Art Deco Seattle.* Seattle: Allied Arts of Seattle, 1979.

————. *Historic Preservation in Seattle.* Seattle: Historic Seattle Preservation and Development Authority, 1985.

————. *The Stimson Legacy: Architecture in the Urban West.* Seattle: Willows Press, 1992. Distributed by University of Washington Press.

————. *West Queen Anne School: Renaissance of a Landmark.* Seattle: West Queen Anne Associates, Ltd. Partnership, Seattle School District et al., Historic Seattle Preservation and Development Authority, First Security Realty Services West, 1984.

Lentz, Florence K. *Centennial Snapshots: Historic Places around King County from the First Twenty-five Years of Statehood.* Seattle: Northwest Interpretive Association, 1991.

————. *Fort Lawton: A Record.* Seattle: National Park Service, Pacific Northwest Region, U.S. Department of the Interior, n.d.

Morgan, Murray. *Skid Road: An Informal Portrait of Seattle.* New York: Viking Press, 1951.

Mumford, Esther Hall. *Calabash: A Guide to the History, Culture, and Art of African Americans in Seattle and King County.* Seattle: Ananse Press, 1993.

————. *Seattle's Black Victorians, 1852–1901.* Seattle: Ananse Press, 1980.

Neilsen, Roy. *UniverCity: The Story of the University District in Seattle.* Seattle: University Lions Foundation, 1986.

Nelson, Bryce. *Good Schools: The Seattle Public School System, 1901 to 1930.* Seattle: Seattle Public Schools and University of Washington Press, 1988.

Nyberg, Folke, and Victor Steinbrueck. *An Urban Resource Inventory for Seattle.* Seattle: Historic Seattle Preservation and Development Authority, 1975 (Includes 16 neighborhood inventory maps).

Ochsner, Jeffrey Karl, ed. *Shaping Seattle Architecture: A Historical Guide to the Architects.* Seattle: University of Washington Press, 1994.

Payton, Charles. *Overview of King County History.* Historical Paper No. 3. Seattle: King County Landmarks and Heritage Program, 1999.

————. *King County Planning Areas History.* Historical Paper No. 5. Seattle: King County Landmarks and Heritage Program, 1999.

————. *Seattle Neighborhoods Bibliography.* Historical Paper No. 6. Seattle: King County Landmarks and Heritage Program, 1999.

————. *King County History.* Historical Paper No. 7. Seattle: King County Landmarks and Heritage Program, 1999.

————. *King County Agricultural History.* Historical Paper No. 9. Seattle: King County Landmarks and Heritage Program, 1999.

————. *King County Transportation History.* Historical Paper No. 13. Seattle: King County Landmarks and Heritage Program, 1999.

————. *The WPA Legacy in King County.* Historical Paper No. 14. Seattle: King County Landmarks and Heritage Program, 1999.

————. *King County Medical History.* Historical Paper No. 16. Seattle: King County Landmarks and Heritage Program, 1999.

————. *King County Theatre History.* Historical Paper No. 17. Seattle: King County Landmarks and Heritage Program, 1999.

———. *School & Education in King County.* Historical Paper No. 18. Seattle: King County Landmarks and Heritage Program, 1999.

———. *Historic Tour Guides.* Open File. Seattle: King County Landmarks and Heritage Program, 1999.

Reinartz, Kay F., ed. *Passport to Ballard: The Centennial Story.* Seattle: Ballard News Tribune, 1988.

———. *Queen Anne, Community on the Hill.* Seattle: Queen Anne Historical Society, 1993.

Sale, Roger. *Seattle Past to Present.* Seattle: University of Washington Press, 1976.

Sale, Roger, and Mary Randlett. *Seeing Seattle.* Seattle: University of Washington Press, 1994.

Schwantes, Carlos. *Railroad Signatures across the Pacific Northwest.* Seattle: University of Washington Press, 1993.

Shorett, Alice, and Murray Morgan. *The Pike Place Market: People, Politics and Produce.* Seattle: Pacific Search Press, 1985.

Speidel, Bill. *Sons of the Profits, the Seattle Story, 1851–1901.* Seattle: Nettle Creek Publishing, 1967.

Steinbrueck, Victor. *Market Sketchbook.* Seattle: University of Washington Press, 1968, 1997.

———. *Seattle Architecture, 1850–1953.* New York: Reinhold Publishing Co., 1953.

———. *Seattle Cityscape.* Seattle: University of Washington Press, 1962.

———. *Seattle Cityscape #2.* Seattle: University of Washington Press, 1973.

Summers, Hearst, and Van R. Pierson. *Columbia City—Back When: Centennial History of Columbia City and Rainier Valley, 1853–1991.* Seattle: Pioneers of Columbia City and Vicinity, 1992.

Takami, David. *Divided Destiny: A History of Japanese Americans in Seattle.* Seattle: Wing Luke Asian Museum and University of Washington Press, 1998.

Thomas, Jacob E., ed. *King County Survey of Historic Places: A Guide to Historic Sites in King County.* Seattle: King County Department of Planning and Community Development, 1979.

Tobin, Caroline C. *Historical Survey and Planning Study of Fremont's Commercial Area.* Seattle: Fremont Neighborhood Council, 1991.

Warren, James R. *King County and Its Queen City, Seattle.* Woodland Hills, Calif.: Windsor Publications, 1981.

Woodbridge, Sally. *A Guide to Architecture in Washington State.* Seattle: University of Washington Press, 1980.

# Index

Page locators for illustrations are in italic. Numbers are alphabetized as if spelled out.

# PHOTOGRAPHIC CREDITS

All people and organizations are located in Seattle unless otherwise noted.

Greg Ahmann: 176 (left)

Bassetti Architects: 159

Dorothy Bullitt Archives: 18, 38 (top left), 45 (right), 61 (top left, right), 172

Bumgardner Architects: 164 (top)

Dick Busher: 94 (left), 152 (bottom), 154

Callison Architecture: 169 (top, Nate Thomas; bottom, Chris Eden)

Friends of Seattle's Parks: 78 (bottom)

Fuller Sears: 170, 171

Victor Gardaya: 32, 52 (left), 61 (right)

Ray and Zita Hichaya: 179 (left)

King County Cultural Resources: 3 (top right), 100 (courtesy Michael Maslan), 114, 120, 126, 131, 134, 135 (left, John Stamets), 136, 137, 138 (left, Mark Ruwedel), 139, 141 (right, Washington State Archives, King County Regional Branch), 142, 143, 145

Kovalenko Hale Architects: 103, 104

Lawrence Kreisman: 8 (top), 47 (left), 50, 54, 58 (right), 70, 89, 91 (top left), 94 (right), 98 (right), 110 (top right), 111 (bottom), 150, 151, 156 (bottom), 157 (top), 160, 161, 164 (bottom), 165 (top), 166 (top), 186 (right), 187, 194

David Leavengood Architects: 47 (right), 168 (left, Deborah Mendenhall; right, Mary Koruga)

Kal Malone: 69, 71, 158 (left)

METRO Transit Division: 79

Museum of History and Industry: 3 (bottom right), 4 (bottom, 2097), 36, 75 (5902 Williamson), 119 (Stewart 1199816011), 122 (5143), 147 (9756), 152 (top, W&S 83.10.309.1), 155 (left, W&S 83.10.3380.5)

NBBJ: 95 (right), 165 (bottom, Michael Shopenn), 167 (Fred Housel)

Olson Sundberg Architects: 93 (bottom right)

Jack and Ginger O'Malley, Preston, Washington: 177 (courtesy Kristina Basinger)

Mary Randlett, Olympia, Washington: i, v, xiii, xiv, 8 (bottom left), 9 (bottom right), 12, 14, 15, 16, 17, 19, 21, 24, 25, 26, 29, 30, 31, 34, 37, 38 (bottom right), 39, 41, 43, 46, 51, 52, 58 (left), 62 (left), 64 (bottom left), 66, 67, 68, 74, 81, 82, 87, 90, 91 (bottom left, right), 92 (top left), 93 (top right), 95 (left), 97 (bottom), 98 (left), 99, 101 (bottom), 102, 110 (top left), 111 (top), 112, 128, 129, 132, 135 (right), 138 (right), 141 (left), 148, 153, 155 (right), 156 (top), 157 (bottom), 166 (bottom), 192

Renton Museum, Renton, Washington: 3 (left, D. Kinsey), 7 (bottom left)

Seattle Public Library: 28

Seattle School District (Lorig Associates): 57, 79 (left, Bassetti Architects), 158

Seattle Times: 174, 175 (Tom Reese), 176 (right, Greg Gilbert), 178 (Mike Siegel), 180 (left, Greg Gilbert; right), 181, 182 (Benjamin Benschneider), 183 (Greg Gilbert), 184 (Greg Gilbert), 185 (Greg Gilbert), 186 (left, Greg Gilbert), 188 (Steve Ringman), 190 (Steve Ringman), 191 (Steve Ringman)

Snoqualmie Valley Historical Museum, Snoqualmie, Washington: 117

Scott Souchock: 52 (right), 59, 60, 62 (right), 64 (top left), 65, 73, 78, 83, 84, 96, 100, 105, 107, 108 (bottom), 110, 113, 127, 179 (right)

Stickney Murphy Romine Architects: 93 (top left), 162 (right), 163

Special Collections, Manuscripts, and University Archives, University of Washington Libraries: 2 (top, Curtis 16394; bottom, Curtis 22875), 4 (top), 5 (top 12013; bottom, Curtis 10279), 6 (top left, Curtis 41637; top right; middle left, Curtis 31258; bottom left), 7 (top left, 2520), 9 (top, Curtis 11202), 42 (14,591), 45 (left, Curtis 25674), 64 (right, Curtis 65146), 85 (top, Curtis 58220; bottom, UW 6587), 86, 97 (top), 101 (top), 105 (left, Curtis 18011), 106 (top, UW 457; bottom, Curtis 881), 112 (bottom, Curtis 14736), 116 (Curtis 14713), 194 (Curtis 11945)

Tonkin/Hoyne/Lokan, Inc.: 162 (left)

Bill and Elizabeth Tracy: 189 (right)

Urban Conservation Office, City of Seattle: 77, 107, 108 (top), 189 (left)

Washington State Historical Society, Tacoma, Washington: 92 (top right, Curtis 15396)